FROM BOYS
TO MEN

"If the vast sums currently spent on trying to keep
teenagers in a failed and punishing school system were
spent on projects such as this, a major step toward social
health would unfold. Buy this book, put it to use, and
spread the word."

JOSEPH CHILTON PEARCE,
AUTHOR OF MAGICAL CHILD AND
THE BIOLOGY OF TRANSCENDENCE

"This book builds a much needed bridge between
contemporary knowledge and the wisdom of indigenous
elders, utilizing tools that are familiar to the western
experience and infusing them with ancestral spiritual
wisdom."

MALIDOMA SOMÉ,
AUTHOR OF HEALING WISDOM OF AFRICA AND
OF WATER AND THE SPIRIT

"A brilliant and practical resource and guide for
stewarding adolescent boys into responsible leadership
and manhood . . . a must for parents, teachers, leaders,
and managers."

ANGELES ARRIEN, PH.D.,
CULTURAL ANTHROPOLOGIST AND AUTHOR OF
THE FOUR-FOLD WAY AND SIGNS OF LIFE

FROM BOYS TO MEN

Spiritual Rites of Passage in an Indulgent Age

Bret Stephenson

Park Street Press
Rochester, Vermont

Park Street Press
One Park Street
Rochester, Vermont 05767
www.ParkStPress.com

Park Street Press is a division of Inner Traditions International

Library of Congress Cataloging-in-Publication Data
Stephenson, Bret.
  [Slaying the dragon]
  From boys to men : spiritual rites of passage in an indulgent age / Bret Stephenson.
    p. cm.
  Originally published: Slaying the Dragon. [South Lake Tahoe, Calif.] : Adolescent mind, 2004.
  Includes bibliographical references and index.
  ISBN-13: 978-1-59477-140-8 (pbk.)
  ISBN-10: 1-59477-140-5 (pbk.)
  1. Initiation rites. 2. Indigenous youth—Rites and ceremonies. 3. Teenage boys—Psychology. 4. Teenage boys—Attitudes. 5. Teenage boys—Conduct of life. I. Title.
  GN484.3.S84 2006
  305.235'1—dc22

                                                              2006020973

Printed and bound in the United States by Lake Book Manufacturing

10 9 8 7 6 5 4 3 2 1

Text design by Ginny Scott Bowman and layout by Jon Desautels
This book was typeset in Sabon with Senator used as the display typeface

To send correspondence to the author of this book, mail a first-class letter to the author c/o Inner Traditions • Bear & Company, One Park Street, Rochester, VT 05767, and we will forward the communication.

This book is dedicated to all the boys whose paths have crossed with mine, and to those boys yet to enter my life. Thanks for the education and for sharing your lives with me.

You all know who you are . . .

Contents

Foreword

For years we have followed Bret Stephenson's work as he tackled one of the most difficult areas in our immature culture: the lack of a grounded and effective passage to manhood for adolescent boys. Scholars such as Campbell and Jung have pointed out that this absence leaves the psyche open to self-initiation—but often in destructive or pathological ways. *From Boys to Men* thus steps into a cultural and existential gulf, to help the lost young heroes of our world and time find their way out of the labyrinth, their luminous shamanic path through the zone of perils, their personal "path with heart" (even as this book seems to us to be Bret Stephenson's "path with heart").

Stephenson makes it clear that the rewards are equal to the difficulty of travel in this cultural "no-man's land." The way is littered with the lost young souls wearing labels such as ADHD, autism, oppositional-defiant disorder, and Youth at Risk, as well as downright criminal sociopaths who murder their schoolmates. Stephenson's work shows that it takes not only guidance and mentorship, but extraordinary personal courage, and access to the time-honored mythic maps (the "Hero's Journey," the "Shamanic Initiation") to thread such a zone of perils.

This book fills an important psychological and mythological need of our time. Parents, counselors, and educators can all profit by its commonsense and timeless wisdom. Stephenson takes the reader through this zone with expertise, compassion, and some darn good storytelling!

STEPHEN LARSEN, PH.D., AND ROBIN LARSEN, PH.D.

Stephen Larsen is psychology professor emeritus at the State University of New York, Ulster, and the author of *The Healing Power of Neurofeedback, The Shaman's Doorway,* and *The Mythic Imagination.* Robin Larsen is an exhibiting artist and art historian and coauthor, with her husband, Stephen, of *Joseph Campbell: A Fire in the Mind* and *The Fashioning of Angels.* The Larsens co-direct the Center for Symbolic Studies, a nonprofit organization that works with youth at risk and offers educational programs for young artists, dancers, and athletes.

Preface

This book may be a difficult read for some of you. Why? Because it makes us adults take a hard look at the state of our children. In my opinion, it's a state of emergency. I'm an adolescent counselor, and I make my living helping twelve-year-old girls who have had two abortions, fourteen-year-old heroin addicts, boys who have been punching bags for their fathers, and kids on medications who have never spoken to the prescribing doctor. I've worked with kids whose father taught them how to steal and paid them to do so, and kids who grew up in the backseats of cars. I've also had a lot of success with such kids, and I am constantly amazed by their resiliency and their ability to still have a sense of humor after all they've been through.

What I do for a living is a twentieth-century invention. My job didn't exist in America a few generations ago, nor did it have a counterpart in native cultures throughout history. I tell my clients and those who attend my workshops and seminars that my overall career goal is to actually unemploy myself. My goal is for no parents to need my skills to get their kids off drugs or out of the gang. My goal is for teens not to need counseling therapy. My goal is for kids to be able to perform in life without mood-altering drugs. If we could fix these problems, I think to myself, I'd be happy to be out of a job and moving on to something else.

Awhile back my wife commented on the fact that after a career filled with damaged, difficult, and often violent kids, the only thing I ever bring home with me is frustration with *adults*. She's right. In a world filled with challenging teens, my only problem is with the adults who limit my ability to help the kids. I see the machinery of the system—schools, social services, juvenile justice—as an impediment to really helping kids.

The cure for adolescent problems in America, like so many other modern cultural issues we're dealing with such as homelessness, environmental destruction, and pollution, will come from a consciousness shift in the country. So I'm trying to help create that consciousness shift. Along with great youth workers like Aaron Kipnis, David Oldfield, and Michael Gurian, I'm trying to tell America it's time to rethink how we interact with and guide our boys into adulthood and manhood. And, as you will see, I propose that we look to traditional initiations and rites of passage to provide models for this transformation.

A number of people close to me have remarked about how passionate and even obstinate I am about teen issues. My soapbox never seems to be far away. Am I zealous and opinionated? Yes, I admit that. Am I driven and demanding? Yes again. In the eighteen years I've worked in counseling I've known too many kids who self-destructed on drugs and alcohol, were abused and neglected by their parents, were viewed as rebels and failures because they didn't fit the one school model we offer them. I've had too many kids commit suicide. I've had kids who have been shot and who have shot others. One kid I worked with actually killed another kid I was working with.

The plight of our children must rise higher on our adult priority lists. My sincere hope is that this book will help you see the problems teen boys face and gain some skills and techniques to help you deal more successfully with them. We grown-ups need to respond to the cultural emergencies facing our teens and recognize the need for implementing a different approach to molding our young men. In this book we'll look at traditional ways of promoting teens to adulthood by using time-honored rituals and concepts.

Acknowledgments

This book would still be floating around in my head if not for my wife, Patty. When I met her twenty-something years ago, I was jobless, homeless, car-less, and rather clueless after bailing on a corporate career. Sometime later she told me that what she saw most in that young man was "potential." She's followed me back into corporate work, then out of corporate work again for the more aesthetic vocation of woodworker, and on into the world of wild teenagers. I hope this book helps convince her she made a good decision so long ago. Patty also helped me get started on the writing aspect of the book a few years ago by donating some money from our meager everyday budget to my cause so I could pay myself a small stipend to type and not feel like a slacking husband and father.

Similarly, my best friend of more than forty-four years, Bob Becker, helped out back then, adding to the stash of money that made me feel, while typing, that I was taking care of business by generating a little income. Bob has also helped me, through countless conversations, like a whetstone helps a knife: he made me sharper. Thanks, Uncle Bob.

This was originally a self-published book, as I had difficulty for more than five years trying to get agents and publishers to produce a book about teen boys that was not specifically a parenting book. The first edition, titled *Slaying the Dragon: The Contemporary Struggle of Adolescent Boys,* was made possible by a donation from Mark Brady, a colleague from the Institute of Transpersonal Psychology and Stanford University. Mark donated much of the money for the first round of publishing, for which I will always be grateful.

And after trying for years to find a publisher interested in my flavor of work with teens, I'm thrilled to add my thanks to Inner Traditions for bringing the self-published book to a more professional level. I appreciate Jon Graham for originally acquiring the book, and my editor Vickie Trihy for crawling deeper into the book than I had ever hoped for in an effort to make it as good as possible. Vickie did a tremendous job sifting through my rambles and rants, adding much needed cohesion and flow to the book. My beliefs and visions are passionate, and she has done a remarkable job bringing out the best of my work. I honor her efforts.

Much of this book was written in the space of my daughter, Cailin. Thanks to the invention of laptops, we've spent many hours together, she working on her little projects and I on this big one. Thanks, Little Girl. My parents have continually given me support, even though I suspect they scratch their heads at my passion for "bad boys." Thanks as always . . .

Thanks to Ruth Cox, mentor extraordinaire, who reminded me to look at this book from a parent's perspective. I also appreciate the narrow-minded people in my life and career who prompted me to be creative, malleable, and persistent. Finally, my gratitude to Lisa, Jay, Diane, and of course Mer, who helped keep the feminine alive in a book inundated with boys.

Introduction

The boy is the father of the man.

G. STANLEY HALL (1904)

I was a great thief when I was a teen. I was successful in my illicit endeavors for several reasons. I was smart and patient. I was a wholesome local boy, a sports star whom everyone thought of as a good kid. But what really made me a good thief was that I enjoyed the risk factor, the exhilaration that made the fear of being caught acceptable.

However, as time passed I began to realize I was getting bored with stealing, and I couldn't understand why. As always, the universe is a great teacher if you live long enough. When I was about fourteen, I found myself at a shopping mall in another town. After casing the situation, I saw the potential for my biggest caper yet: to steal one thing from every store. I proceeded to carry out this plan, even stealing from the stores that held no purpose in my young boy life, such as the women's lingerie store. Slowly, relentlessly, I meandered throughout the mall, completing my task.

When I was finished, rather than basking in my success, I felt empty, dissatisfied. Was this not challenging enough? Was I so good I needed to move on to bigger and better projects? The answer came in a flash: put it all back! That would be the ultimate challenge, and challenge was what it was all about.

So I proceeded to risk being caught a second time, not to increase my bounty but to rid myself of it. When I'd finished, I felt much more content with myself, but not for the usual reasons. I felt good that I didn't have stolen stuff I needed to hide or throw away. I felt good because I had done something good, although of course I neglected to focus on the fact that my good deed was preceded by stealing thirty to forty items in the first place.

As I thought about the whole process, it occurred to me that I was most interested in the risk and the challenge involved in stealing. The actual merchandise and my sense of entitlement were just a means to justify this end. I now saw how the risk factor was really the driving force.

This is a book about risk: the need for experiencing appropriate risk and the taking of inappropriate risks. In case you hadn't noticed, adolescent boys are masters at taking risks, many of them unhealthy.

Boys have risk built into most facets of their lives. They risk their bodies, reputation, and pride in athletic pursuits. As the gender that more often pursues the opposite gender, boys risk refusal and rejection in asking girls out. Caught up in peer pressure at an early age, the words *I dare you* can make a boy do just about anything, even something self-destructive and dangerous.

I've mentioned the term *appropriate risk,* and some of you might be wondering what an appropriate risk is, if there is such a thing in the first place. Risk is not inherently bad. Risk often leads to growth—we learn from our challenges and mistakes. As the old saying goes, "No risk, no reward!" For example, if you are a downhill skier and you never fall down, you are probably not taking the risks that are necessary to attain the next level of proficiency in the sport. To get faster, cut a tighter turn, or catch more air, you've got to risk going past where you are currently comfortable.

I've often wondered in my career why if being drawn to risk is so inherent in boys, we hold this propensity for taking risks against them. Rather than helping them to create acceptable and even necessary risks, too often we adults try to prevent their risk-taking behavior entirely. The challenge for us as parents, teachers, counselors, and mentors of adolescent boys is to find ways to honor their innate need to challenge themselves and to help them experience a genuine transformation to manhood. My aim in this book is to enable you to create initiations and rites of passage appropriate to the times and conditions we live in.

ARE OUR KIDS DIFFERENT?

I've been working with and fascinated by adolescents for more than eighteen years now. A number of years ago I thought I had teen issues pretty well figured out. I subsequently had the opportunity to work at six international projects that exposed me to youth from one hundred countries. Generally I found teens from most other cultures better behaved and more responsible than our local kids. The non-American teens were more willing to take healthy risks, like sharing their feelings or trying something that might not be "cool," and they didn't seem to have the propensity of American youth to engage in so many unhealthy or dangerous risk-taking behaviors like joining gangs and using drugs. I started to wonder why our kids should be so much hungrier for risk and so much less interested in the responsibilities that come with adulthood.

Other observations I'd made about teen behavior also intrigued me. Awhile back I was driving through town, a four-lane road with a double turn lane in the middle. Traffic typically moves briskly here, and three teenage boys were standing in the middle lane waiting for an opening to finish crossing the road. I heard a few motorists yell at the boys, who were laughing in spite of the obvious danger, and they actually looked somewhat bored. It seemed to me that we see so much of this adolescent disdain these days, a mentality wherein to be cool, boys have to act as though they don't care what's happening. I remember the disdain act from my own youth, pretending that what I was doing wasn't really that big a deal. That's an interesting paradox when the point of risk-taking behavior is to test oneself, particularly in front of others.

I've also done a fair bit of work with men's groups, because after all, men are just former boys. Many men I've known and interviewed through the years confided that they weren't sure they were men, even though they were certainly adults. Most of my teen boys definitely felt they were not men—except, interestingly, for gang members, who were adamant and possessive about their masculinity. I wondered how so many successful and otherwise healthy men, including myself, could be so unsure about whether or not they were men. Why were gang youth so much more certain of their manhood than regular teens? Why were 90 percent of my clients fatherless boys, most of whom had moms who were trying very hard to raise their sons right?

All of these questions led me to think I needed to learn more about adolescence itself—not just the American version I was so wrapped up in but also how it was experienced in other times and in other cultures. I spoke to teens from other countries that I got to work with. I devoured all the men's movement literature I could find, trying to learn from former generations of teen boys. And I made my way through mythological stories, fairy tales, and anthropological and sociological models from throughout history and across the globe. That's when it all started to make sense.

I began to notice some interesting similarities among the diverse cultures I was researching. Most traditional societies, such as Native Americans, Australian Aborigines, Polynesians, Eskimos, and Africans, didn't have any juvenile halls, gangs, juvenile violence, or addiction problems. They never had to lock up their youth, try them as adults, or worry about their children being killed by other children.

What became clear to me was the fact that most of these older cultures had time-honored, tried-and-true practices for working with their teens. Even more interesting was that cultures who never knew of one another's existence had developed, over countless years of trial and error, essentially the same approaches. While the delivery often differed, the underlying dynamics were always the same. It was this universality, this common thread through multiple cultures, that really opened my eyes to looking at adolescents from a more archetypal perspective.

THE LOST ART OF INITIATION

The practices used by these diverse cultures were rites of passage, or initiations. They were designed to help guide the youth through the process of adolescence. These societies did not fight adolescent development but instead worked with it for the greatest positive growth. They used boys' propensity for risk and channeled that into an elaborate structure designed to help a youth expand his physical, intellectual, and emotional capabilities, transcend childhood, and follow a healthy path into adulthood—and, even more important, manhood. I had come full circle back to the concept of risk and growth.

Rites of passage were key for survival in our human history. Rites of passage helped ensure the growth of teens into healthy adults, and prepared each generation of adults to fulfill their role in keeping the community vibrant and growing. The adults in a village or community were very deliberate in their efforts to mold their adolescent boys into healthy men. All older cultures learned that if you leave adolescents to fend for themselves, they often take the wrong path. They need to be led through adolescence and put in a position that begins with a boy but requires a man for completion, thus encouraging the youth to grow up quickly yet solidly. Native cultures kept adolescence as short as possible, for it drove everyone crazy. Modern American adolescence is now the longest in history, with no end point and a steadily earlier starting point.

Modern society has all but eliminated these rites of passage. The ceremonies and rituals that cemented their impact on the youth of the past have been abandoned and discarded in our quest for a "civilized" lifestyle. Ironically, American teens now lead the rest of the world in dysfunction, including incarceration, drug and alcohol problems, violence to themselves and others, prevalence of gangs, teen pregnancy, and suicide—hardly a hallmark of "civilized" life.

While running a discussion group for fatherless, middle school-aged boys a few years ago, I was focusing on topics of men and manhood, fathers and the archetypal Father figure who provides and protects—a stereotype found in all cultures. We talked of initiations and rites of passage, how one got to be a man and what that might look like. One day, one of the thirteen-year-old boys, dressed in his usual all-black attire, suddenly spoke up excitedly. "What's up?" I asked.

"I got it!" he exclaimed. "I know what it takes to be a man!"

"What's that?" I asked curiously.

"Well," he said, "you gotta slay a dragon and rescue that there fair maiden." I nodded my understanding and approval.

"Dude," he continued, "there's only one real problem with that."

"And that is . . . ?" I asked.

"There ain't no dragons in Lake Tahoe in 1994."

It was a powerful moment for both of us. Not only did he understand what was at the heart of the stereotypic, mythologically flavored rite of passage, but he also recognized that in modern society it was impossible to experience it. He realized that although the demand for him to achieve manhood is still there, the path has been removed.

My intention in this book is to restore that path for our young men. For everyone living and working with teen boys, I will explain original models for working with adolescents and compare those to modern approaches. I will offer suggestions on how to use time-tested, universal techniques for helping our boys have an authentic experience of coming of age.

In the work I do, we speak of traditional and alternative approaches. What's interesting yet frustrating about this is that what we consider "traditional" approaches are barely a hundred years old. Many of us who work from alternative models are applying techniques and beliefs that are tens of thousands of years old. It is my contention that most adolescent problems could be prevented if we brought back a unified, community-based approach to helping teens through this great developmental period of life.

THE KIDS ARE *NOT* ALRIGHT

The Masai tribe of Africa is a proud, fierce people. Great warriors and cattle farmers, they are one of the most prosperous groups in Kenya and Tanzania. Their everyday greeting, their equivalent of our hello, translates to "And how are the children?" This is a conscious check-and-balance system they use to monitor the well-being of their society. They believe if they cannot respond with a positive answer, they must see to the needs of their children that are not being met.

I have taken to sharing this example with my audiences. Without fail, when I ask them "And how are our children?" they have unanimously answered "Not well."

I've been accused of having a distorted view of teens, allowing my experience with high-risk youth to cloud my vision of the overall picture of adolescence. To some degree this is true, I suppose, for most of the teens I work with are not mainstream, to say the least. But I see evidence that teens in every stratum of society are struggling. Columbine showed us that middle- to upper-class youth are at risk of violence. School performance continues to decline, even for many of the kids we think of as low risk. When 50 percent of all nineteen-year-olds move back into their parents' home at least once, that tells me that a lot of motivated, healthy kids are not making it in the adult world. When half the college freshmen in America have to take remedial reading or math, that confirms that it's not just "delinquent" teens who are being short-changed by our culture's misguided approach to adolescence.

My goal before I die is for no one to need my skills at fixing damaged and broken teens. That day, I have come to realize, will be when I ask how the children are and everyone answers back "Just fine!"

WHAT YOU'LL FIND IN THIS BOOK

Chapter 1 is a broad overview of the nature of adolescence and the issues that have characterized this developmental stage everywhere and in every time. In chapter 2 we trace the emergence of adolescent discontent in the twentieth century and take a look at how American teens are faring in a number of areas at the beginning of the twenty-first century. Chapter 3 discusses the disappearance in our culture of an authentic initiation process to support teen boys, and what that void has cost us as individuals and as a society.

Chapter 4 describes the process that traditional cultures developed for guiding their boys through adolescence into manhood. Chapter 5 introduces the Hero's Journey, a template of sorts for guiding and tracking a youth's progress on the journey from boyhood to adulthood. The challenges boys will face on that journey that are inherent to the culture and times we live in are examined in chapter 6.

Chapter 7 provides suggestions for dealing with the typical problem behaviors of teens using communication strategies and behavioral science approaches, while stressing the limitations to these models. Chapter 8 offers a series of transpersonal approaches for structuring meaningful initiation and rite-of-passage dynamics in modern society. With these practices we can prevent acting-out behavior, and get teens to respond in a positive way to us grown-ups.

Finally, chapter 9 offers a firsthand look at The Last Resort—one of the facilities for segregating and treating the boys who have the most extreme problems navigating the turbulent waters of adolescence. It is my hope that by focusing on providing solid guidance and genuine initiation experiences for adolescent boys, we will no longer have to send boys to such places.

1
Adolescence 101

What a man is . . . is far less important than what he is becoming.

CLARENCE KING

DEVELOPMENTAL ISSUES OF ADOLESCENT BOYS

Adolescence is a period of tremendous emotional and intellectual growth in our lives, second only to the period from birth to two years old. During this time a boy is shifting from dependency to independence, from childhood to adulthood, from irresponsibility to responsibility, and from boyhood to manhood. That's a lot to ask of such a short period of life. As adults who want to help our boys complete this transition successfully, we need to have a clear understanding of what all boys experience during this time. Whether we focus on teens in middle school, teens from the 1940s, or teens from Aboriginal Australia ten thousand years ago, we can identify fundamental concepts of what is normal for this developmental period.

It's amazing to me that with adolescence such a powerful and influencing dynamic in our lives, one that every adult human on earth has been through, we still treat it like an illness to be cured of. Many people in Western societies look at the modern stereotype of the teenage boy as the norm: irresponsible, unmotivated, and antagonistic toward the adults around him. But working with youths from more than one hundred countries, I have found that typical American teen behavior is the exception to the rule, rather than the global and historical norm. I have learned to look at modern teens from the perspective of a universal and archetypal model of adolescence, to determine what is truly "normal" for a teenager.

From that perspective, the developmental issues all boys work through during adolescence can be summed up this way:

- ▶ The Search for Identity
- ▶ Individuation and Leave-Taking
- ▶ Dealing with Paradox and Abstraction
- ▶ Egocentrism
- ▶ Idealism
- ▶ A Sense of Pride
- ▶ Puberty
- ▶ Sexuality
- ▶ Seeking Non-Ordinary States of Consciousness

In this chapter we will discuss the needs of teenage boys with regard to each of these developmental issues and examine the modern dilemmas and attitudes that work against, rather than with, those needs. And we will begin to contrast modern approaches with time-tested models for initiation that enabled generations of adolescent boys to make a strong and safe passage to adulthood.

THE SEARCH FOR IDENTITY

The search for identity is one of the major dynamics of this time of life. Since this process is quite familiar to most adults, I will focus on only a few significant aspects of what this journey looks like for our boys.

It's important to understand how much this natural process has been culturally distorted. As teens become more and more the driving force behind media and fashion, their personal and collective identities become obscured by the current trends. As David Oldfield explains, "In early adolescence, the development of identity is easily confused with the creation of a persona, or social mask one can use as a front to the world." A youth's identity may be obscured or hidden by the persona mask he or she wears.

With our cultural adolescent identity so confusing, teens have gravitated to smaller groups or cliques in which to find a place of belonging. One need only look at the stereotypic cliques common in high schools to see how many variations of adolescents there truly are. When I was in high school, we had about four cliques to choose from. Now, we've got jocks, preps, skaters, theater geeks, stoners, geeks, dweebs, gangbangers, shredders, band geeks, punks, SHARPS (Skin Heads Against Racial Prejudice), goths, losers, and loners topping the list of unofficial clubs to join. Many adolescents experiment with different identities by joining and quitting various "clubs" as they see fit. A youth may try being a prep for a while, then see how he is accepted by the skaters. Clothing and hairstyles shift as the teen tries to find a group that fits.

Many who work with adolescents would say this is not only common but also healthy behavior in the search for identity. From my perspective, though, having such arbitrary expectations to choose from is chaotic if not traumatic. Often, shifting from one clique to another is not as simple as just showing up. In essence, each clique has its own initiation. There are formal or informal expectations and requirements, and kids who do not fit in walk away even more confused, often with less self esteem as they continue to fail at fitting in. If there's one thing the recent teen shootings have taught us it is that no one likes to be on the outside. The Columbine High School tragedy in 1999, as well as others in Southern California, Oregon, and elsewhere, was a sad but poignant example of how one group of young men felt so alienated by other cliques that they felt compelled to harm them.

Adolescents will change their clothing, hairstyles, religious preferences, and social cliques in an attempt to find a place where they fit. Kids will wake up one day dressed all in black, listening to depressing music. A few weeks later they might sport green hair while seeing how a butterfly tattoo works for them. Will they fit into the jock club or the computer geeks? The preppies or the stoners? The skaters or the punks? As teens attempt to find out who they are and what they believe, change will probably be the only certain thing during this time.

In traditional cultures, identity was not something to be stumbled into but a gift to be given to young people. It was understood that teens need to be guided into their adult identities rather than left to "find themselves," as the common saying for adults goes. Initiations helped speed up the search for identity versus the modern model of waiting for teens to figure it out on their own.

What Does It Mean to Be Masculine?

> *I'm full of fire, full of anger, and full of hate.*
> *I'm haunted by the dreams that keep me up late.*
> *I'm full of love, full of happiness, and full of joy.*
> *But I still am confused if I'm a man or just a boy.*
>
> FROM THE POEM *My Native Warrior*
> BY MIKELA JONES, 18

The concept of masculinity in our culture has shifted dramatically over time. As we become less and less clear with each generation on what healthy masculinity is, it becomes hard to agree on what is expected of boys as they mature. Differences in just a couple of generations serve as testament to this.

For example, in the world of movies there have always been heroes for us to identify with. Typical movie heroes of the 1940s were Bogart, John Wayne, Cary Grant, and Clark Gable. They were strong and tough, but not necessarily the biggest and baddest guys around. They often portrayed fairly ordinary men; their personification of ideal masculinity arose from their confidence, their values, and their resolve. Contrast that with the profile of modern heroes like Arnold Schwarzenegger in the eighties and nineties and Vin Diesel and The Rock today. The current model of a hero is truly larger than life, often assisted by technological invention such as bionics, genetic manipulation, and/or some serious weaponry. This new breed of hero, unlike those of yesteryear, is an image unattainable by the common boy who doesn't have personal trainers and mega-million-dollar computer effects to enhance him.

The need for a men's movement, sexual abuse issues, emotionally displaced fathers, workaholics chasing the culturally approved dollar, and spousal abuse all reflect a decline in healthy cultural masculinity. Men are gaining stereotypic reputations in many areas, and few if any reflect a healthy shift. Mention the words *twelve-year-old girl* and *step-father* in the same sentence, and many people automatically think of sexual abuse. Books for women with titles like *Women Who Love Too Much* help create a negative stereotypic view of men in America. Robert Bly says, "The new equation, male equals bad, has given rise to a loss of identity for a whole generation of men." The masculine identity in America and other Western nations is confusing, nebulous, and arbitrary, and often seems politically incorrect in modern society.

Thus our adolescent boys are faced with a very confusing interpretation of what it takes to be a man.

A fear of the feminine is another factor in our unhealthy masculine identity. It's common for the feminine to be used to threaten masculinity, particularly among boys, young men, and uninitiated men. This is most commonly manifested in verbal disrespect, wherein a boy's performance is strongly connected to how masculine he is (or isn't). Almost every coach I had, regardless of the sport, seemed to translate any physical or mental error on the part of us boys as a lapse in masculinity. In their effort to make us tougher, any weakness or transgression was usually treated as a lapse into the feminine. Boys grow up being repeatedly called sissies, fags, pussies, queers, wimps, and a bunch of other names designed to make them act and be tougher, and the result is a negative association with anything feminine. Why, I wondered so often, was I called "a girl" rather than "clumsy" when I missed a ground ball?

This approach is and was common in other cultures as well, but with important differences. Most cultures taught their boys to be tough, preparing them for a life of hard work, danger, and difficult decisions.

But older cultures took time after the initiation to blend more empathic and compassionate dynamics into their youth to temper the full expression of the traditionally masculine traits. They helped their young men learn to embrace both their masculine and their feminine qualities—to be a whole person. For boys who are initiated in a healthy way, there seems not to be such a need to belittle someone else's performance.

In Native cultures, masculinity was not perceived to decline with age as it is in our current culture. In modern society the worth of a man is based largely on his job productivity; one of the first questions men ask of each other is what they do for work. Retirement at the end of a productive career essentially tells men they are through being productive, no longer the men they were. Traditional societies did not view elderhood as nonproductive leisure time, but rather as a time to give back to the community, to teach and mentor young people.

What Does It Mean to Be an Adult?

> *A son asking to know the sacred [archetypal] father is*
> *asking, "What is manhood, and what kind of man should*
> *I become?"*
>
> MICHAEL GURIAN, THE PRINCE AND THE KING

John Taylor Gatto, former New York City and State Teacher of the Year, observed, "The children I teach are indifferent to the adult world. This defies the experience of thousands of years. A close study of what big people were up to was always the most exciting occupation of youth, but nobody wants children to grow up these days, least of all children; and who can blame them? Toys are us." Gatto's play on Toys "R" Us reflects his belief that modern teens are largely irresponsible and drawn to frivolous distractions like younger children rather than toward adult or mature responsibility. When I see so many teens spending countless hours playing video and computer games rather than being more productive, I have to agree with him.

Unfortunately, our culture presents a wealth of reasons for our young people to feel only disdain for the adult world. Consider these messages I saw recently on T-shirts for sale at a popular store:

Shut up Brain! Or I'll Stab You with a Q-Tip

My state bird is the finger

I've upped my standards. UP YOURS!!

I'm immature, unorganized, lazy and loud, BUT I'M FUN!

DO NOT DISTURB I'm disturbed enough already.

Why even bother with marriage? Just find a woman who drives you nuts and buy her a house.

If at first you don't succeed, GIVE UP! No use being a DAMN FOOL!

Don't work too hard.

He who dies with the most toys wins.

I'd rather be golfing.

The worst day fishing is better than the best day at work.

Adults are inventing and marketing these dubious goods for our kids, apparently to make light of their "normal" negative behavior. When our products and our advertising relentlessly send the message that being an adult is a joke, is it any wonder our children will think twice about joining our club?

The Music Connection

As anyone who spends time around adolescents will know, modern teens search for who they are in music. Until the 1950s or so, music was not written specifically for teens. Music, as well as clothing and other trendy products, was designed for grown-ups, and the teens did their best to make it their own. It has actually been quite a short time in the scope of the world that music has been written for youth and targeted toward them as consumers.

Since adolescents are caught up in concrete, black-and-white thinking and often overwhelmed by struggles with identity, lack of control in their lives, and so on, the lyrics they spout so freely fill in a necessary communication gap for them. Similar to using various photos to create a collage, teens use other people's words to speak for them. They use song lyrics to express what they think and feel, as often they are unable to synthesize and express it so well themselves.

Because so much contemporary music is intended for adolescents, many adolescent dynamics are played out in their lyrics and overall sound. Starting in the 1960s, adolescent feelings of frustration, rebellion, and anger began to permeate the music industry. As adolescents feel more and more isolated from society, as each new generation feels more in limbo, their music has reflected this and seems to be heading toward some sort of critical mass.

I think our culture and the media in particular are interpreting the meaning of this trend backwards. While it is arguable that kids are influenced by angry, violent music, I believe the music is more a symptom of their cultural struggles than it is the cause of those problems. If the music did not reflect how they feel, it would not have such an impact on them. Gangsta rap and other violent and negative genres of music do not create the animosity in adolescents; they represent the cultural rage our teens are feeling more and more each year. It's interesting that the majority of gangsta rap consumers are white middle-class boys.

One of the tools I regularly use to gain insight into the boys I work with is to discuss lyrics with them. I learned the value of this approach when one of my favorite thirteen-year-olds kept badgering me to listen to his Metallica tape. I kept refusing, telling him I had heard and didn't like Metallica. One day he brought me the cassette cover with each song's lyrics. He told me to read the words to such and such song, and then talk to him. Even as I read the lyrics, I knew they spoke volumes about this particular boy. Our conversation after that opened up to a level not previously reached. Now, I ask boys to bring me the lyrics that "speak for them," and they never fail to paint me a picture of how they feel.

A Country in Its Own Adolescence

Searching for an identity as a future adult is that much harder for American teens, because America itself is an adolescent country in many aspects. Being the newest, youngest nation, we have often acted like adolescents in disregarding our European parents (elders) as we continue to strut around the world telling everyone the way things should be. We reflect typical adolescent idealistic and magical thinking with regard to our own environmental problems, homeless and hunger problems, racial inequities, depleting natural resources, overpopulation, and so on. Thomas Hine, author of *The Rise and Fall of the American Teenager,* puts it like this: "Ours is a culture that is perpetually adolescent: always becoming but never mature."

The identity issues of our teenage boys are enmeshed within the dynamics of multiple generations of uninitiated men. "Finding yourself" has become a buzzword in our culture, and has given many adults permission to act immaturely under the guise of pursuing personal growth. Generation X and now Generation Y or the Echo Boomers, often labeled as directionless, are searching hard for identity in a culture uncertain of its own identity. As the lines between the generations become less clear, and men continue to have identity problems within our culture as a whole, male youth will obviously find the path to healthy masculinity unmarked and uncertain. As Hine declares, "Being a teenager isn't an identity but a predicament most people live through."

INDIVIDUATION AND LEAVE-TAKING

Individuation is the process of becoming an individual, of conceptually separating yourself from your parents. This is getting more difficult for youth who don't know their fathers and don't have a sense of their ethnic or cultural heritage. It is hard to know who you are when you don't know where you come from.

A related aspect of adolescence is that it is the beginning of "leave-taking" from the home and family. Kids and parents are getting their first glimmer that junior will one day be leaving. Teens start to expand their distance and time away from home, while parents normally try to keep them close and safe. Of course, whereas the idea of leaving tantalizes the youth, it terrifies the parents.

America now has the longest period of adolescence of any country. This is in direct contradiction to the wisdom of hundreds of cultures over thousands of years—which held that adolescence works best if kept as short as possible. Historically, one of the primary indicators of adulthood for boys was moving out of their parents' place. But our extended adolescence only makes the normal act of leaving more difficult now than it was ever intended to be, as a boy has to wait so long and the parents and other adults have to put up with the youth's frustration. Looking back, I have to admit that my own unconscious behavior set me up to get kicked out of my parents' house. I couldn't find an acceptable way to get free, so I misbehaved until my father made the decision for me.

For a growing number of young adults, adolescence seems to be continuing indefinitely. In early 2002 *Newsweek* ran an article on the rise of "adultolescents," those young people now in their twenties and even their thirties who have found it difficult to leave the family home.

PARADOX AND ABSTRACTING

I think, therefore I am.

RENÉ DESCARTES

Western thinking is steeped in logic, rational thinking, the need to quantify anything for it to exist or be true, and the desire to control all aspects of our lives. Though this trait certainly has advantages in certain fields, it stumbles when it collides with the uncertain world of paradox. Paradox describes something that seems impossible, yet is clearly evident. Adolescence is full of paradox, which is one of the reasons the split between teens and adults in this culture is widening. Paradox creates tension in a logical, "prove it" adult society. The paradoxes of adolescence are difficult for them and trying for us, to say the least.

To deal with paradox requires abstract thinking. Abstracting is the ability to think in terms that are not concrete, not just black or white, yes or no. Ironically, this ability to understand and deal with abstract concepts generally is just beginning to develop during adolescence.

Adolescents are often confusing and frustrating, even on a good day. One reason for this is that they are caught up in their own paradoxes without realizing it. For example, while they will seldom, if ever, ask for structure and boundaries, they usually do want them. In fact, they have to have them in order to test and rebel against them. If parents give their kids too much freedom, the kids flounder because they have nothing to come up against. Here are two analogies that illustrate this point.

In order to sharpen a knife, you have to hone it against something of equal or harder substance. If we want to "sharpen" our kids, then we have to provide some resistance for them to push against. If we don't, they'll never know how "sharp" they can be. Thus, parents who always say yes give their teens no opportunity to test themselves.

We can also look at boundaries and structure as a boxing ring of, say, fifteen feet square. Our job is to set the ropes or boundaries, and the adolescent's job is to push up against them and see how firm they really are. If you don't let your teenager test your values, ethics, and beliefs, then how is he supposed to decide if those values are as real as you say, and if they work for him personally?

A familiar adolescent paradox is the fact that although they want to be independent and unique, they often act and dress alike. While consciously they want to be different, unconsciously they want and need to belong and be accepted, which forces them into some levels of conformity, at least among themselves. Just because adults no longer subscribe to the community model doesn't mean that teens don't want to. I firmly believe that teens have replaced the old concept of community with their peer groups, which fill an archetypal need for belonging. If we wait too long to invite them into our club, they'll look elsewhere for membership.

Another interesting paradox is that although there is an unspoken "us against the adults" bonding and camaraderie among teens, they create many of their own problems by the pressure they put on each other. Teens often unite to deal with adults and authority, yet as often as not, they divide themselves by cliques and fragment their efforts.

One of the paradoxes or dilemmas we adults put adolescents through has to do with confusing messages they get from us regarding whether we want them to act like children or adults. I call this the yo-yo effect, and it is further complicated by extending the period of adolescence. Often boys complain that while older people frequently exhort them to act like a man or an adult, just as often they are relegated to childhood again when the adults do not want them to expand too far. Parents, concerned and afraid their children are growing up too fast, will attempt to curtail this shift by imposing curfews, dating rules, and other limits. The resulting confusion often manifests in anger and frustration from the teen, who can't ever seem to figure out who he is supposed to be. This dynamic is particularly difficult and damaging in single-parent homes. On the one hand, the youth will be expected to act as the man of the house, but on the other, he almost certainly never gets all the rewards associated with that role.

Let me give you a metaphor for this dance we do with adolescents, and remember, it takes two to tango. Imagine you are on one baseball team and your teen is on your opponent's team. You are the pitcher for your team and your son is a runner on first base for the opposition. Your job, which you are good at, is to keep that runner from stealing second base. You have a variety of techniques and tricks to help you do this. You might try to pick that runner off first base, step off the pitcher's mound to change your timing, or set up a pitchout with the catcher to catch the runner in the process of stealing.

Now change the positions in your mind. Imagine you are a teen on first base; what is your goal? To steal second base, of course, and like the opposing pitcher, you have a number of tricks to help you be successful. Adolescence is like this analogy. This mind-set also helps keep your testing procedures in your ballpark, so to speak, rather than out in public. You can try not to play the game, but you'll probably end up getting called in when your teen acts out elsewhere. As I described above, if you win, he loses. If he wins, you lose. Thus, this is about balance. Because the game really only ends when adolescence ends, here's another reason older cultures kept adolescence to a minimum.

Michael Gurian explains the difference between a boy in an older culture compared to a modern teen: "This adolescent knew the boundaries going in, and he did what adolescents do: he challenged them. He suffered for challenging them but was not shamed for challenging them." We too often shame our teens when they test us, but the testing is part of the process. The challenge, and the healthy reframe to rebellious adolescents, is to understand that this is a game of sorts, with two sides and two roles. As David Oldfield has pointed out, adolescence is a "necessary crisis" to go through. This is another reason why overprotecting our adolescents as a group is backfiring.

The best adolescent workers I have seen learned this early on. And once you see how adolescent resistance is a game, and a necessary one to play, it helps you to not be so reactive to or frustrated with the testing behavior. Every time I say no to a teenager or set some other boundary, I fully expect him to test it somehow. That is the game, and by expecting it, the frustration and stress level I normally experience are diminished.

EGOCENTRISM

I've mentioned before that teens are egocentric. As they did when they were toddlers and preschoolers, teens believe the universe revolves around them. Everything that happens, such as Dad's new job or a move to a new town, initially gets run through a "What does this mean to me?" filter.

Being egocentric often means teenagers will have little empathy for others. This is a long and tedious time for most parents. The best cure for egocentrism, although not an easy one, is to try and set up your teenager to experience or feel what others are feeling. For example, if your son is always leaving dirty dishes in the sink despite your frequent reminders to put them in the dishwasher or wash them himself, try leaving his dirty dishes on his bed or on the chair he sits in when he uses his computer.

IDEALISM

*I don't want things to be they way they used to be, I just
want them to be the way they're supposed to be.*

GEORGE WASHINGTON HAYDUKE,
CHARACTER IN EDWARD ABBEY'S
THE MONKEY WRENCH GANG

I believe that adults too often misread adolescent disgruntlement with
the way of the world as being a negative point of view. On the one
hand, that may be true, but there is another way to look at it. Having
just awakened to the concept of thinking for themselves, they now see
the world with new, idealistic eyes. Robert Bly tells us that a boy entering adolescence "tests his 'I' now to see how strong it is: he may decide
to stay up for three nights, or to drink only water for a week. Thinking
becomes a joy; he invents great systems that put in place all civilization
since the beginning of time; he invents a new theory every day." Bly
adds that, searching or hoping for a perfect world, "He has given up on
his parents; he still wants society to be perfect: so he becomes a rebel."
This idealism, which many of us adults also suffer from, gives teens a
powerful sense of the way the world should be. Is it any wonder that
they are indeed negative and judgmental when they see how the world
actually works?

It's as though teens wake up one day with a blank canvas in front
of them. Their experience in life has largely been dictated by being told
what is right and wrong from parents, teachers, relatives, and other
adults. Now they have to see if this is true for themselves. The easi-
est way to fill in, or paint, this new blank canvas is with the way they
believe the world "should" be. It makes perfect, black-and-white sense,
and their logic is difficult to fault.

Perhaps the best example of this idealism was the '60s revolution
against the Vietnam War and the "establishment." Youth woke up to see
death and dying, political corruption, and police brutality in the world's
freest nation. They envisioned a different, better way: People should love
one another, open their minds and consciousness to other possibilities

and paradigms. The world would be a nicer place if everyone painted flowers on himself or herself instead of carrying clubs and guns.

The problem, of course, is that the world we all live in is certainly not simple, nor is it black or white. Much of life takes place in the gray, murky areas. Because kids in their early teens are usually still stuck in concrete, black-or-white, either/or thinking, this is where the clash takes place. "That's not fair!" becomes the standard reply to a reality that does not fit their idealistic expectations. Many parents compound this already confusing situation by making teens feel guilty for having or expressing these feelings. The challenge is to actually help them see the complexity of the world, and not to instill guilt, shame, or blame when they miss the mark. Guilt coupled with an already idealistic feeling will further alienate your teens—they will remain resolutely attached to their version of reality because it feels better.

Many of the youths I've known claim to be anarchists. The concept of no rules appeals strongly to their new idealistic view of the world. Everyone should be able to do what he or she wants. However, like communism, anarchy looks good on paper but fails when put to the human test. Every culture known has followed some set of rules and societal norms, for without them you get chaos.

Anarchy fails most dramatically when its members are egocentric teens, who view everything in the world from a perspective of how it affects them personally. Many teens feel it is all right to steal or follow all their other hedonistic impulses. But when they are the recipients of such behavior, they are outraged.

A SENSE OF PRIDE

This turf is small, but it's all we got!

WEST SIDE STORY

Pride is not just a teen issue. All humans need to have something to be proud of. But for teens, who worry constantly about how they look, how they are perceived, and how they are accepted or not accepted by their peers, having a strong source of pride is especially important. Teens need to feel needed; they need to feel valued for what they can contribute. They need to experience a sense of their competency.

Some of the best counselors, teachers, and, of course, parents have learned to help their teen boy find something he can have pride in. A club, a sports team, a hobby—anything that can fill that void in a healthy way will do.

A few years ago I was giving a presentation at the Association of Transpersonal Psychology's annual conference. On the agenda was a teen theatrical group I knew I'd just have to check out. They were from a small town in northern California. One night, the local high school drama teacher had seen a bunch of teens "hanging out" on the street. Rather than be fearful or judge them, he invited them into the school theater to get warm. After a little resistance, they agreed that it would be all right to just sit and get warm. The teacher told them they were free to use the stage or props if the mood struck them, and went about his business.

Soon, he noticed they were making up impromptu skits that were quite good and intense. With no script to follow, they slipped into the subject they knew best: their families. The kids began doing skits on their drunken fathers, bad living situations, and anything else that came to them. The teacher was so impressed that he offered to help. By the time I saw them, they were touring nationally, putting on skits and teaching creative impromptu exercises to improve communication. All this came about because one man saw a potential for trouble, and offered a solution without judgment or blame. With a little encouragement and mentoring, the young people rose to the occasion, as I have so often found them capable of doing.

If people need to be proud of something, and they have trouble finding that something in their habitual surroundings, they will understandably search elsewhere for it. This is one of the driving forces behind joining gangs: to have pride in something. Gangs are notorious for not only having pride but also backing it up. After all, as the thinking goes, what good is pride if anyone can easily take it from you? The vast majority of gang kids I have known have told me they joined a gang for the feeling of family. One boy in a gang once told me, after I had asked, that he was in his gang because of the safety he felt, which is ironic when you consider how violent many gangs are. He said, "My homeboys, they'd step in front of a bullet for me. My old man certainly wouldn't." The question of belonging and having something to have pride in was simple for him, as with so many other kids in gangs. If you can't get it at home, get it elsewhere. Not every disgruntled teen will join a gang, but he might join another dubious clique or peer group for the same reasons.

PUBERTY

Puberty is the term for the biological and physiological changes that occur in adolescence and can continue for many years. Boys grow larger muscles, longer bones, and hair under their arms and on their groin, as well as on their face and possibly the rest of their body. Their voices deepen, and we wonder where our cute little boys suddenly disappeared to. Girls, too, grow taller and stronger. They develop breasts, also grow more body hair, and begin their menstrual cycle.

These changes are exciting for our teens but also confusing and sometimes humiliating. They also put our children in danger of engaging in relationships that they aren't emotionally ready for, having children of their own far too soon, and contracting sexually transmitted diseases.

Although many preteens crave adolescence and bigger, better bodies, it is very common for these radical changes to be difficult for the youths to integrate. Boys become embarrassed at being so tall and gangly, or having their voice squeak and break in the transition from childhood to adulthood. Peer pressure takes its toll, with some fourteen-year-olds needing to shave and some seventeen-year-olds wishing they could. The physical, hormonal changes come in shifts or cycles, and can drive everyone mad. I remember waiting impatiently for my body hair to grow while in junior high, and then when I finally had two little hairs in my pubic area and about three under my arms, I was suddenly the target of relentless humiliation.

Girls become more sexually identified as their bodies mature. Suddenly, those long awaited breasts seem to bring only embarrassment and become a target for curious boys' desires. Too big, too small, too soon, or too late, puberty is difficult for even well-adjusted teens. In an image-based culture, these changes radically impact how a young person looks at himself or herself.

But even the rules for puberty are changing. Whereas the average age worldwide for a girl to start her menstrual cycle is about fourteen, the average in America now is about 11.8 years. My friend's nine-year-old daughter already has breasts enough to warrant a bra. An eight-year-old at my daughter's gymnastics class has already started developing breasts. I had a twelve-year-old client a number of years ago who had already had two abortions.

The problem with this for girls is that the physical changes that have historically corresponded with their mental and emotional growth are now outpacing that growth. Quite simply, girls are starting their menstrual cycles earlier than they have been programmed to for millennia, and the brain is not keeping up with the body. Girls who are still playing dolls and dress-up have no frame of reference for these adult changes.

Boys, too, are entering puberty earlier than previously. In 1850 most boys began puberty at about sixteen; nowadays, our boys are beginning the process closer to twelve.* As Robert Bly explains, early puberty "stirs up the sexuality before the psyche has been properly prepared."

A related development is the emergence of tweens, or tweeners, a term that is being used more and more frequently by those who work with youths. These are the eight- to eleven-year-olds, give or take, who see the power and influence teens have and want to emulate that. Tweens are often seen with the expensive hip-hop type of clothing, usually with a set of CD headphones on, sporting an expensive skateboard or cool scooter. They are too "old" and advanced for typical childhood desires, and are growing up much too fast.

The splitting of tweens from childhood results in an even longer

---

* *Raising Cain: Protecting the Emotional Life of Boys,* by Kindlon and Thompson.

extension of adolescence in our culture. With no end criteria to mark the passing of adolescence, which is what rites of passage did, and a dropping entry age into the adolescent club, the process of adolescence in America can now run from age eight or nine until the early twenties or even beyond.

SEXUALITY

If there's one thing that really scares parents, it's the thought of their formerly cute little children having sex too early. It helps, I have found, to take the long view or perspective about teens and sex.

First, we have to realize that we humans are the products of countless generations. Depending on whether you believe in evolution or creationism, we've experienced thousands or even possibly millions of years of experiences and biological and cultural programming. Sexual practices and attitudes have evolved throughout history, often changing drastically in just a generation or two. Just look at the difference between the Victorian period and the flapper era. Remember how strict we were in the '40s and '50s, not even showing married couples in the same bed in movies? Compare that to "free love" in the '60s and casual sex in the '70s. Nowadays, R-rated movies continually push the envelope with regard to what kind of sexual relationships society will sanction and how explicitly they can be portrayed onscreen.

Thus, teens at this point in history are dealing with a version of sexual morality that dates back to a time when the risks involved in being sexually active were different from how they are now. Teens in the '60s and '70s enjoyed great sexual freedom. The Pill was everywhere and easy to get, and AIDS had not manifested yet. Sexually transmitted diseases were mostly benign. The right to abortion had cleared some major legal hurdles, and the operation was readily available. Today, teens are confronted with the risk of contracting AIDS, HPV or human papilloma virus (which can lead to cervical cancer), and genital herpes, as well as dealing with the renewed vigor of the antiabortion movement. Never before did we have to worry about sex leading to death.

It is no coincidence that the average age for traditional initiations and rites of passage for boys is about fourteen, for that is the average age for the onset of puberty in boys. For thousands of years, young teens have been physically capable of sexual activity at that age, and participated in sex. Traditionally, this was through marriage, for in most older cultures young marriages were and still are common. Even in America in the late 1800s and into the early 1900s, it was not uncommon for the sixteen-year-old boy to marry the fourteen- or fifteen-year-old girl down the road.

What all this leads to is the frustrating fact that teens are *programmed* to engage in sexual activity. Just because we live in a period of history in which the rules have changed doesn't mean teens will lose that desire. Many people put their hope and effort into the abstinence model, hoping that teens will get on board with the idea of zero sex. I don't disagree with this approach in theory, but I haven't seen it to be at all effective thus far.

Along with the earlier menstrual starting point for girls, emotional and socioeconomic patterns contribute to the incidence of teen pregnancy. As Sharon Brown-Dror points out in *Crossroads: The Quest for Contemporary Rites of Passage,* ". . . impoverished and dysfunctional families are often unable to create and maintain [a healthy and supportive] environment. As a result, an adolescent girl, lacking the psychological tools, confidence, and motivation to give birth to herself, will tend to resolve the issue of identity by giving birth to a baby instead." Having a baby can be a very appealing direction for some girls to take in their search for identity. Girls coming out of troubled, chaotic, and often dysfunctional homes also have children because it gives them someone to love, and to be loved by. As teens struggle to break out of adult control, in the absence of effective initiation rites and guidelines and amid changing cultural values, having a baby can seem like the clearest path to adulthood.

Boys, on the other hand, are taught from a very young age to pursue females, and much of their growing identity is based on their success or prowess with the opposite sex. In many cultures, a man's worth is based largely on his number of lovers and/or children. Marketing and advertising techniques have been teaching us guys for decades that if we wear the right clothes, drive the right cars, drink the right beer, we'll get the pretty babes. As a person with an undergraduate degree in journalism specializing in advertising and public relations, I was appalled and insulted by how, as a man, I was perceived to be so easily manipulated by such techniques. One of the basic Marketing 101 techniques I was taught is that "sex sells."

Let me be clear here. I don't want my own daughter engaging in early sex any more than other parents do. However, the more we understand why our teens are so driven toward sex, the better chance we have of diverting that energy. Having so much history driving them is only one reason. Another is extended adolescence, which makes teens wait an unbearably long time to play grown-up.

In our culture, most contemporary parents seem to believe that sex is appropriate, or at least expected, after age eighteen or so. However, kids in our culture are also often expected to go to college. Thus, we are asking kids programmed to have sex at about fourteen to sixteen years of age to wait until eighteen, or even better until after college at twenty-two or twenty-three. Quite simply, most won't wait.

One-third of all children born in America today are born to unwed mothers. That is a staggering statistic, and clearly must encompass children born to many young women who are neither delinquent nor dysfunctional. Just in my lifetime, society's attitude toward unwed mothers has changed dramatically. I remember when they were frowned upon, scorned, and hidden with obscure relatives; now it is more acceptable to be an unwed mother. Many high-profile adults such as actresses Susan Sarandon and Goldie Hawn have declined to marry the fathers of their children. Also, if you look at the teen pregnancy statistics, they are particularly high for certain cultures such as Latina girls. In their native culture a couple of thousand miles south, marrying and having children young is still appropriate even in this day and age. Unfortunately, when teens living in this country bear children, odds are the fathers will not be engaged in their children's lives, creating a generation of fatherless boys and placing an enormous parenting burden on single mothers. (To get the full effect of the single-parent dilemma, I can't recommend enough that you read David Blankenhorn's *Fatherless America*.)

A recent study revealed that about 85 percent of all sex portrayed on television is among unmarried adults. Recent hit shows like *The O.C.*, *Grey's Anatomy*, and scores more drive home the point that unmarried sex is great and, ironically, that married life is not sexy.

The first time I gave a teen a condom, I felt I was selling out morally and ethically. However, there were so many kids who simply were not going to resist sexual temptations, like the twelve-year-old mentioned previously who'd had two abortions already. I figured that protected sex was better than unprotected sex. Abstinence is like anarchy and communism in that it looks great on paper but seems to fail the human test. No religion or government has been able to stop people from having sex, and with the way we Americans use sex for everything from selling cars to selling TV shows, I don't see that happening in the near future.

NON-ORDINARY STATES OF CONSCIOUSNESS

Non-ordinary state of consciousness (NOSC) is a currently popular term for an altered state. It may seem surprising to include this topic as a developmental issue, but I believe it definitely falls into that category because it is so prevalent in the lives of teens. NOSCs seem to be found in every human culture. Every society seems to have some sort of inebriant—a beverage, mushroom, or plant that alters consciousness. It appears to be a universal human need to occasionally alter one's perception of the real world. In most cultures, NOSCs are associated with ceremonies and rituals invoking Spirit or the Divine. Because this use of NOSCs is monitored and occurs in a healthy and community-sanctioned context, most of these cultures have nowhere near the drug and alcohol problems we experience with both youths and adults in America.

In our quest to become modern and civilized, we have let go of many rituals and ceremonies that seem quaint nowadays. In doing so, we have taken away acceptable ways for our youths to get "high" and left them with only alternative, illegal ways. Teens readily see the contradiction behind legal alcohol and illegal everything else.

America produces the most legal (prescription) drugs of any country while also having the most drug- and alcohol-abuse problems. With approximately 6 percent of boys in America currently on Ritalin or some other behavior modification drugs, are we teaching them to abstain from chemicals or that drugs are acceptable and necessary in order to function?

In France, they are sending alcoholics and chemical addicts to Africa to experience Ibogaine, a local medicinal plant that has a good rate of success with those issues. It's interesting to me that they are using one drug to cure another drug's problems. Even in America, there remains a strong underground for this type of work with medicinal plants, which are not used just for partying but are also being provided by some very reputable psychologists and other healers who see the benefit of these age-old approaches. Many are risking their careers and freedom to help their patients through these time-honored means. Both young and old people use NOSCs in an effort to expand their wisdom and health.

Remember the effect of Prohibition? Not only did it not eliminate the use of alcohol in America, but it spawned the growth of bootlegging and gangs as well, only one of which went away when Prohibition was repealed. American adults preferred to break the law rather than give up their "escape."

Adolescents love escaping reality and experiencing different states of consciousness. Instead of trying to create an unenforceable "Just Say No" policy that kids laugh at, my suggestion is to give them healthy alternatives. If you don't, it's an even bet that they'll find unhealthy ones.

By "healthy alternatives" I mean guided imagery, visualization, hypnosis, and storytelling. These approaches give the youth an escape from everyday life, without creating hangovers or illegalities. Fasting cleanses the body and helps induce altered consciousness. Many older cultures wove together all of these components to create a healthy yet powerful experience.

CEREMONY AND RITUAL

Where ritual is absent, the young ones are restless or
violent, there are no real elders, and the grown-ups are
bewildered. The future is dim.

MALIDOMA SOMÉ

The need for ceremony and ritual among humans is universal. Without them, life is empty and meaningless. Ceremony and ritual invoke Spirit into everyday life, and are based on faith in the unprovable. With our predilection for the scientific, we have deemed ceremony and ritual outdated and old-fashioned. But Malidoma Somé, an African-born writer and lecturer on community rituals, points out that ceremonies and rituals are not supposed to make literal sense. They are a symbolic understanding and representation of dynamics going on in people's lives. They indicate a belief or faith in something not readily apparent at the time.

Someone once asked Joseph Campbell his definition of a mythology. He laughed, then said that it had been his experience that a mythology is usually what one person calls another's religion. Religion and mythology both function on a faith or belief system, as so little of either one is provable.

The illogical honoring of Spirit has been losing the battle to logic and rational thinking for decades. But that doesn't make the desire go away. Even the agnostics or atheists usually have some sort of personal ceremonies and rituals they perform, even though they may not recognize them as such. Many of us say grace at meals; others attend a yearly family reunion. Sports stars are notorious for being superstitious with their rituals for dressing, batting, scoring a touchdown, and so on.

Most of us observe some public rituals such as July 4th and Veterans Day, or private ones like the annual family reunion. What are these exercises and experiences supposed to do for us? These nebulous things called ceremonies and rituals, whether a traditional Latin Catholic mass or a Native American sweat lodge, represent our hopes and beliefs that we will get some assistance in this difficult thing called life. Just as athletes improve their ability to perform by visualizing success, we have to believe that we can wish and hope for things to be in our favor.

It's worth noting that most people in the world would have been pretty busy at survival and getting through everyday life. Thus, they seldom had time to waste on things that did not immediately and directly benefit them. Ceremonies and rituals became mainstays of organized societies because they had a tangible, measurable benefit for the community.

Through rituals and ceremonies we hope to manifest our intentions. You could say that these rites are our prayers. Larry Dossey, M.D., explained in an interview in the December 1994 edition of *The Sun* that he had noticed that those of his patients who prayed or had prayers said for them seemed to do better than those who didn't. After studying what research he could find on the value of prayer, he decided to literally "prescribe" prayer for his patients, for he felt that not to do so would be tantamount to withholding penicillin or other beneficial drugs. (Prayer is the verbalization of intention, and intention has a powerful way of influencing what we are able to achieve and to endure in our lives.)

In my years of working with youth and families, few words other than *religion* and *sex* have had such a fearsome impact on grown-ups as have *ritual* and *ceremony*. In a society that is sharply divided about whether religion has any place in its government, business, or school systems, is it any wonder that we have culturally decided that rituals and ceremonies are frivolous, superstitious, and vaguely connected with the occult? In our melting-pot country with no agreed-upon religion, we have seen a decline of ceremonial ways.

But I have found that teen boys love ceremony and ritual. Typically they are resistant or embarrassed at first, but I always see the longing for meaning and richness overcome their resistance. They often have ceremony and ritual built into their own worlds. Awhile back I was talking with six teen boys. We realized that each boy had a name for his bong (a water pipe for smoking marijuana), and a highly defined set of steps or rituals he went through in getting high.

Much of everyday life all around the world is difficult, and the ceremonies and rituals we have created for ourselves help give reason, value, and purpose to the everyday mundane parts. Teens, having been programmed for millennia to participate in rituals of initiation, are now going through withdrawal like many of us adults.

What's the Difference Between Ceremony and Ritual?

> If ritual is not frightening, it is only ceremony.
>
> MALIDOMA SOMÉ

Ceremony and ritual are so far removed from our culture and vocabulary that we really don't even know what they are and which is which. My interpretation of Malidoma Somé's quote above is that rituals don't need to be literally "frightening" so much as they need to be intense and powerful. For example, when I was a kid, the Catholic Sunday mass in Latin had me awed and a little frightened by its intensity and seriousness.

A *ritual* is a body of ceremonies or rites, commemorating a meaningful event or idea, that is held in a place of worship or public gathering place. A ritual is usually associated with a special day that is regularly honored. It is the focus, the anchor of the celebration or experience. In almost every culture, there are rituals for harvesttime, fertility, birth, death, and the changing of seasons. Rituals remind us of what is most essential and universal in life.

Ceremonies are the formal acts or sets of acts that are performed as prescribed by the rituals or customs. These are the smaller, individual components of the overall ritual. For example, every 4th of July, Americans celebrate Independence Day—a ritual commemorating the ideal of freedom. Ceremonies may include lighting fireworks, holding parades, displaying American flags everywhere, and making potato salad.

THE LABYRINTH OR THE MAZE?

To enlist. To slam the door impulsively on the past, to
shed everything down to my last bit of clothing, to break
the pattern of my life—that complex design I had been
weaving since birth with all its dark threads, its unex-
plainable symbols set against a conventional background
. . . I yearned to take giant military shears to it, snap!

JOHN KNOWLES, *A SEPARATE PEACE*

The above excerpt perfectly expresses the overwhelming adolescent drive
to shake off all remnants of childhood and discover who one can be.
Because this urge to overthrow childhood and embrace something new
and exciting can so easily lead teens into trouble, we adults need to be
looking out for them and stepping in when they need us to. But we also
need to understand that their urge toward growth will not be denied,
and we must know how to work with it rather than try to eradicate it.

Initiations and rites of passage were designed to channel these undeniable forces in teens, not neutralize them. Rather than forcing kids to
fit an adult concept of the process, older cultures built systems to fit the
clientele, and therefore ran into much less confrontation and resistance
than we currently have.

The difference between the traditional, ritual-based approach to the
developing adolescent and the modern approach is comparable to the difference between a maze and a labyrinth. A maze is built to be confusing
to the participant. Blind alleys and blocked paths confuse and confound
the traveler, making this journey difficult and frustrating. In figure 1.1, a
typical maze, it's clear how a person could wander through it indefinitely
without finding the center or even getting back outside.

Conversely, a labyrinth is a simple guided path allowing a clear
trail to the center and then back out again. Without the confusion
and frustration of a maze, a labyrinth offers a more subtle, internally
focused trip where one learns from the quietness within. (See fig. 1.2)
Note that after you enter from the bottom, you need merely to follow

Fig. 1.1. A typical maze

the path before you and it will lead you into the center and easily back out again.

The scenario adolescents face as they try to become adults in modern cultures is very much a maze that they are expected to get through on their own. The maze is what we create when we look at adolescence as "a phase to get through" and an impediment to productivity. The maze stirs anger and invites failure along the way, often leading the traveler nowhere at all. Getting stuck is common, which often results in quitting. For our youth, quitting the path is quitting the future.

The universal structures of initiations and rites of passage were built on the principle of the labyrinth: to create a clear and simple path to adulthood without all the negativity, difficulty, and arbitrariness of the

Fig. 1.2. A classic labyrinth

maze. This simple path was created by those who had walked it previously and who would also support and mentor those who followed. The guides were the elders who had completed the process themselves, giving back and passing on their knowledge. Sadly, elder mentors have become almost extinct in this day of forced retirement, moving to warmer climates, and the breakdown of extended families.

The labyrinth represents a trail followed by countless others before, marked carefully for future generations to follow, just as a hazy trail may be marked with rock cairns left by a previous traveler. These trails were monitored and maintained for all to use.

Today's teens meander down an unmarked trail, the rock-cairn aids dismantled and discarded. They plow ever forward, stumbling into the blocked passages and closed pathways of the maze, looking for signs or clues to the correct direction but not finding them. There are no clear criteria for them to follow or emulate, and they often become lost or take the wrong path.

Adolescence has an often negative image in modern society, but this has not always been the case. Historically, modern adolescent behavior as we have come to expect it was the exception rather than the rule. There's a reason so many independent and isolated communities throughout history and across the planet all developed a similar approach for helping their adolescents through this difficult coming-of-age period: it worked! Traditional, indigenous cultures did not have the luxury or resources for pursuing and embracing approaches that did not work. Being irresponsible and lazy is a luxury of modern teens only. The universality of these approaches worldwide and historically is an indication of how well they worked and the necessity of providing them.

We, the former travelers of adolescence, are bound by love, history, and experience to create clearer paths for our youth, to provide maps for them to follow, and to remodel our mazes into labyrinths. One of the great crimes in modern times has been to steal these practices from our youth, forcing them into the maze and taking away the responsibility and the rewards of walking the time-honored paths to adulthood. The second greatest crime has been in holding this irresponsibility and lack of guidance against them.

2
The State of the Adolescent Nation

Girl dancing: "Hey Johnnie, what are you rebelling
against?"
Johnnie (played by Marlon Brando): "What have you
got?"

THE WILD ONE (1953)

Since the second half of the twentieth century, the role of teenage children in their families and in society as a whole has become radically redefined, with unfortunate and unanticipated results. In the eighteen years that I have worked with adolescents, I've noticed that they are becoming increasingly disenchanted with the idea of growing up—of becoming like us. In earlier times, even through the first half of the twentieth century, teens looked up to adults and hoped to be like them some day. But modern teens are repulsed by the dysfunction they see in adult life. And because they enjoy many privileges that used to be reserved for grown-ups, the allure of living life in an adult role has diminished.

I believe about half of what all teens go through is always the same, no matter where they live or during what period in history. The other half is what they deal with at their particular place and time in the world. In the early twenty-first century, much of what our adolescents are experiencing is new not only to them, but to us adults as well. The cultural shifts they have been forced to navigate present an overwhelming array of obstacles on the path to a healthy adulthood.

If you ponder the staggering statistics later in the chapter, it will be apparent that not just the "bad boys" are in jeopardy. The amount of dysfunction and distress in overall adolescence is at its worst ever, yet many people seem to accept this breakdown of our youth as an acceptable and necessary cost for modern society.

WHAT THE HECK HAPPENED?

I'm depraved on account I'm deprived.

GANG MEMBER IN *WEST SIDE STORY* (1961)

Our culture has undergone a staggering amount of change in the past hundred years. In this century we went from seeing the occasional horse-less carriage to living in fear of depleting gasoline resources to feed all of our automobiles. We shifted from small-town, rural living to large-scale metropolitan life. Air travel went from being impossible to being commonplace. Divorced children lived then with the breadwinning fathers and now live almost exclusively with single mothers. Not surprisingly, the lives of teenagers have been transformed along the way.

One of the best ways I've found to help explain societal shifts and their impact on teens in the twentieth century is to use a twentieth-century tool: the media. I chose this approach because problems with adolescents were not being seriously documented in the literature or by educators. I believe that the way most of us learned that the rumblings of adolescent discontent were brewing was through novels and movies.

Some will argue that perhaps these media created the adolescent issues, raising the proverbial problem of the chicken or the egg. While I admit that it's possible that movies and books influenced the behavior of teenagers, the scenarios they depicted reflect my own personal experience since the '50s and fit with what little literature there was for us to review. For example, when you overlay the movies of the '50s with the comments of the few authors studying teen behavior in that decade, the correlation is clear. Thus, I will use landmark novels and movies to illustrate how the roles of real teenagers evolved in the last century.

The first juvenile court manifested in Illinois in 1899, a result of the already declining urban environment. Increasing urbanization fostered delinquency in poor areas of town, and the 1920s brought about the first look at gangs, which were like clubs. Early gangs had set meetings, perhaps had uniforms such as matching sweaters or coats, and even shared their hangouts with other gangs. In the mid-1940s, *The Amboy Dukes* was published, a fictional look at inner-city gangs. These gang members wore ties and sport coats, kept clubhouses, and often pooled resources. However, they also cut school, drank alcohol, and smoked pot, and slowly were drawn into more violent encounters with each other. The main character in the book is a decent boy who slowly comes unwound while his parents work double shifts at WWII factories, enjoying the prosperity of employment after the difficult Depression years.

In 1937 James Cagney and Humphrey Bogart appeared in *Dead End,* a classic "good-boy-gone-bad" story. Coming off Broadway and making their first screen appearance were the Dead End Kids, a group of teens bordering on delinquency. They were ill supervised, and seemed to have no functional parents around to monitor them. The boys idolized gangster Cagney, and although they were cute and funny, they had little respect for law, adults, or school. The Dead End Kids went through a few more incarnations through the years, eventually becoming the Bowery Boys.

America seemed enthralled at this new concept of delinquency, flocking to Dead End Kids movies into the 1950s, when the "boys" couldn't pass for boys anymore. In the original movie, one of the boys is pleading with the local priest, a lifelong best friend of gangster Cagney, with what has become a standard dynamic lament in teen culture: "It's not his fault, Father. He was just a kid who made a mistake and got sent to reform school. They made a criminal out of him . . ."

Society had already begun the "geographic cure" process of sending boys into reform schools and other types of incarceration. The movie reflects the reality of "reform" schools: the boys often come out worse than they went in. *Dead End* is almost seventy years old, yet it sadly reflects an ineffective approach that persists today. Many people look at juvenile detention facilities, reform schools, and the like as the graduate schools of delinquency.

Many people fondly remember the '50s as a time of prosperity, wholesome values, and post–World War II tranquillity. Large tract home developments sprung up, giving us kids instant neighborhoods to play in. The economic conditions allowed most families to live on Dad's single income, enabling moms to stay at home and raise their families. Movies remained clean, with married couples still sleeping in separate beds and the issues of sex still mostly left up to our imagination. By and large, music was still pretty wholesome, and though Elvis, Buddy Holly, and Chuck Berry had many parents worried, the content of their music was still fairly benign. Teenagers portrayed in sitcoms and movies were usually clean-cut, wholesome, and well adjusted. But a very different kind of teenager was about to come out of the shadows and cause a sensation.

In 1951, J. D. Salinger published *Catcher in the Rye*, making Holden Caulfield a household name. Holden was one of the first symbols of adolescent discontent to come forth in our post–World War bliss. His disdain for the "phoniness" of adults and his boredom with life were in sharp contrast to our ostensibly content society. It challenged much of what many adults believed to be true of their teenagers at the time. In 1957 an Australian shipment of the books was confiscated although it was a present from the U.S. ambassador. The power of *Catcher in the Rye* continues its impact on us fifty years later. It is still on the list of most challenged books of the twentieth century, and is still banned in some areas.

John Lennon's murderer, Mark Chapman, said he had just finished reading the book when he decided to kill Lennon, claiming that Lennon was only pretending to be the "catcher in the rye" whereas Chapman was the real one. John Hinckley Jr., who attempted to assassinate President Reagan, had a copy of the book on him when he was arrested. In 1999, another former Beatle, George Harrison, was attacked and his assailant was also carrying a copy of *Catcher in the Rye*. It seems clear to me that the book's message struck a deep, psychic chord in America.

The movie *The Wild One* with a young Marlon Brando came out in 1953. The film is about a group of young men who go on weekend motorcycle excursions. Although Brando and his cronies seem to be in their early twenties, and have steady weekday jobs, they are very adolescent in their delinquent behavior and antiauthoritarian attitudes. They intimidate the citizens of a sleepy town, ignore the police, and wear their anger and rebellion very openly. This movie is very difficult for me to watch, because Brando's role is almost sociopathic: he has no regard for anyone's feelings or property. It foreshadows what has since become a reality—teens hanging out on the street and frightening adults for fun, using their sheer numbers to intimidate grown-ups.

Around 1955, James Dean leapt into our lives with his brilliant, and tortured, portrayal of Cal in the film of Steinbeck's *East of Eden*, in which he wrestles with his emotionally distant father. Director Elia Kazan took advantage of Dean's difficult childhood and estranged relationship with his own father, who had also been distant, giving Dean little attention even when he became a celebrated success. Dean would think of his own childhood and work himself into an angry state of mind, and Kazan would start the cameras. Dean would get so lost in his role that he sometimes had to be pulled away physically.

In 1956, Dean filmed *Rebel Without a Cause,* which established him as the consummate teen rebel. His adolescent angst, his trouble getting his father to understand his feelings, and the growing separation of teens from grown-ups lead Dean's character, along with his cohorts in the movie, into a destructive mode. Good kids are heading into delinquent and dangerous behaviors. (If you remember the movie, you'll note the absence of teen culture from a marketing standpoint. In the mid-fifties, even James Dean still wore a coat and tie to school. One evening, after an argument with his father, Dean's character rips off his tie and turns up his now infamous collar. That was all he could do with the available adult clothing.)

Soon thereafter, Elvis showed up in his own movie about a disgruntled teen, *King Creole.* With a father who is essentially useless after his mother's death, Elvis's character must work not only after high school but also early in the morning before classes. Having flunked the previous year, he has the family on pins and needles wondering if he will graduate and have a "real life" or slide into delinquency. He doesn't seem to have many other options.

Early in the movie, Elvis's character, Danny, is preparing to attend his final day in high school. He remarks to his sister, "Boy, it sure don't feel like the last day of school. Everything's so quiet, just like any other day."

She asks, "What were you expecting, a twenty-one-gun salute?"

"Why not?" he responds. "I mean, at three o'clock it's all over. Don't that make it kind of special? Tomorrow they call my name and give me a piece of paper."

While cleaning up a barroom before school, he protects a young woman who is being hassled by a drunk, only to get to school late. His unrelenting teacher takes this as an affront to her authority and flunks him again. Even when Elvis explains the whole story of his mother's death, his father's depression and bankruptcy, and being forced to work both before and after school, the principal claims he's unable to help, and Elvis does indeed flunk. Not surprisingly, after that, his behavior starts to decline, and Elvis, like so many other young men, does not look to adults to help him anymore.

The growing alienation of teenagers was not just the subject of fiction, as I recently discovered in some rather obscure books on adolescence. It's difficult even to find the term *delinquent* early in the twentieth century, but as far back as 1925, German psychoanalyst August Aichhorn wrote in *Wayward Youth* that dissocial behavior in teens was caused mostly by repressed emotions, a typical Freudian view. What is significant to me is the fact that there were enough "dissocial" youth around at the time to merit a book.

Incidences of delinquency were relatively rare before the 1950s. In 1950, only 170 teens older than fifteen were arrested for serious crimes. Between 1950 and 1979, the serious-crimes rate for teens increased more than 11,000 percent!*

The Sibling Society, by Robert Bly.

In 1956 Paul Goodman first published *Growing Up Absurd*, commenting on the increasing numbers of "boys and young men disaffected from the dominant society." His basic premise was that youth were no longer interested in the traditional "social message." Next, Edgar Friedenberg published *The Vanishing Adolescent* in 1959, pointing out that "the adolescent becomes the favorite rebel without a cause—causeless because society seemingly asks so little of him, merely that he 'grow up,' finish school, and get on the payroll." He felt that adolescence as it had always been known was disappearing in modern society. Taking away teen responsibility, as I pointed out earlier, simply made many teens irresponsible.

Friedenberg followed up in 1963 with *Coming of Age in America: Growth and Acquiescence*. This book examined how schools were focusing more on controlling student autonomy and creating good citizens than on actual education. According to Friedenberg, "The 'teenage' market is big business. . . . The school is interested in keeping him off the streets and in its custody. Labor is interested in keeping him off [out of] the labor market. Business and industry are interested in seeing that his tastes become fads and in selling him specialized junk that a more mature taste would reject." In a particularly telling analogy, he remarked that "the 'adolescent society,' like that of other colonies . . . is a costly drain on the commonwealth and a vested interest of those members of the commonwealth who earn their living and their social role by exploiting it."

Whether you agree with Goodman and Friedenberg's explanations is less important than what they were trying to explain: the growing disdain of teens, the decline of teens' interest in school, their lack of trust that education will truly improve their lives, and the removal of youth from the daily ritual of work and responsibility. Fifty years ago they made these observations at a time when most people were still innocently enmeshed in *Donna Reed, Father Knows Best,* and *Leave It to Beaver.*

The year 1961 brought the spectacular movie version of *West Side Story,* an adaptation of *Romeo and Juliet* that placed the lovers in a modern setting, with a backdrop of racial inequalities, rival gangs, and street life. The movie was celebrated for its unique style that included the choreographed fighting of gang members. Clearly gang influence at the time was apparent and interesting enough to use as a background plot.

Throughout the movie, the delinquent boys refer to their prostitute sisters, addicted mothers, and drunk fathers. None of the street boys, neither the Anglo Jets nor the Puerto Rican Sharks, has any father figures around. One of the great quotes from the tough boys is that "juvenile delinquency is a social disease," a big concept for that period in history. Aware they are enmeshed in inner-city poverty, dysfunctional parenting, and apathy from "the system," the boys do what so many other boys have done in the twentieth century: form a gang for protection and connection.

Until the early '60s, adolescent discontent was a growing undercurrent. Once the Beatles hit America, teens never looked back. The tone of rock music shifted as the relatively mild Big Bopper and Buddy Holly gave way to a new group of musicians fueled by anger and drugs, including Jim Morrison and the Doors and Jimi Hendrix. Coupled with growing unrest about Vietnam and racial inequality, this essentially blew open the doors of rebellion. Hippies decided that adults were useless, and that anyone over thirty couldn't be trusted. Youth was encouraged to "make love, not war." We teens of the time were admonished to "tune in, turn on, and drop out!" Most of us know the rest.

Teens have been rebelling against adults for thousands of years as part of the adolescent process. This time, however, they crossed a line and did not come back. Since the emergence of the Flower Power generation in the early to mid-'60s, teens have had more decision-making authority, more marketing clout, and more unified resistance to adult agendas than any previous generation. Corporate America took advantage of this new market to create the goods and solidify the youth culture in which we are all submerged right now. A line in the movie *Almost Famous* puts it bluntly: "Adolescence is a marketing tool." Many of the teen crazes that currently irritate or scare adults, like gang-style clothing and music requiring a Parental Advisory, have not only been adopted by teens but also are created and manufactured specifically for adolescents. American industry and marketing has offered them rebellion on a platter. We'll see later how granting this unprecedented power and knowledge to youth runs counter to traditional rite-of-passage models.

THEM VERSUS US

Boys need to compete and to combat, they need to be field tested in the physical and interpersonal world. Our job is to help them navigate—not squash—this need.
    MICHAEL GURIAN, THE WONDER OF BOYS

Anyone who ever "hung out" as a teen will remember the unspoken rule of teens against adults. I've been fascinated by how teens who would normally have little to do with each other will band together, particularly in group homes or residential placements, to form a united front against the adults. For example, I've witnessed opposing gang members in placement quit fighting each other and agree to a new bond: gang members vs. grown-ups. I've seen the same thing among kids of opposing racial groups: they will often put aside their animosity until later to form a stronger union against the authority figures called adults. One of the developmental differences I've observed in teens in the world of addiction and chemical dependency is that whereas adult addicts need to *create* a network of support to function daily, teens have a "built-in" system of support. Kids who don't even know each other will cover for one another, lie out of principle, and protect each other against the bad guys: grown-ups.

The fact that our culture treats teens as an "other," a demographic group unto themselves, exacerbates our inability to communicate and resonate with them and reinforces their perception of adults as the enemy. The separate cultural identity foisted on teens, coupled with their intellectual tendency to see everything in very concrete, black-and-white terms, further widens the chasm between teens and adults.

SOBERING STATISTICS

Teens act as a mirror for society. They serve a valuable and critical role in any culture, for their idealism and passion tell us, often continually, what they perceive to be right and wrong, good and bad. I have come to value this input. I believe our role as grown-ups and parents is to listen with open minds to our teens, and to try to see what value their perspective offers us. We need to be thoughtful when we hear their pleas and decide which ones merit attention and which ones are just groundless complaints.

Since teens, especially boys, have a difficult time expressing in words how they feel, we also need to "listen" to their behavior. The violence in our schools and on the streets, the high incidence of drug and alcohol use, their declining success in schools, and other problematic teen behaviors tell us volumes about how they feel. Teens as a culture today are screaming out to us parents and adults that things are not right, that they are not healthy and safe, and that "the children are not well."

So let's take a look at what statistics can tell us about our teens' lives at this point in history. Like many people, I take statistics with a grain of salt. But my professional experience and observations lead me to believe that those I include here deserve our attention.

Teen Violence and Crime

> *White man turns the corner, finds himself within a*
> *   different world*
> *ghetto kid grabs his shoulder, throws him up against the*
> *   wall*
> *he says would you respect me if I didn't have this gun*
> *'cuz without it, I don't get it, and that's why I carry one.*
> FROM THE SONG "BOTH SIDES OF THE STORY"
> BY PHIL COLLINS

One of the points I make in trying to bring back initiation-type approaches for teens is that, paradoxically, while we let go of such approaches partly to protect our teens from getting hurt, the process has really backfired.

American teens have become the most violent on the planet. And the vast majority of the offenders as well as the victims of teen violence in America are boys.

- ► In 2002, one in twelve murders in the United States involved a juvenile offender.* The rate of fourteen-year-olds or younger who commit murder in the United States is five times higher than for the other twenty-five industrialized countries combined![†]
- ► Nearly one million adolescents between twelve and nineteen are victims of violent crimes each year. Teens are twice as likely to be assaulted as are twenty-year-olds.
- ► In 1993, boys aged fifteen to nineteen were more than six times as likely to be murdered as were girls the same age, and they were twenty times more likely to kill someone else.

Here's another statistic that I find disturbing: only 13 percent of juveniles who have violated probation go to juvenile court as a result.[‡] Another way to say this is that 87 percent of the time, they get their hands slapped, so to speak. I am not a fan of teen incarceration; however, I understand from a behavioral standpoint the futility of using threats that aren't backed up. If the threat of serious consequences for criminal behavior is going to have any preventive value, we have to follow through and make those consequences stick.

Depression and Suicide Among Teens

Martin Seligman, an expert on depression, contends that this disorder has increased tenfold over the past fifty years and that the average age of onset is now early adolescence, making what used to be an adult disorder into a childhood illness.

Juvenile Offenders and Victims: 2006 National Report, Office of Juvenile Justice and Delinquency Prevention.

†*Angry Young Men: How Parents, Teachers and Counselors Can Help "Bad Boys" Become Good Men,* by Aaron Kipnis.

‡*Juvenile Offenders and Victims: 1999 National Report,* Office of Juvenile Justice and Delinquency Prevention.

Suicide rates for teenagers have more than tripled since 1950. And most of those who take their own lives are boys. Boys account for 86 percent of suicides among older adolescents and 80 percent among younger teens.[*]

The Media

Having grown up in the 1950s and '60s, I admit to being addicted to TV, and I'd guess many of you reading this book are in the same boat. As someone who is old enough to remember the first color TV on the block, I've seen the huge growth in the influence that the media have on modern lives. Many people I talk to, including parents, lament the time their kids spend in front of the TV and/or playing video games. What's troubling to me is how hard it is for us parents to say no, fearing our children will be seriously deprived somehow if we disconnect them from their electronic entertainment. Of course, most of us know the opposite is actually true. Many teachers I know report that they can easily tell which children in their classes were not raised with a TV because they have a longer attention span, greater creativity, and better social skills. With this in mind, let's look at some facts about kids and television:[†]

- ► The average American household has its television on 6.7 hours each day.
- ► By the time the average American kid reaches age eighteen, he will have spent 22,000 hours watching television, double the time he will have spent in classroom instruction and more than any other activity except sleeping.
- ► Some 66 percent of American households have a TV set on while they are eating dinner.

---

[*]Dan Kindlon and Michael Thompson. 1999. *Raising Cain: Protecting the Emotional Life of Boys.*
[†]Statistics in this section were found in *A Fine Young Man: What Parents, Mentors and Educators Can Do to Shape Adolescent Boys into Exceptional Men,* by Michael Gurian.

- The average kid in America spends five or more hours a week seeing television commercials. By the time he is twenty-one, he will have seen *one million commercials.*
- By the age of sixteen, the average American kid will have seen 200,000 acts of violence on TV. Of these, 33,000 of those will have been acts of murder.
- By the time a kid graduates from high school, he will have spent more time watching TV than he spent in school.

The Changing Face of the Family

Life has always involved dealing with change. However, many social scientists agree that change nowadays is coming faster and faster, too fast for us as a society to properly integrate it. As we'll see in chapter 6, these changes have had a dramatic effect on the structure and dynamics of family life. For the moment, I'll just let the statistics speak for themselves.*

- In the early 1920s, the divorce rate was only about one-fourth of what it is now. Today, 50 percent of all marriages are remarriages for at least one person. Of these, about 60 percent will divorce again.
- In 1997, 72 percent of single divorced parents with custody were mothers.
- One-third of all kids born since 1980 will live in a stepfamily at one point.
- Single mothers endure a poverty rate three times as high as the national rate.
- More than half of divorced kids have never been inside their father's new home, and 42 percent have not seen their father in a year.

Drugs: Legal and Otherwise

Technology and our desire to live as long and healthy a life as possible have made America a pill-popping culture. The behavior we model for our kids is that drugs are a legitimate solution to many problems.

---

*These statistics appeared in *The Prodigal Father,* by Mark Bryan.

This trend takes a particularly ironic turn when it comes to the use of prescriptions like Ritalin for our kids. Some children undoubtedly have a genuine need for this medication, but many of us in the youth industry feel that medicating our children is reaching epidemic proportions. Consider the following statistics.

▶ The amount of Ritalin manufactured in the United States rose 500 percent in the second half of the 1990s.

▶ U.S. doctors write over 11 million Ritalin prescriptions a year, five times that of the rest of the world combined!

▶ About 5 percent of American boys are currently on Ritalin or another behavioral-control drug. If current growth rates continue, by 2010, 10 percent of all American students will be prescribed behavior-controlling drugs.*

Think about this: we put a boy on Ritalin for half a dozen years to help moderate his behavior, then when he becomes an adolescent we try desperately to teach him *not* to use drugs to moderate his behavior!

Mood-altering drugs are becoming big business. The question is, are all of these prescriptions necessary? How did kids with Attention Deficit Disorder (ADD) and Attention Deficit Hyperactivity Disorder (ADHD) manage in previous generations? Many in youth care think that we are creating much of the need for Ritalin and its counterparts with too much TV, video games, and other distractions that make kids hyper and/or diminish their attention span. My sense is that we are trying to medicate adolescence out of teens, that the process of adolescence takes more time and energy than many modern parents and others who deal with teenagers have.

Of course, teenagers also use illegal drugs and abuse legal ones. Between 1980 and 1996, deaths from drug overdose climbed by over 540 percent. This reflects the proliferation of designer drugs and abuse of legal drugs such as antidepressants. In 2001, in a government survey called The Monitoring the Future Study, 19.5 percent of eighth-graders,

---

*Aaron Kipnis's *Angry Young Men.*

37.2 percent of tenth-graders, and 41.4 percent of twelfth-graders reported use of an illicit drug in the past year.

HOW IT'S BEEN DONE ELSEWHERE

Older cultures did not have the kinds of adolescent problems we are now experiencing. However, since adolescence is a universal process, they did have to deal with typical adolescent dynamics and, frankly, they fared better than we do with all our technology and resources. Even in ancient times and primitive cultures, parents wrestled with their adolescents' moods, desires, and rebelliousness. I can imagine a young African boy hounding his father for his own spear, a Native American youth begging constantly to go on the next hunting trip, or a Polynesian boy demanding to have his own canoe.

Traditional cultures seemed to realize even better than we do that adolescence is a trying time, to say the least, for both the youth and the adults. One of the ways they minimized the stress of dealing with their blossoming teenagers was to confine adolescence to a short period of time. Rites of passage and initiations were created not only to foster a healthy transition from boyhood to manhood, but also to put a limit on the time required for the whole process to unfold, and to give it a definite end point. Promoting youth to adulthood quickly enabled our forebears to avoid years of head-butting with teens.

In most older cultures, parents needed to teach their children survival skills while they were young. With the onset of puberty and the beginning of adolescence, the adults realized the need to get their youths grown up and involved with the adults. Teenagers were deemed big and strong enough to do adult work, and they were able to have babies. Rather than make them wait for years to engage in adult behaviors like sex, the older cultures thought it wiser to prepare their teens for adult work and marriage sooner rather than later. Thus they allowed short periods for adolescence, not the number of years we now subject them to. They were given an initiation, and those who successfully completed the test were promoted into the general population.

Older societies seemed to have learned, by trial and error, that fighting the adolescent process was harder and more time consuming than working with the process. While the Western mind thinks it can control adolescence like it tries to control other phenomena, older cultures knew you could not control or fight the process. From my experience with adolescence I draw this analogy: It's like rafting a river. Once you get into it, there's really no stopping and certainly no going backward. Ironically, your only real semblance of control is to actually release control and go with the river. Older cultures acted like very experienced river guides; they knew the process was difficult and dangerous but had learned you can't fight the current. The more you work with it, the more actual control you have.

An example of this "go-with-the-flow" approach to adolescence can still be seen today in one African village. For generations, when the boys in this particular village start getting typically adolescent, which includes becoming independent, rebellious, and thinking they know it all, the adults have a fascinating way to deal with it. About a mile from the main village is a camp built especially for adolescents. As a boy starts demanding more control and autonomy in his life, the adults invite him to go live with his other adolescent friends for up to a year. Imagine, a whole village of teenagers! The deal includes the requirement that after one year, the youth must agree to come back into the community and act like an adult. Looking at a year of hanging out with his friends, the boy always says yes. But then something amazing happens.

When the boy gets to his new teen village, his first bachelor pad, everything seems like a big party. But very soon reality shows up. There are no adults to provide food when the boy gets hungry, or to build a fire when it gets cold, or to fix the roof when it rains. Almost instantly, the boys learn that to really be autonomous, they have to act like grown-ups. It usually doesn't take long—about three days—to see that they're probably better off in the main camp where there's food, girls, and other amenities.

Rather than fighting the normal drives of their boys, this society has learned to flow with them and let the reality of everyday life do the lecturing for them. If these African parents did what many of us do—lecture to their children about showing responsibility and how one day they will have to get their own food and their own firewood—then their kids would ignore them like many of ours do. One reason for this relates back to the developmental fact that adolescents are not very good at abstracting, and trying to imagine how their lives might be in the future is an abstract concept. Thus, these parents learned to put the kids in a concrete situation they could easily understand: reality. Certainly things may have gone wrong, accidents may have happened, but it was learned that withholding this process from youth actually backfired. While we may not like the "survival-of-the-fittest" concept, the ones in any culture or species who learn and grow are the ones who survive, and, just as importantly, thrive.

We are not set up in modern America to send our teens to such a camp, but the lesson and the message are important. The adults in that village realized that lectures are not the best way to relay information. Those of us who have read what behavioral science can tell us about teens understand the need for logical consequences, and logical consequences are just what the teens in the camp experience. The information the adults are trying to pass along is not some vague, abstract "you'll use this one day," but instead lessons in the here and now.

I believe it is crucial to bring this principle into practice with our young men. Where possible, allow your teen to experience situations in which he is responsible for the results of his own decisions: working part time outside of the home or managing his own money. One of the hard jobs we have to do with teens is to give them a little leeway and see if they move forward appropriately or slip up.

3
The Loss of Initiation

*When the roles of life are assumed by the improperly
initiated, chaos supervenes.*

JOSEPH CAMPBELL

Initiations and rites of passage have been the mainstays for transforming boys into men since we first became reasoning human beings. Essentially, every culture the world has known—some come and gone, others still thriving—realized the need to initiate its boys in a structured and timely manner.

Initiations were designed to help a boy stretch his thoughts, feelings, and beliefs. They helped determine who was ready and who was not ready to move up in community standing. The initiation created an opportunity for a young man to test himself, to learn what he really believed, and to prove to himself and his community that he was indeed ready to act as a man. A youth's overall maturity, regardless of his age or physical growth, was the factor that determined whether he was ready for such trials. As Malidoma Somé points out, "Anatomic maturation is insufficient for manhood or womanhood." In other words, just growing taller, or getting body hair, or being able to create babies does not get you there.

Initiations were structured challenges or tests. They might be physical tests, like enduring pain or long ordeals. To be fair to all participants, they were largely tests of mental fortitude and persistence. They were designed so most would succeed, not fail. A boy might do a vision quest, sitting alone in an isolated spot for three to five days, fasting and praying until his exhaustion led him to a vision of who he was meant to be. Many rites of passage involved bloodletting of some kind. There was a twofold reason for this. First, the boys had to get used to shedding and seeing blood. Life as a man involved physical danger and the boys needed to be tough when they were injured and not wince when they were hunting. Second, bloodletting practices mimicked the female process of the menstrual cycle and coming-of-age completion of childbirth. To a modern parent, these practices seem cruel and archaic, but there is much to be learned from their successful dynamics.

It was universally agreed that the process for moving boys through adolescence needed to engage everyone. Thus, initiations involved not only the boy but also his whole community—so the youth felt supported and confirmed in his transition from boy to adult. That universal concept of community is now seen as only a quaint old tradition. As Somé observes, "The first consequence of westernization has been to make initiation private. In the old days, initiation was a village matter that mobilized the energy of every person."

Ceremonies and rituals wove together all the aspects of initiations. They celebrated the challenges overcome and affirmed the growth and confidence of the successful initiates. They officially welcomed the initiates into the adult community. These celebrations included elaborate music and dance, handed down for generations. Initiates shared their experiences, made symbolic representations of their experiences, engaged in self-ornamentation, and immediately began acting like adults.

The village or community knew that young people initiated in a healthy way grow up to be healthy adults. As our Western culture became more civilized, more concerned with avoiding risks and prolonging life at any cost, we determined these initiation ceremonies to be pagan and foolish, not in keeping with the advanced model we were setting for ourselves, and dangerous to our boys.

The loss of initiation in Western culture, and increasingly in older, traditional societies, is having a devastating impact on our youth. In turn, as these uninitiated youth, particularly adolescent boys, grow into adults, the cost of not being properly initiated into men is expensive indeed. Though we modern Westerners may not think that any of these old practices have any value in our current society, I believe the declining emotional health of our boys, as well as of our men, is directly related to the decline of effective initiation practices.

This chapter deals with the effects of loss of initiation on our boys, how these issues impact our men, and how our culture is faring after having eliminated these processes from our way of life. The loss of initiation has had a far-reaching and multidimensional effect on all of us.

ADULTHOOD VERSUS MANHOOD

Hold on to 16 as long as you can,
Changes comin' round real soon
make us women and men.
JOHN MELLENCAMP, *JACK 'N' DIANE*

Initiations were designed to help create a healthy and successful transition for boys from adolescence into manhood. One of the underlying concepts to these practices is the understanding that there is a marked difference between becoming an adult and becoming a man. In Western society we tend to lump them together, which does not serve our boys well.

Becoming an adult is reasonably easy in our country. One need merely live long enough to gain the appropriate age-related reward or responsibility: getting a driver's license at sixteen, signing up for the draft or, in some states, drinking at eighteen, or getting the whole package dropped in your lap the day you turn twenty-one.

While it may seem harsh, I contend that this philosophy of "everyone succeeds" builds false self-esteem and conflicts with the reality of survival of the fittest. The recipients of these modern rewards and responsibilities "earn" them by merely collecting enough birthdays.

There is no trial, no test to show that a young person has the maturity and understanding to use his newfound privileges wisely. The driver's license test does challenge your memory of the manual you studied, and the driving test shows you have skills enough to control the vehicle. But nowhere in that process is a design for testing your responsibility or comprehension of the ramifications of getting behind the wheel. In a similar vein, many people have commented with regard to the declining health of families and parenting that, while we require training and passing a test to earn the privilege of driving a car, we don't have the same requirements for becoming parents. Initiations served as this training and testing process.

Becoming a man is a whole different game from becoming an adult, and if we don't acknowledge this as a society, we certainly recognize it privately. Of all the men and boys I have worked with, not one truly felt that getting a driver's license, being able to vote, being eligible to get drafted, or being allowed to drink alcohol made him a man. These milestones brought a measure of independence on the path to manhood, but they were not the criteria for manhood. More than one of these young men participated in risky ventures such as using drugs, driving fast, engaging in indiscriminate and unprotected sex, and fighting as possible initiations into manhood. In every case, though, there was confusion as to whether those activities made him a man.

Becoming a man requires a deep emotional and spiritual transition, an internal shift that cannot come from an arbitrary bestowing of legal rights. This self-transcendence is most likely to take place in the course of an extraordinary experience, often in a single, memorable moment in time. (I'll say more about this in chapter 4, Rites of Passage.) In our Western culture, we have lumped together age-related rewards and self-transcendence, mistakenly believing that one naturally leads to the other.

So what are the results of allowing arbitrary, age-based signposts of manhood to replace authentic initiatory practices? One is that we get a never-ending version of adolescence, for without any clear finish line, boys are really never sure when they make that transition or if they ever do. Another is that we are now seeing multiple generations of uninitiated men. It's similar to making a photocopy of a photocopy of a photocopy: each copy loses a little bit of clarity and quality from the one before it. Without a culturally accepted norm for the transition, how can anyone know if he has made it or not? If a boy, or an arbitrarily rewarded adult, is uncertain of his manhood, how can he know how to behave? Without an accepted picture of how and who they should be, many men tend to wander aimlessly down the path toward manhood. There is no closure, so the process persists.

The ramifications of this murky sense of adult identity can be serious for individual men as well as for society. Men who are uncertain of their manhood and their masculinity often manifest these feelings in a variety of negative behaviors, including spouse abuse, divorce, molestation, and addiction.

A DUBIOUS ROLE

When I was a child, I spake as a child, I understood as a child, I thought as a child: but when I became a man, I put away childish things.

1 CORINTHIANS 13:11

In essence, teens today are considered a drain on their families and their communities, rather than as contributors. But this is not the way it has always been. Historically, teens have had much more responsibility, as that was necessary for family and community survival.

In chapter 1 we discussed the importance for teens to feel that they belong and that they are needed. But our model of adolescence does not accommodate these needs. As Joan Lipsitz, educational program director of the Lilly Endowment, sees it, "We give youngsters few opportunities to feel competent at a time in their lives when they need to feel competent. When we tell them to act responsibly, do we only mean take out the garbage?" And Bill Kerewsky, editor of *The Early Adolescent Magazine,* writes:

We are the only civilization in history to have created a whole category of people (adolescents) for whom we have no real use. In
times not long gone by, fourteen-year-olds helped on the farm. They
assisted with the animals, cared for younger siblings, and helped get
the crops in before the frost. If they lived in the city, they got into
the shops and found jobs as apprentices, helpers, stock clerks, or
custodians. They had a role in society—and they understood that
hard work and responsible behavior were the keys to future success. They were in partnership with adult mentors.

Now, however, we have "protected" them out of jobs, and relegated young adolescents to the roles of pizza consumer and vid-
eotape junkie . . . Children this age need to be needed, but we have
institutionalized our rebuff to their pleas to be of service.

Taking away our teenagers' responsibility has simply made them
irresponsible. By effectively eliminating initiations and separating adolescents out from the general population, we have extended adolescence
into a process lasting much longer than it ought to. Rather than bringing teen boys into the fold of adulthood, we have made them a driving
consumer force, mostly of items adults find frivolous and childish. But
more importantly, encouraging the establishment of a private "youth
culture" has left our teenagers no desire or need to participate in our
adult culture.

This is one of the growing dynamics with adolescents I have watched
closely through the years. More and more each year, they seem less willing to simply buy into the adult world as they perceive it. Whereas for
thousands of years children and adolescents wanted to grow up and be
adults, nowadays they are seeing entry into the adult world as a dubious step. Scores of teens I have worked with have looked at our environmental problems, political corruption and scandals, economic trade
deficits, homelessness, racism, propensity for war, and the proliferation
of nuclear weapons and basically decided "Thanks, but no thanks!" It
seems clear that instituting the initiation process will not solve all of the
above problems, but I believe that if young people are brought into the

adult fold while they are still enthusiastic and curious, we could use that positive youth energy to work on these problems together.

ADOLESCENCE IS A PROCESS, NOT A PHASE

Children have more need of models than critics.

MILTON

If boys are not initiated as men during adolescence, how and when will that happen? I sense that our culture has allowed itself to slip into a false belief that these things will somehow work themselves out. Too often in adolescent work, we hear parents and other grown-ups remark that "it's a phase he's going through." There's a very dangerous assumption that many adolescent issues will simply go away one day, which reflects our Western propensity toward individualism. Quite the opposite approach evolved from the older, traditional societies.

It was apparent to our ancestors that these "phases" do not necessarily go away of their own accord. Many cultures from all over the planet came to the same realization that this process needed to be contained and managed, have a definite start and finish, and have an unmistakable end product—healthy and motivated adults to join the community. Trusting kids to figure it all out for themselves obviously did not work; successfully navigating the tumultuous waters of adolescence required help.

Societies that initiated their boys were attempting to address specific developmental issues that all boys needed to work through. For example, in most patriarchal cultures there is a frustration or anger between the son and the father. The father holds the "job" the boy wants and the boy competes for it, and that is a normal process and changing of the guard, so to speak. But with more and more fathers disappearing from their sons' lives, father longing is replacing father anger, and this changes the rules of the game. Father anger was fuel for the young boy to drive forward toward his potential and destiny. By not having fathers to healthily pursue and replace, as a prince replaces a king, boys do not strive so much to grow.

In a country with increasing numbers of uninitiated men, many men act like boys. With the adults acting like adolescents, the teens, observing this, have little desire to become adults. The result is the so-called Peter Pan syndrome—a generation of youths who don't want to grow up.

If boys are not initiated into men, what does that mean? Sadly, the obvious answer, as Robert Bly observes in *Sibling Society,* is that we have a society of uninitiated men, which creates a multitude of personal and cultural problems.

Multiple generations of uninitiated men have developed a deformed and diminished view of their own manhood and masculinity. As I have stated earlier, with no community-sanctioned or culturally accepted initiation into manhood, many former boys simply do not know if they are men or not. My experience has taught me that many uninitiated men have a tentative if not fragile grasp on their masculinity. This very often manifests in misguided attempts to instill manhood in their sons by teaching them to be homophobic, to treat women poorly, to be aggressive fighters, and so on. When healthy men anoint their boys into men, it strengthens the older men's feeling of masculinity, manhood, and the way things are supposed to be. Each generation needs to go through this process of receiving and then passing on the mantle of adulthood. But the path to manhood has become blurred and the criteria for becoming a man are based more on arbitrary ages than on maturity and capability.

A father's insecurity about his own manhood can have an impact on his ability to successfully initiate his son. It stands to reason that if a boy or man is unsure of his own masculinity, he finds it difficult to "let go" of it or pass it on. The feeling from such men at the critical anointing moment is that if they "give" their masculinity to their sons, they will be somehow diminished, have less than they had a moment before. It's hard to give away something you're not really sure you have.

Initiations were designed not only to help boys, but also to help adults move beyond their current roles and developmental stages. So it should be obvious that in addition to helping the boys move forward, this process also helped the adult men move through their own passages. As always in life and family, everything is interconnected.

The men's movement evolved as an attempt to explore and address how some of the above dynamics affect men in their relationships and everyday lives. In the mid-1990s I was involved in running men's groups, setting up male-only workshops and activities, and tying together the interrelated dynamic between boys who want to be men and men whose issues often stem from boyhood. During a conversation I had in 1995 with Keith Thompson, editor of *To Be a Man,* he posed this question: "Whatever became of the Men's Movement?" I quickly and defensively replied that it was alive and well, as the proliferation of men's groups and related books would attest. He responded that his sense was that the movement had stalled somehow, and he asked me to think some more about it.

Pondering that question ultimately led me to conclude that the men's movement had stalled at the emotional realm. While in 1995 there was an abundance of men's movement literature and activities, there has been very little new material in recent years. Having gotten the psychology down, which comes rather easily to reasoning and rational minds, men seemed collectively unable or unwilling to cross over into deep emotional work. That reluctance or resistance made me look more deeply at the stereotype of men being emotionally detached or removed, which does not seem to be the case in traditional cultures still initiating their males.

I wondered what happened to the "sensitive males" of the 1970s, exemplified by the Alan Aldas of the world. Many women have told me that the reason the sensitive male of the seventies did not endure was that although women were pleased that the men were more in touch with their softer and feminine sides, they missed the healthy warrior energy that makes a man a man. Women wanted a sensitive man, but one with power as well. Initiation allowed for a blending of the strong masculine traits with feminine attributes like empathy and intuition.

It became obvious to me that our culture is actually creating males, both boys and men, who are unable to express healthy emotions. It also occurred to me that this had to be connected to the high divorce rate, the growing incidence of sexual abuse and incest, and the alarming amount of domestic violence going on. For a two-month period, I followed the traumatic kidnappings of about half a dozen young girls in our country by obviously warped men. Tiny Lake Tahoe has had at least two young girls kidnapped and killed by men in recent years. It struck me that this had to be related to questions about healthy masculinity. The high incidence of such deviant behavior in our country underscores my belief that emotion and emotional trials are important in establishing one's ability to express feelings in a healthy and appropriate way.

Initiations helped boys learn how to think and feel more maturely. Once the initiation, which might have lasted only a few days, was over, the training would go on for years. Elders would teach initiates about important aspects of life not previously shared, such as relationships, marriage, procreation, parenting, religion, creation mythologies, and so on. Childhood training was about survival skills; post-initiation skills were more about feelings and interpersonal relationships within the community. Simply put, boys were being groomed to be feeling and healthy men. Sadly, our culture has been teaching men that their main job is to provide for their families financially, and that emotional responsibilities are of secondary importance.

ELDERS: THE MISSING LINK

They [elders] teach us that rites of passage impart a form
of self-understanding that is felt in the heart rather than
learned in the head. . . . In ancient cultures, people under-
stood that the wisdom of the heart is accessed by the
imagination; that imagination is the thought of the heart.
DAVID OLDFIELD

Traditional societies transmitted to the young not only lineage and survival information but also the beliefs and expectations of the culture. This system perpetuated the health, longevity, and survival of the community and its values. To do this, it was critical to have strong interconnection among three generations: grandfather, father, and son. The wisdom and legacy of the community was passed along through the elders.

Elders were the original television, the original textbooks, and the original radios. They were an integral piece of the initiation puzzle. And as valuable as the actual transferred information was to the initiation process, the feeling of being part of a community, the intimacy of sitting at Grandfather's knee, and the ambience and safety of sitting around a fire together were priceless.

In addition to benefiting the young people, this generational hierarchy helped clarify the role of the elders. As they aged and became less able to help with more day-to-day survival chores, their importance did not diminish, as is generally the case in modern Western society. Elders were still responsible for the training, nurturing, and molding of the young, particularly the adolescents.

Rather than seeing adolescence as a time when it was best to ignore their teens or give them a wide berth, elders arranged to provide the greatest level of interaction and personal training during these years. However, they actually kept their young people in the dark regarding nonessential skills. They knew not to give children all the information before they were ready for it, that holding some back created a hunger for knowledge—creating mystery creates curiosity. Elders used the curiosity and intensity of adolescence to entice teen boys into manhood and adulthood.

Robert Bly talks about how, rather than a generation gap—a split between the generations—we have a generation boundary problem. Teens are allowed too often to act like adults before they are ready. If they get the rewards of adulthood, the sex and booze and money, what will be their motivation to venture into the much harder world of adult responsibilities?

In a social system that included authentic initiation, it was important that children heard only what parents wanted them to hear. Television, the Internet, and movies have seriously altered how we relay information to our children. Unlike the traditional model of keeping youth in the dark about adult affairs until they were initiated, we now share everything with them. This period in history is often referred to as the Information Age, and we are inundating our kids with more information than they can process. This information overload diminishes their curiosity about adult life. Older cultures were wise to use curiosity as a leveraging tool to encourage teens' desire to become adults.

One of the continuing complaints from parents and adults about typical teenagers is that they act as if they know everything. My experience has been that in a world where global communication is the goal, where pornography is readily available to all ages on the Internet and television, where wars in all their blood and glory are depicted on the evening news during dinner, it's no wonder the kids nowadays feel they do indeed know it all. What haven't they seen?

Keeping kids in the dark until adolescence seemed to work for countless cultures across time and across the globe. When I was a young teen, I had to steal a *Playboy* to glimpse a naked female body. Now, all kids have to do is stay up and watch HBO or do an Internet search for porn. Young people who are exposed to adult themes and material have no frame of reference for what it all means. And, quite often, they are dismayed by what they view the state of the world to be. David Oldfield, in a personal correspondence, looked at it this way: ". . . it seems to me that taking the dreams away from the young is a particularly pernicious form of child abuse. . . . And we have done that so totally in this culture, it seems, almost surgically removing dreams for them."

The modern model of kids staying out of the way, men working away from the home, and elder men sitting around or removed to some remote paradise has created a devastating separation of the generations. I think our concept of retirement, particularly mandatory retirement, is almost criminal on some levels. Taking away older people's right to perform and contribute to society diminishes their feelings of worth. Even in retirement, we control how much extra money they can make, keeping them dependent on the system. Disregarding the inestimable and time-honored role they have played in helping create healthy adolescents and men, and banishing them to Ft. Lauderdale and Sun City, has been a sad and costly societal mistake. Is it any wonder that elderly men and teenage boys have the highest suicide rates in the country?

WHERE ARE THE FATHERS?

We no longer define fatherhood as the norm, but we struggle to salvage something called child support; we no longer count on marriage, but we strive to improve our procedures for divorce.

DAVID BLANKENHORN, *FATHERLESS AMERICA*

As a specialist in at-risk and high-risk adolescent boys, it struck me a number of years ago that about 90 percent of them were coming out of homes without fathers. It certainly made me rethink what the causes of their troubles might really be. Recurring generations of uninitiated men have altered the way our culture perceives fathering. Although there are a lot of theories on how the prevalence of fatherlessness started to manifest, I believe it can be traced to the major shift of our society from an agriculturally based lifestyle to an urban one. The Industrial Revolution pulled fathers away from families to work in the cities and factories, creating a dangerous precedent for Dad providing the money in one place and Mom doing the parenting in another.

Also, rather than father going out every day and returning at the end of the day with a bushel of corn, a deer, or a load of oats, modern fathers began bringing home this new thing called a paycheck. Rather than putting food on the table, literally, they now received an abstract payment for their services. Thus, dads necessarily became most interested in dollars.

What is clear is that the father presence has been declining for years. The stereotypical workaholic dad resides in the home but has little time or energy for his son. Our culture, focused on individual achievement and financial prosperity as criteria for success, has allowed the importance of fathers and creating healthy men to fall by the wayside. TV shows and standup comics talk about men's inability to commit to relationships. "Deadbeat dad" is now a common term everywhere in the country, with many communities posting photos of delinquent dads on milk cartons or in the newspaper. Think about the stereotype of a deadbeat dad: what we hold against him is *not* that he is absent from the home but that he has not provided enough money.

A 40 to 50 percent divorce rate, unprecedented anywhere else in history, has created a cultural norm in which a large proportion of fathers do not stay in the household. And our social programs actually create and support some of those splits: Think about the cultural message that is sent out to single mothers who are supported by government welfare funds and penalized financially for having a man in the house. That policy, along with the long-standing practice of awarding the vast majority of custody cases to mothers, has confirmed to the men that they are not needed in the home and that it is all right for them to be elsewhere. Ironically, in Western society, up until the early part of the twentieth century, custody of children in divorce cases nearly always went to the fathers, largely because women were not allowed to work and children were seen as the "property"of their fathers.

Settling on a better version of divorce, creating more Boys and Girls Clubs, or changing legislation to get better financial support from estranged fathers addresses only the symptoms of the problem. Putting our energy, resources, and belief in the value of fathers, and helping them get recommitted to the family, is the best way to address the cause of the problem of absent fathers.

THE BURDEN OF SINGLE MOMS

I've alluded to single mothers a number of times thus far, and I'd like to spend some time looking at how the loss of initiation has affected them. In modern society we've begun to believe that because moms are capable of both holding down a job and raising children alone, dads are not critical to this process. I believe the universality of marriage in all cultures and throughout history suggests that a family runs best with two parents.

Single moms cannot do everything; and there are some things they were never intended to do. How can we ever reasonably expect a mother to provide her son with a clear sense of what it means to be a father? How are boys supposed to identify with the archetypal concept of Father when there isn't one around?

One of the basic dynamics in a boy's initiation into manhood is a breaking away from the mother. All traditional societies were quite aware of this, and built that criterion into their ceremonies and rituals. This is not a negative reflection on mothers, but rather a universal belief that a boy's coming-of-age process should involve only initiated men.

For many years I worked hard to help all the frustrated single moms I was working with try and manage their boys. I helped devise contracts, behavior management models, and a myriad of other approaches to help them control their young boys. In an embarrassing reflection, I realized that not all single moms were dysfunctional in their parenting skills. Many, indeed, were right on the mark with what we feel usually works. They struggled with the thirteen- or fourteen-year-old's desire to go live with the abusive or neglectful father. They struggled with the youngster's propensity to hang out with older, more "experienced" males or even gangs. What finally struck me was this: If it truly takes a man to initiate a boy, how can we expect single moms to accomplish this feat? Even in older cultures where the men were not so involved in daily and early-childhood parenting, they were always expected to tap back in during adolescence and fulfill their role as initiator. I now see these motivated, powerful, compassionate single moms in a game they can't win, with their boys being the losers. Quite simply, a mother cannot make a boy into a man. Mothers represent safety, not risk.

LIFE, DEATH, AND REBIRTH

Initiation traditionally dealt with death, both symbolic and literal. In times past, initiates sometimes were accidentally killed in their effort to become men. Many rites of passage had the potential for something this serious to happen. In modern times we certainly don't want our kids risking their lives, so the focus of initiation is on a symbolic death, heralding rebirth into something else—the boy dies so that the man might live.

At the actual moment of initiation, an ego death occurs. *Ego death* is a psychological term to describe when a developmental stage is completed or an older aspect of a person gives way to a new, expanded version. Many rite-of-passage models used the concept of ego death to provide closure for the time of being a boy, allowing for the new man to be born from the boy's ashes, so to speak. In many tribal ceremonies, this dynamic is explicitly expressed in the initiations.

This "death" effects a twofold change. First, ending the reign of the boy severs his childhood relationship with his mother. Most cultures believe it is necessary for boys to be separated from their mothers to attain manhood. Mothers stand for safety and nurture, not helpful attributes for a boy trying to gain autonomy and become a strong man. Men are perceived as not needing a mother anymore, so symbolically the boy is "killed" and he is literally forbidden to live with his mother anymore. Second, by putting boyhood behind him, the initiate closes that door firmly so that he may enter the world of men with no looking back.

It's pretty clear that our Western thinking entails a deep fear of death and of aging. This is manifested in the vast technological and economic efforts we employ to keep people alive at all costs and to keep looking younger than we really are. I strongly believe it has been this growing fear of death in our culture that has made us fearful of initiation practices.

Part of becoming what we perceive as civilized is the ability to control aspects of our environment—such things as death, weather, aging, the natural world, and human nature. With death as the ultimate failure, so to speak, of controlling our environment, the Western mind has become obsessed with trying to foil it. Our obsession with cheating death and old age also derives from the modern image of manhood that as our bodies grow older, weaker, balder, and get more gray hair, our value as men is diminished.

In initiated societies, death is not seen as the adversary of life. Initiation is about the birth of a greater person from the death of the younger person. Although this death is symbolic, not literal, it stirs our cultural fear of dying. Malidoma Somé explains that in his native Africa, "Elders . . . interpret people's refusal to get initiated as the first sign that death is being evaded."

Being afraid to get hurt makes you afraid to take risks. I remember growing up playing all available sports, and one of the adages I heard in a number of ways was that if you play scared, you get hurt. The point is you have to play all out and hope for the best. Worrying about getting hurt will take your mind off what is important, and you'll probably make a big mistake that may actually hurt you. Our fear of death, and our view of death as some sort of personal or cultural failure, has made many of us unwilling to take risks, or to let our children take the necessary healthy risks they need in order to grow.

Teenagers have an innate drive to bring about their symbolic death as children, to give birth to their adult selves. And as we know, they are also compelled to take risks to test themselves. If we don't provide structure and containment for these symbolic deaths and risk-taking propensities, adolescents will continue to pursue unconscious archetypal instincts built into them for so long. Without positive guidance, they will be forced to take their best guess. As Michael Meade, a noted expert in mythology and symbolism, points out, "Instead of little symbolic deaths, young people will help towns and cities burn . . ."

Meade offers this explanation regarding the teen propensity for taking drugs: "Seen with an eye for initiation and mystery, addictions are rites of substitution, where 'tortures and death' occur on a junk level that can't quite create a breakthrough. The ritual revolves around a 'cracked quest' for spiritual relief, but keeps repeating the alchemical mistake and moves toward actual death when real change was the desire." I have seen this longing, this craving for a healthy symbolic death in so many teens. They have shown me how hungry they are for it and how remiss we are as their guides in not furnishing a safe passage that provides it for them.

It doesn't seem coincidental to me that the two highest age groups for suicide are teen boys and elder men. As teens become more confused, and as elders find themselves considered less useful, is it any wonder they question their value to society? Every time I ponder symbolic versus literal death I think of the Columbine High School tragedy in 1999, and the subsequent ones in San Diego; Eugene, Oregon; and so on. I look at these tragedies from a different perspective from what was presented by the media or by clinicians trying to explain those events. To me, they seem to be classic examples of the shooters confusing symbolic death with literal death. If we are not going to provide these ego-death opportunities for our adolescents, they are going to continue to try and create them on their own, with mixed results at best and in the worst cases, tragedy.

EMBRACING MYSTERY

It is the dim haze of mystery that adds enchantment to the pursuit.

ANTOINE RIVAROL

Even if a culture has decided that initiations are no longer necessary, that does not mean the mental, emotional, and psychological processes of the boy will change. His inherent drives and cravings cannot be eliminated by culture, laws, and psychology. Denying these ingrained, innate desires and needs has an effect similar to taking away an addict's drug—we have actually created more of a craving for some kind of initiation.

One function of the initiation was to help the participant find his own beliefs, his own understanding of values and ethics. The initiation helped him learn who he was. It was determined by our ancestors that one cannot simply tell an adolescent what is what and expect him to buy in to it. Since the search for identity is one of the major dynamics of adolescence, teens need to ground their beliefs in their own experience.

Lacking a clear, well-marked route to self-discovery, teens try to puzzle out their identities by observing the examples they see around them. And what do they see? Many adult men who are not content with our current cultural model of success. Not only does the American Dream fail to materialize for everyone, but when it does, it often still leaves people feeling empty. The stereotypical midlife crisis occurs as a man, after finding personal success and financial security, still feels like something is missing. The huge self-help, spiritual-growth movement in our culture reflects that people feel the need to invent meaning for their lives. For an adolescent, who has trouble making sense of the world even on a good day, his father's inability to find meaning and mystery is confusing and make the teen reluctant to grow up.

Thus teens are caught in a huge, interconnected weave of dynamics struggling to find balance. Changing the rules in the middle of an ancient game is obviously not working, and some of the consequences are severe indeed.

Failing to have acknowledged and supported initiatory ceremonies, kids often follow their archetypal impulses while driving blind, so to speak. And sadly, sometimes the ramifications of those ill-planned deviations from healthy models become the new criteria for "normal" teen behavior. I recently read an essay written by a teen in John Nikkah's *Our Boys Speak* in which he remarked, "dysfunctional is now orthodox." What happens when the abnormal becomes the norm? For many young men, being in trouble is seen as normal, inevitable, and even cool. I would have to say that the majority of youth I've talked to in the past ten years or so have no fear of juvenile hall, and indeed look at it as a test or challenge to face. Many young boys I know have actually said they want to go to the hall to see what it is like. Rather than a culture of healthy boys and men who don't even need jails and prisons in their community, we have more and more teen boys who see serving time *as the initiation itself.*

Louise Mahdi, editor and contributing author for *Crossroads: The Quest for Contemporary Rites of Passage,* once called prisons "houses of failed initiations." I find her statement most intriguing and, sadly, true. In the course of my cross-cultural studies, it struck me that while so many people continue to view the ancient and traditional indigenous cultures as backward and primitive, they operated very well without a lock-down prison, jail system, or juvenile hall. Native Africans, Native Americans, Australian Aborigines, Aleutians, and Polynesians who created ways to initiate healthy and productive members had no need or desire to "control" other people's behavior. They felt no need to use community resources to continuously pay for unproductive systems and people.

In the absence of legitimate rites of passage, gangs will continue to initiate needy boys into the waiting arms of violence and drugs. Prisons and juvenile halls will continue to house uninitiated men and boys, who will surely face trials, ordeals, and risks within those walls, but will not come out the other end as healthy men.

Ironically, in our society, when real initiations happen unexpectedly, they are likely to go unnoticed or to be misconstrued or misinterpreted. Boys who find themselves faced with "man-making" moments and decisions, as in the case of the boy at Columbine who threw his body over a girl when the shooting started, are treated as victims by the press and therapists, and the significance of the moment passes by unnoticed and unused. If the survivors of Columbine, both boys and girls, had been treated as though they went through an initiation, they would have an entirely different image of their role in that tragedy. Many of the men I spoke of who are unsure of their manhood offered story after story of things they had gone through that should have cemented their manhood, but there was no one around who could help structure and confirm that transition. It's terribly sad and backward that the only public way a boy is generally acknowledged to be a man is by committing a serious crime for which he can be tried in court as an adult. In essence, instead of "promoting" our teens for good behavior, as the initiation process did, we are now promoting them for bad behavior.

Initiation is a way of life, or at least it used to be, and American youth seem as determined to experience it as their primitive ancestors were. The question remains whether we will allow them to keep trying self-initiation via overt risk-taking, or if we will respond to their cries and help to restructure healthy initiations that everyone can be proud of and participate in. In protecting our kids from the "harm" of initiations, we may just have damaged them at a deeper level—an injury they will carry into adulthood as boyfriends, husbands, and parents.

4
Rites of Passage
Then and Now

A man who "cannot get it together" is a man who has probably not had the opportunity to undergo ritual initiation into the deep structures of manhood. He remains a boy—not because he wants to, but because no one has shown him the way to transform his boy energies into man energies.

ROBERT MOORE AND
DOUGLAS GILLETTE,
KING, WARRIOR, MAGICIAN, LOVER

Initiation, which we discussed in the previous chapter, is the overall process of guiding and acknowledging a boy's journey into manhood. Rites of passage are the tools for implementing that process—the specific events that transform the boy and celebrate the community's recognition of his new status. This chapter will focus on the rites themselves—what they're commonly like and what they're supposed to do. We'll look at the Hero's Journey, the classic conceptual model or map for the coming-of-age-process, in the next chapter.

THE ESSENTIALS

Rites of passage were created and designed to guide and mark transitions from one stage of life into another. They announced a developmental advancement achieved, a personal transition accomplished, and a movement from one social position to another. They chronicled the growth of the individual within the community.

The point seems to have been to take what and who somebody was at a pivotal time in his life and provide the optimum conditions to help him expand into something more. Life transitions were not left to happen by chance or in isolation, and once they had occurred, everyone rejoiced in that growth.

In older cultures, the adolescent boy's rite of passage was usually treated as importantly as a birth, marriage, or death. Elaborate rituals and ceremonies were created to support these transitions. Remember the developmental issue of the search for identity? Rites of passage helped adolescents fill in the blanks during that critical search. They helped announce to everyone the initiate's new identity. Considering the relative difficulty of our ancestors' daily struggle for existence, it seems logical that they would not have supported these processes, or wasted their precious resources, if there was no return in it.

Ingredients for Transformation

Our global forefathers had a system for their initiations and rites of passage, prescribing the sequence of events and the context in which they would be used. The two main ingredients in a rite of passage are risk and community acceptance. What a boy must go through should provide enough challenge to make him transcend his boyhood self to become someone stronger and more mature. And his community must witness and affirm his growth and accept him as an adult. Without the recognition of the community, a boy can doubt his own transition, which nullifies the whole process. It does no good for a boy to perform some feat and return home only to be perceived the same way by those around him. This is why the "geographic cures"—group homes, wilderness treatment centers, and boot camps—fail, because nothing new happens at home.

Let's look at what some prominent thinkers on the topic of rites of passage consider to be essential ingredients for these experiences. I've included a range of perspectives, each of which provides insight into this process.

According to Christina Grof, addiction expert and author of *The Thirst for Wholeness*, there are four main components to a rite of passage:

- ▶ There is an essential shift in attitude from the people who are doing the initiating. They must look and act differently toward the initiate.
- ▶ The spiritual needs of the youth are addressed.
- ▶ The initiate attains a non-ordinary state of consciousness. This might be a result of fasting, lack of sleep, drumming, exhaustion, and so on.
- ▶ The ritual incorporates psychological symbolism of death and rebirth.

As we mentioned previously, some of these components are not necessarily embraced at this moment in history. *Spirituality* is a term that can create a lot of concern in a society committed to keeping church and state separate and honoring religious diversity. In my experience, talking of spirituality in the clinical world or school setting often fosters animosity among the adults. Also, Americans tend to be uncomfortable with the term *altered states* even though an altered state does not have to come from an illicit drug. Although the literal information is obviously important, it's also imperative to read between the lines, to look for the reason and purpose behind the events and their sequences.

Probably no one synthesized more information on this topic than did mythologist and educator Joseph Campbell. Investigating the universal need for initiation and rites of passage, Campbell condensed his findings down to the simplest common denominators:

▶ Separation
▶ Initiation
▶ Return

Essentially, the boy is separated from his community and uninitiated people. The initiation takes place, followed by the boy's return as a new person into the community.

An important purpose of these initiatory practices was to cue other members of the community to treat the initiated boy differently, as Grof's model states. A set of rules everybody followed helped all participants handle the changes. The return stage was as critical as the other stages of initiation—the former boy must apply what he learned from his initiation in his new role as an adult. He must find a frame of reference from which to share what he now knows of himself and his value to the community.

David Oldfield, strongly influenced by Campbell's work, sees the rites-of-passage stages break down this way:

▶ Separation
▶ Isolation
▶ Trials and Obstacles
▶ Transition/Transformation (Symbolic Wounding, Symbolic Death, Symbolic Rebirth)
▶ Incorporation

Oldfield expands on the significance of the symbolic wounding, death, and rebirth aspects of traditional initiations. Boys received ornamental scars, underwent circumcision, or received ornamental tattoos or other physical woundings for a reason. These emotional and physical wounds helped show teens, who are prone to magical thinking and denial about consequences in life, that pain is a real and tangible part of the adult world they are entering. Most adults are keenly aware of how fragile and short life is, but teens, especially modern teens, often feel bombproof and think they'll live forever.

Of course, in modern times we don't actually wound a child. But youth are symbolically wounding themselves in an innate drive they probably do not totally understand. Nowadays, we explain this process to teens. We help them look at the risky and wounding behavior they are engaged in from this archetypal perspective and help give structure and meaning to their internal drives.

Likewise, the symbolic death of the child in an initiation conveyed a couple of important messages. Many cultures looked at a child's typical attachment to his mother as a second, figurative umbilical cord that needed to be "cut" to allow the boy to move upward with his peers. But symbolic death also served to bring the reality of death into a teen's awareness in a healthy way. Not intended to traumatize them, symbolic deaths got teens used to the fact that death is a common theme and occurrence in everyday life.

Oldfield approaches symbolic death using a number of powerful and experiential exercises that have youth look at images of death they have picked up from family and the media. For example, boys are asked what a gentle or unfair death would be. They ponder a "death worth dying." Or they can do more metaphorical work such as describing what death would look like if it were an animal or time of day. This also helps teens learn to abstract, a developmental challenge. Similar to the ego death explained earlier, we can use masks and symbolic gestures to help youth see how they are letting go of childhood. Artwork and stories can be utilized as well to help boys process these internal changes.

Oldfield sees more everyday life lessons in symbolic rebirth. Like the phoenix that rises from the ashes, an initiated boy experiences an inner rebirth. From a developmental perspective, this helps to cement the search-for-identity process in a hurry. This process also helps to prepare the boy for the understanding that everything in life changes. Seasons come and go. Friends appear and disappear. Family members are born and die. Nothing in life is static, although it may have seemed so when the boy was living in the protective sphere of childhood. Life is a never-ending cycle of growth and change, birth, death, and rebirth of the new.

We can create rebirth dynamics through sweat lodges or guided imageries that allow youths to let go of childhood thoughts and feelings while embracing more adult concepts and issues. Masks can be used to document who a boy used to be, or who he has recently become, or how he now looks at himself. Stories, particularly mythological ones, can supply this part of the initiation process, since their plots commonly involve themes of death and rebirth. Interestingly, when I discuss death with teens, many of them do not have a negative or scary belief system about the subject. Many teens see it as natural, or soft and filled with clouds or light. We adults have to remember not to project our own beliefs or fears about death onto teens, who may already have a healthy approach to the topic.

All three of these symbolic acts in initiations were intended to show teens the ways of the world, to bring them into adulthood with a true understanding of what they were to face. As someone who has spent untold hours with thousands of teens, I commonly see that modern teens, both disadvantaged and over-advantaged, have a skewed sense of adult reality.

Malidoma Somé, one of the few men walking around this country who has been through a formal rite of passage, lists these criteria for an initiation:

► It must take place outdoors.
► It must have a high degree of risk.
► It must include community acceptance.

In this model, man's history with nature cannot be overlooked. Somé does not believe an effective initiation can take place inside a building, where initiates feel safer than when they are exposed outdoors.

Somé's inclusion of risk as a required component of initiations is echoed by many who work with adolescents, but it is the biggest obstacle in trying to create modern initiations. Contemporary parents and mentors have a very difficult time accepting that we need to literally risk our children's health or safety for them to grow, although historically this was the norm across the planet. But to be truly transformative, the risk or challenge in an initiation must be experienced as powerful enough to create an ego death, to "kill" the boy so the man can be born.

These days, acceptable means of offering this necessary element of risk are found in wilderness settings. In wild places a youth can set out on a vision quest and sit alone for a number of days, dealing with his fears. Rites of passage can also be structured around activities such as rock climbing and river rafting.

This is very difficult to achieve in a metropolitan environment, particularly in a melting-pot society like that of the United States. For the past few years I've been helping families to create micro-communities for a number of youth to work within. Based on the popular adage "It takes a village to raise a child," I suggest getting together perhaps twenty families with the same goals and values. They can act like a small village to create and support rites of passage for their teens, and can provide the community acceptance so critical to this process.

I don't think it's possible to overstate the importance of community acceptance in a boy's initiation into manhood. Too often in this work I've seen a boy or teen do something that is personally remarkable for him, only to have his experience diminished by those around him who minimize or don't understand the process. For example, as good as Outward Bound, Vision Quest, and other wilderness-based models might be in creating healthy challenges and tests for their participants, if the community at home does not recognize or accept the experience of the boy, then the whole process fails to take hold. These wilderness programs only ensure that the youth completes the risk part.

Many adults have argued with me that it is up to the boy to maintain his own needs and growth. This "do-it-on-your-own" stance reflects our Western propensity for emphasizing the importance of the individual and minimizing the role of the community. But I believe that we are asking too much when we expect a fourteen-year-old with a dubious self-image to find his own way to manhood, and we are only going to see more boys get lost on the way if we don't provide the guidance they need.

Ego Death

As explained earlier (see p. 71), one of the basic dynamics behind rite-of-passage ceremonies was to cause an ego death. To accomplish this ego death, to help actually create and promote a developmental shift in the boy, he would be removed from the nurturing and protection of his mother and usually subjected to some trial or test. Surviving the test, which called upon the boy to demonstrate the skill or courage of a man, empowered the boy to put away his childhood and enter the world of adults and men.

Rites of passage are based on the concept that what one experiences directly affects what kind of person one will become. If you put someone through a rigorous, challenging test, you'll get back a strong, healthy individual. Many of these tests were brutal and painful, and often included the possibility of literal, physical death. The underlying rationale was that if it is very difficult to be a real man, becoming one should also be difficult, requiring new strengths and abilities. According to mythology expert Joseph Campbell, the ordeal itself is what enables the ego to "put itself to death" so that a serious, life-changing shift can occur.

Most people I talk with about adolescent rites of passage have difficulty accepting the idea of this need to face an ordeal. Our Western minds resist this risk-taking, this challenging of safety. Yet most people will admit that we humans learn from our mistakes and unpleasant experiences. How many times have we looked back at a bad situation, only to gain an understanding from it that makes us wiser or more mature? The ordeals embedded in rites of passage accomplish the same thing; the difference is that they are planned and structured rather than random occurrences.

While we certainly do not want to brutalize or harm our boys, we need to skirt the risky edge as close as possible. For example, many vision quests for boys do not really work because instead of the original model where boys had to go a couple of days without food or water, we keep them fed and hydrated. We check them at regular intervals to see if they are cognizant and focused. This, of course, detracts from the actual goal of getting exhausted and experiencing altered consciousness to produce his vision.

Actual rites of passage were intended to be unique and life-changing. If they were easy, the experience would not be special or have the power to transform. Thus, the trick in modern settings is how to make the initiation challenging but not overly dangerous. Long hikes are a good solution. Multiday backpacking trips that are physically demanding and take place in unusual surroundings can work. We can't risk our boys' safety, of course, but we still need to push them to their limits. We're looking to get them out of their comfort zone.

One need only look at how communities come together during a flood or other destructive event to see how we actually thrive on responding to challenge. Many childcare workers I have known have noticed that in a group home where peers do not get along with the staff or other peers, they are often brought together by some unforeseen catastrophe or difficult circumstance. For example, on a backpacking trip one of the staff from a group home injured her ankle. The boys split up her gear among themselves and carried it for her with no hesitation. Boys want to feel like men and be part of a community, and often will rise to the occasion if they are allowed and encouraged to do so.

Why Must Boys Be Tested So Hard?

> *The aim of the initiation, some practices of which are*
> *stupid, some brilliant, some brutal, some mediocre and*
> *ineffectual, is imagined as a way to complete the develop-*
> *ment of the being from a neutral genderlessness to a state*
> *of genuine masculinity.*
>
> ROBERT BLY, *THE SIBLING SOCIETY*

Girls and boys both have the need to be tested and to grow into expanded versions of themselves. Why, then, have so many cultures come up with such scary, painful, often bloody rituals for their boys to go through? Part of the answer comes from nature, which has provided girls a relatively clear path into womanhood.

Typically, for girls in traditional cultures the onset of menses marks the beginning of their rite of passage or initiation into womanhood. The pain and blood, the symbolic wounding, which are common ingredients in boys' rites of passage, occur naturally for girls. The beginning of the menstrual cycle announces to everyone that the former girl is now capable of having children, which is considered an adult function. Later on, when she actually has a baby, this becomes her full-fledged initiation into womanhood, her rite of passage.

I've heard that until a hundred years ago, there was about a fifty/fifty chance of either the child or the mother dying in childbirth. The trials of childbirth, the pain and blood and fear, as well as the undeniable understanding that death can be a reality, plainly marked and continues to mark this event as entry into womanhood. (This helps explain why the teen pregnancy rate is so high. For a young girl in America struggling to find her adult identity, having a baby is an age-old way to achieve this.)

David Oldfield observes that there are two universal themes in storytelling that are related to rites of passage, and they reflect archetypal differences in how boys and girls experience coming of age. The main character follows one of two distinct types of paths or directions. Generally, boy characters and girl characters take different paths to get to the same place. The first path is that of an inner awakening, which is usually done by the girls. They tend to shift perspective, to become subtly aware of an important change that must occur. The second path is that of outward mastery, which requires one to prove oneself, and this is the path most often followed by boys.

Many people wonder why boys set themselves up to get hurt, to get wounded as in football or motorcycle racing. This is not simply thoughtless high-risk behavior, nor is it a death wish. For many boys, injuries or scars, and the stories of how they occurred, are like badges of honor. They reflect our desire to prove ourselves, to test ourselves and see how we measure up. Girls, on the other hand, are reminded monthly of their pending or continuing womanhood. Since boys have no clear wounding to deal with, they create it.

This leads us once again to the difference between literal death and symbolic death. Boys set themselves up to be tested as men, which should be a symbolic action but too often becomes a dangerous, literal one. Boys want desperately to act as men, and if there is no structured path for them to follow, they will take whatever path presents itself, often with unhealthy or even deadly results.

Have you ever noticed the fascination boys have for large, prominent scars? For many boys and men scars are seen as a sign of masculinity. Scars function as ornamentation commemorating trials we have gone through, and serve as proof we did something "manly." When I was a boy, and even into young adulthood, we considered scars as testaments of a man's courage and trials. After our mothers warned us not to pick at our scabs or we would get scars, that's exactly what we did.

For boys there is no obvious trail to manhood. Since nature did not provide a clear path comparable to what girls have, older cultures recognized that they needed to orchestrate something that would serve that purpose for their young men. While there is great diversity in the specific rituals and ceremonies developed worldwide, what's most important is that the general approach works. A thousand years ago, there were no psychologists, social workers, or therapists, but it seems that most cultures had a good grasp on adolescent development.

Traditional Rites of Passage

By modern Western standards and values, and probably even to the participant about to engage in them, traditional rites of passage practices were often harsh indeed, even brutal. However, they needed to be. In fact, that was the whole point. If being a man was the supreme goal to be achieved, it couldn't be done easily. To create an ego death, to make possible a moment in time in which a boy had to transcend himself, could be accomplished only in the midst of something unfamiliar and difficult. A boy needed to face risk and fear, look inside, and find the resolve to step forward.

This is one of the most difficult aspects of initiation to explain to the parents or advocates of modern-day teens. No parent, including myself, wants his or her children to get hurt. But many who work with adolescents have reached the conclusion that was universally evident among diverse and isolated cultures of the past: To initiate boys into healthy men, we need to push them to the edge. And I can say that in my personal experience, archetypal approaches to personal growth are the most easily accepted by boys and by far the most effective.

Although the following examples of traditional practices would be unacceptable in modern Western societies, they do serve to paint us a picture of how the original process functioned. I'll present a variety of ways to safely mimic the essential dynamics of these traditional practices in chapter 8.

The variation and severity of traditional rites of passage are vividly described in David Gilmore's *Manhood in the Making*. For example, Gilmore points out:

> In East Africa young boys . . . are taken away from their mothers and subjected at the outset of adolescence to bloody circumcision rites by which they become true men. They must submit without so much as flinching under the agony of the knife. If a boy cries out while his flesh is being cut, if he so much as blinks an eye or turns his head, he is shamed for life as unworthy of manhood, and his entire lineage is shamed as a nursery of weaklings.

In New Guinea, boys are taken to an all-male sacred site in the bush and subjected to numerous tests and hazings, often including physical beating or bloodletting. One test is "nosebleeding," in which stiff, sharp grasses are thrust up the nostrils until the nose bleeds copiously. The grown men, having terrorized the boys into submission, celebrate and let out a war whoop to greet the blood. The boys are expected to learn fortitude and to show disdain at letting their own blood.

Bloodletting is done for a couple of reasons. Men are expected to deal with blood in their lives, either through hunting or other work they do or as a result of injuries and accidents that occur in the course of the typical activities of men. And once again, it mirrors the girls' monthly bleeding and childbirth, so boys can be perceived as equal to or stronger than girls.

On the Greek island of Kalymnos, men dive deep into the waters to collect sponges. Divers using any kind of equipment are considered effeminate, and are thus scorned and ridiculed. Even though many get the bends and are crippled and some die, they are willing to take that risk to preserve their masculinity.

Near the Puget Sound, one Native American tribe would take their initiates, both boys and girls, about a mile from shore in a boat. They had to swim back to shore in the frigid water. While not so bloody or painful as some of the practices already mentioned, the results were stark and clear. Make it to shore, and besides being alive, you would be recognized as being a man or woman. Don't make it to shore and it's a moot point.

Regarding the hazing New Guinea boys go through for their initiation, Gilmore points out that "[t]hese Highlanders believe that without such hazing, boys will never mature into men but will remain weak and childlike. Real men are made, they insist, not born." This statement seems to synthesize the fundamental meaning behind rites of passage. In many cultures, if a boy did not successfully complete the test, his future was limited, to say the least. Here are a few examples of the way different societies view the inability to perform the difficult rites:

- ► The Dagara, Malidoma Somé's West African tribe, believe that unless initiated, one remains a "child forever."
- ► The Bedouin of the Sahara believe you become either "real men" or "no men."
- ► The Fox tribe of North America calls true manhood the "Big Impossible."
- ► Even to the peaceful !Kung bushmen of southwest Africa, "manhood is a prize to be grasped through a test."

Boys and Men at Risk

> *You never stood in that man's shoes or saw things*
>   *through his eyes,*
> *stood with helpless hands, while the heart inside you dies.*
> *So help your brother along the way, no matter where he*
>   *starts,*

for the same God that made you, made him too, these
men with broken hearts.

HANDMADE POSTER AT A LIQUOR STORE

In our civilized culture, of course we would consider these practices barbaric. The whole purpose of civilizing oneself is to avoid getting dirty or getting hurt. We simply don't take such risks. However, it appears that, while extending everyone's physical life span, we have inadvertently and seriously impeded teens' ability to participate fully in life with a clear understanding of who they are.

I repeat, I am not advocating hurting boys. But I do advocate trying to understand how this age-old practice worked and which dynamics we can safely adapt to current times. I don't believe it will permanently harm a boy to have him go without food for a few days, be exposed to the cold for a little while, or walk farther than is comfortable—especially if he understands and agrees with these conditions. As we have seen, a certain desire for risk is in his nature to begin with.

As someone who specializes in work with "high-risk" youth, it has struck me time and again how misguided we are in actually holding teens' propensity to take risks against them, rather than structuring and monitoring healthy risk-taking for them. Ironically, "high-risk" boys are the ones who seem most ready, willing, and able to test themselves. The problem is, we have removed the testing grounds. We penalize them for taking risks, a behavior that is ingrained in their psyches deep enough to keep driving them toward test after test, usually unconsciously.*

I often feel that this conflict is a key factor in the high percentage of male teen suicides. They have decided there is no way to win the game they are playing. The struggle to grow, to become a man, and to grab a new and healthy identity must seem too difficult for them to keep pursuing.

---

*For a deeper look at how risk-taking is inherent to the adolescent process, I suggest the following: Lynn Ponton's *The Romance of Risk: Why Teenagers Do the Things They Do* and Cynthia Lightfoot's *The Culture of Adolescent Risk-Taking.*

I have seen this unconscious desire to create a test countless times not only with boys but quite often with men, myself included. I always struggle with my cultural training to avoid unnecessary risks versus my seldom acknowledged desire to see if I can "take it." Adventure, the flavor of rites of passage, is the opposite of what we do in our civilized lives. After a boyhood of playing war and cowboys, I have often wondered if I "had what it takes" in real life. What would I do in the face of a life-or-death challenge? Scores of men have told me they ask themselves the same thing. Not knowing the answer is a source of never-ending doubt. Having proved yourself helps put the question to rest.

We boys and men were bred for many generations to test ourselves, and despite our attempts to civilize one another, we still feel the drive to see if we've got what it takes. Almost every man I know has had this feeling at various times. We wonder if we have the "sand," the "mettle," the "true grit" to do what the other guy has just done. As most of us know, if you do not honor or deal with something consciously, quite often it will manifest unconsciously.

So how do boys and men manifest this unconscious drive in their day-to-day, ordinary lives? One answer can be found in the statistics related to men and industrial accidents. We all hear stories of men working on high-rise structures who scoff at the need to be harnessed or to take other safety precautions. Think of how high the teen drinking and driving statistics are. That is the number one killer of male teenagers. How about the guys who work in the coal mines without respiratory equipment, disregarding the high probability they will contract black lung disease? How about the inherent danger in joining a gang? The guy who drives a difficult shortcut that will probably break down his car? The stereotypic man who will not ask for directions? The group of adolescent boys crossing a busy boulevard while laughing, seemingly oblivious to the physical threat? The gang member walking in the wrong part of town, knowing on one level that this is pretty dangerous but driven unconsciously to do so anyway?

This, I believe, is how the uninitiated boy or man tries unconsciously to set himself up to be tested. Behind each of the examples above, and the countless other stereotypical ones we can easily imagine, is the concept of disdain for risk. Men seem to know unconsciously that they must ignore the unpleasant or dangerous ramifications of their situation, and that they must stoically cope with whatever the universe throws at them. The key point here is that unless this need to be tested is created and delivered in a healthy, structured way, boys and men will continue to manifest it inappropriately.

PSEUDO-INITIATION

We are a country of "something-aholics," ranging from alcoholics to workaholics to shopaholics to chocacolics. We even have a large population labeled codependents, sometimes described as being addicted to another addict. What is the real craving at the heart of all these addictions? It seems to me it's a desire to feel whole, to be sure and content with who you are and how you fit into your community. People, and especially boys, try to fill the need but have no idea how to do so. Rites of passage used to fill this need. Without the ability to perform these rituals consciously, and the appropriate setting in which to do so, boys and men will follow their unconscious desires and unfulfilled longings in a variety of ways, many of which will be unsatisfying and unhealthy.

Craving Wholeness

I find it no coincidence that America, at the forefront of Western thinking, is struggling with more addiction problems than most other countries. We have more drug use and drug-related problems than anywhere else, as evidenced by the large numbers of people in prison for drug-related crimes. As Aaron Kipnis points out in *Angry Young Men,* we lambaste other countries for their lack of human rights, yet we continue to incarcerate more youth than all other countries except Russia, and more adults than anywhere else except China, which has four or five times our population.

A recent government report shows that one out of every thirty-two black Americans is either incarcerated, on probation, or on parole. This cannot be the right direction for us to follow. I believe we are misguided in committing so many resources to attempts to stem the flow of drugs into the country, and punishing drug traffickers, as opposed to eliminating the need or desire for the drugs.

Why doesn't a more civilized, rational, pragmatic approach to drug use work with teens? In her book on addiction, *The Thirst for Wholeness*, Christina Grof explains:

> "Just Say No" is not enough, nor is fighting violence with violence. Slapping teenage addicts into jail will not quench their spiritual thirst. If we as concerned community members aim at the deep sources of the conflicts, I feel that we have an excellent chance of curtailing or even preventing much of the destructive acting-out during the teenage years.

Addiction issues seldom respond to behavioral methods. What's more, the legal system's approach to working with teen offenders is inconsistent and ineffective. Most adjudicated youth I work with have clauses in their probation prohibiting them from using drugs and alcohol. One boy I worked with had thirty-two positive drug tests while on probation. He received consequences for just a few of them. When I told this story to another boy, he told me he had twenty-one positive tests thus far while on probation, and remembered actually getting additional consequences only three or four times. The vast majority of youth who violate probation receive no further consequences for that action, except more empty threats and bluffs. We just keep telling them what not to do, and fail to follow through when they break the rules. Instead of putting them to a test that strengthens their sense of pride and accomplishment, we reinforce their pattern of unhealthy risk-taking and failure.

Many of the boys I work with are required to attend AA or NA meetings. Through the years I have seen the Twelve-Step approach help many adults but very few teens. I believe the reason is a developmental one. One of the basic tenets of Twelve-Step work is to surrender to a higher power, to acknowledge that you need more than your own power to battle addiction. This works well for many adults. But it conflicts directly with the developmental issues of individuating, making choices and gaining control, and the search for identity. Boys who are desperately trying to acquire autonomy and control of their lives are most resistant to relinquishing that to an abstract concept requiring faith. I'd say 95 percent of the boys I've worked with do not relate to the Twelve-Step approach.

The truth is, making drugs illegal will never take away the need to try and fill oneself up somehow. A look back at Prohibition will confirm this. The poor results of our drug-enforcement efforts make it clear that it doesn't matter how many new laws we pass: to stop drug use and abuse, you must take away the need to use.

Most Native cultures have nowhere near the drug and violence problems our boys exhibit, until they are forced or encouraged into Western models of living. The older cultures that are currently experiencing some of the same problems as we are in the West have also recently relinquished their traditional rite of passage ceremonies in lieu of more "civilized" approaches. The "first world" cities in many Third World countries, such as Buenos Aires, Mexico City, and Rio de Janeiro, and in a number of African countries are all experiencing increasing teen delinquency with the growth of urbanization.

Life as a teenager in America is no longer simply trying and chaotic; it is downright dangerous, as we saw from the statistics in chapter 2. From that perspective, I have to wonder if the risks we fear in rites of passage might actually be the lesser of two evils. If indeed our departure from more established forms of initiation was meant to protect our children from harm, I fear we have failed them miserably.

Gangs and Rites of Passage

Man, you don't understand. My homeboy, he'd step in
front of a bullet for me. My dad, he certainly wouldn't.
INTERVIEW WITH A GANG MEMBER

On the other side of the coin, an example of a situation in which the rite-of-passage process is quite effective, although used inappropriately, is in adolescent gangs. I am constantly amazed by how much more adamant and proud gang kids are about their manhood and masculinity than are most of their mainstream counterparts. This, I've come to believe, is a result of having gone through an initiation into the gang that incorporates the universal, archetypal dynamics we've been discussing in this chapter. Ironically, gangs have gravitated to dynamics used successfully for tens of thousands of years to transform adolescents into productive adults.

To get into a typical gang, a boy (and a growing number of girls) in essence separates from his mother and his community. In joining the gang, he leaves home, at least on an emotional level, and the general community on a social level. Many gangs demand you get "jumped in"—meaning you get a frightening beating from the other members. Some gangs even go so far as to demand a killing by the initiate, often of an innocent or even random person, to prove his worth and desire to join. These violent actions, of course, are the trials and ordeals, and stepping up to actually perform them creates that intense and transformative moment. If you recall the lists of initiation components we discussed earlier in the chapter, you'll recognize that gang members separate out from the overall community, isolate, and initiate, but fail to return to the overall community, choosing instead to create a micro-community or subculture instead.

The gangs have elaborate ceremonies and rituals, history and lineage to be passed down by their version of elders, the O.G.'s. The O.G.'s are "original gangsters," or "old gangsters," but sadly are often young themselves and initiated in a negative and inappropriate way. The initiates take on new names, signifying new identities. They adopt a new tribe, adorn themselves with the gang clothing, tattoos, or other body art, use the language, and adopt the demeanor of their new "village." You could say they have reverted to a smaller, tribal and homogenous community.

In many gangs, there is no exit. Gang members are usually forbidden to leave under threat of bodily punishment or even death. Almost every gang member I have worked with has said that he is unable to leave the gang. Even more interesting is that when offered a relocation and removal of their identifying tattoos, they almost always refuse.

One boy I know, though, came up with a creative way to get out of this environment. A fifteen-year-old Crip from the Los Angeles area, he was about to rob a mini-mart with some of his "homies." He told them he would do the robbery alone and that they could wait in the car. Impressed by his courage, they agreed and gave him an AK-47 machine gun to use. The boy went up to the counter, pointed the gun at the clerk, and, confident his peers could not hear him, told the clerk to "push the alarm button." The clerk did so, while the boy pretended anger at the clerk's stalling. When the cops arrived a few minutes later, his friends drove off and he was arrested. His crime got him sentenced to a facility out of state, and out of his neighborhood. More often than not, however, the strong sense of community and belonging overrides a gang member's common sense. With multiple opportunities to go elsewhere, this boy eventually chose to return home to the same environment.

The rite-of-passage dynamic these boys continually miss is the incorporation back into the community at large. Of course, from a societal viewpoint, these gang members are inappropriate in their violence, stealing, and drug involvement. Thus, they will always be viewed as outside of the general community, and never be fully accepted. But I've found it fascinating how, given to own devices, which include not following many of our current social norms, they gravitate back to the universal rite-of-passage dynamics. They know what works, what causes transition and transformation, what creates a deep bond and a belief in one's self and one's (sub)community. They have simply reverted to the old ways, and have established their own culture within our larger one.

Almost every gang member I have known, regardless of race, neighborhood, or economic status, when questioned about why he joined answered that the gang makes him feel like he "belongs," like he is part of a tighter family. This is a sad reflection on our parenting, for these youths are simply telling us they are not receiving what they need, emotionally, at home.

Another reason why teens who might otherwise be productive citizens are drawn to gangs is a lack of employment and adult responsibility for teenagers who don't want to be kids in school anymore. Since these young men have no economic base to fall back on, they have created their own economy fueled by drug sales. Many of the teen drug dealers I have known would make great businessmen, if they were allowed into the workforce at large.

Fraternities

We also see many inappropriate and adolescent dynamics in fraternity initiations and hazings. While trying to initiate the new members, the older ones, self-initiated at best, usually come up with bizarre if not dangerous means. Hank Nuwer chronicles some of these alarming incidents in his book *High School Hazing*. It's as if groups of terminal adolescents know *what* to do, but with no healthy guidance and direction from authentically initiated men and elders, they don't know *how* to do it. As we have read too often in news reports, the results of these ill-conceived initiations are sometimes tragic.

Sports as Rites of Passage?

Many in our culture would say that sports are a healthy way to prove oneself and to experience initiation. However, there are some inherent flaws in that argument. For one thing, most sports are set up so that half the participants lose. In individual sports like golf and tennis, you get one winner and *dozens* of losers. From an initiatory viewpoint, traditional cultures would never have allowed so many to fail.

In addition, most sports are also set up in a hierarchical fashion with some roles or positions more important than others. Many players feel a great sense of failure for not reaching the top, which of course only a few can actually achieve. Someone might be great at baseball in high school, only to feel like a failure if he doesn't make his college team, or start, or star. And on it goes up the ladder into the world of professional sports, where the definition of success becomes narrower and narrower—win a world championship, and preferably become the most valuable player in that effort.

What would happen to a community if only half its boys became healthy men? Small communities of people needed all the healthy and qualified men they could get, and put much effort into structuring initiations that certainly tested them but were designed for most, if not all, to succeed. The rites of passage were set up so that all participants could succeed, not just the tall or strong ones. That's why, though the tests were usually physical challenges, they were about perseverance and courage, internal attributes. This is an important understanding when we try to create contemporary rites of passage, for although we cannot physically risk our children's lives, we can put them in situations that require or accelerate a change in their thinking, making a life-altering decision, or even ego death. This will be explained in more detail when we start looking at transpersonal approaches (see chapter 8).

Below are a few examples of slogans found on a line of T-shirt that is popular with guys. They make it vividly clear how sports are used to judge the masculinity of a boy or man, not based on growth, but on success:

There is no final four. There is only the final one.

It's simple, you lose, you go home.

If at first you don't succeed . . . you lose.

Perception: You Fought Really Hard for Second Place. Reality: You Were the Fastest Loser.

Blessed are the losers, for they determine the winners.

You just do it, I'll just win.

Do what losers didn't.

I didn't come here to play, I came here to win.

The Military as a Rite of Passage

The military has long been viewed as a way to "make a man" out of someone, although it generally happens at a later age than the initiations of earlier cultures. The military also follows most of the basic rite-of-passage dynamics in creating its soldiers. Boot camp helps to separate and isolate the participant from Mother and the old community. The trials and obstacles help create an internal shift, while the demeaning and verbal onslaught from training sergeants helps break down the individual ego. Age-old ceremonies and rituals help cement and commemorate the events. And once the boy is broken down, he is "reborn" in a stronger version and returns to the platoon—the community.

However, since Vietnam, being in the military has not been as publicly admired and respected as it has been in earlier times. Public sentiment toward soldiers who have served in Iraq seems to be generally favorable. But the welcome for returning soldiers seems confined to loved ones and the military "family"; the greater community is not really paying much attention.

Self-Ornamentation

One of the inherent components of rites of passage is self-ornamentation. Once a boy has been initiated, he gets to look like the other adults. For the Masai of Africa, this includes dying their hair red. For the Maori of New Zealand, this means elaborate tattooing.

One of the trends that has been going on for some time in Western countries that has many grown-ups concerned and confused is our teens' propensity for bleached hair, tattoos, and body piercing. According to various sources, between 8 and 16 percent of American high school students now have tattoos. The average age of tattooing is dropping, with more and more incidents of hepatitis, HIV, and other infections being reported.* And the trend does not stop with teens. Obviously, hair dying, tattooing, and body piercing are forms of self-ornamentation. But why now, we might ask?

All of these activities make sense when you look at them from the point of view of the absence of real rites of passage in the lives of teenagers. First, I believe the current forms of trendy self-ornamentation are symbolic of our teens' unconscious drive to experience initiation. These kids, and many older people as well, are making a statement about who they are, and who they are not. Although cliques remain an important means of expressing identity, teens seem to be searching for more than that. I think self-ornamentation, as a statement of a new identity and of belonging to a separate community, is another example of how adoles-

---

*According to the Public Health Agency of Canada and the Palo Alto Medical Foundation.

cents are trying desperately to grow up in a culture determined to keep them children too long. In this culture, every day, more adolescents are acting collectively and at an unconscious level. I call these small bands of youth not fully buying into modern norms and expectations and separating out from the larger community "the New Nomads."

Second, I believe the self-ornamentation is a substitute for actual initiation. If no one will initiate boys into the community, then like gangs, they will self-initiate. Body piercing contains several of the rite-of-passage attributes we've discussed: fear, pain, blood, and stress. Most of the boys I have spoken to about this also allude to the disdain element, the requirement to be stoic in the face of pain and discomfort. Indeed, they even have to joke about it while in the process of having their body pierced and not look weak to their peers. Tattooing creates the same possibilities. Rather than the self-ornamentation supporting the initiatory process, the self-ornamentation is *becoming* the initiation.

PUBLIC OR PRIVATE?

Responsibility for providing rites of passage and initiations has largely been removed from the domain of community and relegated to the nuclear family. This decision to leave it up to individual families to initiate their young is not working. We have seen how initiation is most effective when it is a community effort. Not only did this process help the initiate succeed and feel supported, but, as Somé asserts, it also energized the community. It served to pass along values that emphasized and strengthened the individual's sense of responsibility for his community's well-being.

We can see how not having clearer community and cultural values has backfired as the government and now private enterprise spend incredible amounts of money to control and incarcerate those people unable or unwilling to play by cultural rules. Ironically, it seems that the more there is no one around to witness and approve of their actions, the more boys and men are compelled to prove themselves in ill-advised ways.

5
The Hero's Journey

I'd rather die while I'm living than live while I'm dead.
JIMMY BUFFETT

If we imagine that the goal of a boy's initiation is to get to the other side of a river, and his rite of passage is the physical crossing of that river, then the Hero's Journey would be the vessel he uses to cross the water. The Hero's Journey is a mechanism for envisioning and understanding the path he is on—where he is now, where he has been, and what lies ahead. It is a conceptual map of the essential phases of personal growth and change that comprise a rite of passage, and it applies just as well to unplanned rite-of-passage situations as it does to formalized rituals.

This chapter's goal will be to explain the Hero's Journey as a means of interpreting the adolescent boy's experience of rites of passage, both formal and informal. Why do we need a section on the Hero's Journey when we just talked about boys' rites of passage? Because many things happen in a boy's or a man's life, outside of his structured, official initiation, that can act as a rite of passage. At any time, the universe can set you up in a powerful, challenging situation.

I believe my own unnoticed rite-of-passage moment was overlooked and discounted in a well-intentioned effort to soften its impact on my fourteen-year-old psyche. One Sunday night in winter, my cool twenty-five-year-old mentor, who lived across the street, stuck a deer rifle in his mouth and pulled the trigger. He had been having dinner with his mother and girlfriend when he excused himself from the table, and then from life.

My parents and older brother helped drive the traumatized women to the hospital and I was volunteered to stay behind to guard the house. A policeman had told us that many bad guys listen to police scanners for incidents such as this, so they can break in to the house while everyone is at the hospital. Okay, I thought, I can do this.

After my family had left, the final policeman on the scene came up to me. He pointed out that sooner or later the young man's mother was going to come back to the house. Yes, I agreed, that made sense. "You don't get it, do you," he continued. "She's going to see her son's brains splattered all over the wall and bed." Realization suddenly dawned on me. Oh, I replied, I should clean up the room. "You got it," he said, and left.

I remember watching the movie *Patton* while trying to bolster my courage to face that room. I looked in at it a number of times, but quickly walked away. I had very mixed feelings, including wanting to do the right thing but wondering why it had to be me, and if an immature and scared boy like me was the right person for the job. I eventually got up the nerve to clean that room, and did a pretty good job for a boy who didn't do much cleaning other than picking things up. I remember steeling myself for the task, then working quickly but efficiently because I did not want to do it twice.

Later, when the adults returned, nobody said anything; everyone just looked at me like I was some sort of victim, and apparently they all decided, as is common with suicide, that the less said the better. I recall being disappointed that no one gave me any credit for what I had done. Not aware of the stigma surrounding suicide at the time, I wondered why everyone just ignored the process. Because essentially my community did not accept this effort as a rite of passage, I never knew what to make of it, so I put it in the back of my mind. It was thirty-five years before my father ever brought up the incident, and complimented me on my actions.

Sometime when I was in my thirties I was looking at my actions in life and wondering if I was really a man or still uninitiated. I came to an inner understanding that this extraordinary event had indeed been a coming-of-age moment and allowed myself to hold it that way ever since. If any of the adults had honored my action in words, I believe I would have felt much more mature at a younger age and not searched around so long for validation.

This is a good example of why initiations were invented and structured as they were. While everyday life can indeed put a young boy through a rite of passage, what happens when the adults don't notice, when the community does not acknowledge the achievement? Native cultures created structured and consistent rites of passage for just this reason, to be certain every boy got a fair chance to be initiated.

AN ARCHETYPAL MODEL FOR
RITES OF PASSAGE

The Hero's Journey model that I use is based in part on the work of Joseph Campbell. In the course of reading thousands of mythological stories from diverse cultures, Campbell began noticing patterns and common themes. He first described this in what he called the Monomyth Model. The Monomyth Model visually portrays a distinct cycle of separation, initiation, and return, which can repeat over and over throughout one's life. It illustrates how a person encounters and deals with challenge. When the person completes the cycle, he or she is set up for the next challenge in life, which will follow the same pattern. Campbell ultimately simplified his model and coined the term the Hero's Journey, or Hero's Adventure. Each time the Hero's Journey cycle is completed, a person emerges more complete and mature than when he or she began.

Why is the Hero's Journey so important if it is really only a representational model of real life? Like the labyrinth metaphor described in chapter 1, it offers us a framework that can provide direction and grounding, and supplies a path for us to follow that is based on universal, nonjudgmental principles.

The process of adolescence is a journey, which is why this model fits it so well. Each stage of the cycle is a developmental hurdle to be cleared. As we'll see later in this chapter, refusing to follow the path can be more costly than facing all the scary and difficult elements along it.

The Hero's Journey model I use is a simplified version of Campbell's Monomyth, with terminology from Roger Walsh's *The Spirit of Shamanism* as well as some subtle influences from David Oldfield. In this chapter I will explain how this model can be utilized to chart and interpret the coming-of-age experiences of all adolescent boys. I will also describe how I use it in my work with high-risk adolescent boys, and how it can be woven into treatment plans and therapeutic models.

STAGES OF THE HERO'S JOURNEY

The Hero's Journey defines a series of stages along the path to personal change and growth. Because we humans are resistant to change, having a model that establishes clear markers for one's progress along the path encourages and expedites the inevitable change. The stages in this model are:

- ► Conventional Slumber
- ► The Call to Adventure (including Crossing Thresholds of Difficulty)
- ► Discipline & Training
- ► Culmination of the Quest (including Crossing Thresholds of Difficulty on Returning)
- ► Return and Contribution

We'll examine each of these stages in a moment.

Boys are constantly involved with the Hero's Journey whether they know it or not. I learned long ago that once they understand how it works, they will readily use this ancient model of growth as a pattern or template for their own lives. The Hero's Journey gives them a frame of reference for the struggles or challenges they will be dealing with at various stages and times in their lives.

Conventional Slumber

The Hero's Journey begins with Conventional Slumber. At this first stage, the man-to-be is essentially "asleep" to the bigger picture going on around him—stuck in conventional, status quo thinking. Teens in Conventional Slumber often fail to see or acknowledge issues that are clearly necessary to deal with. This stage can sometimes take the form of denial.

But there is something in a boy's world that needs to be looked at differently. It is time to grow up. While the boy is sleeping comfortably in conventional thinking, something happens to wake him and give him an opportunity to test himself and grow or to remain stuck where he is. This lure, this challenge to change, is the Call to Adventure.

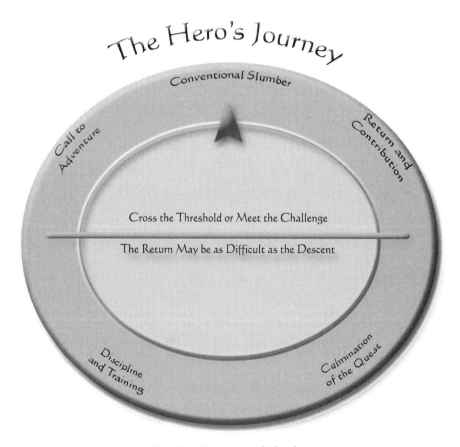

Fig. 5.1. Conventional Slumber

The Call to Adventure

> *I hate to have to tell you this, but whether you like it*
> *or not you're a man! You're stuck with it. You're gonna*
> *find yourself standing your ground and fightin' when*
> *you oughta run, speaking out when ya oughta keep your*
> *mouth shut, doing things that will seem wrong to a lot of*
> *people, but, you'll do 'em all the same.*
>
> JOHN WAYNE IN *THE TRAIN ROBBERS*

The Call to Adventure challenges a boy to do something different, change his ways, or act more responsibly. It can be a positive challenge like getting

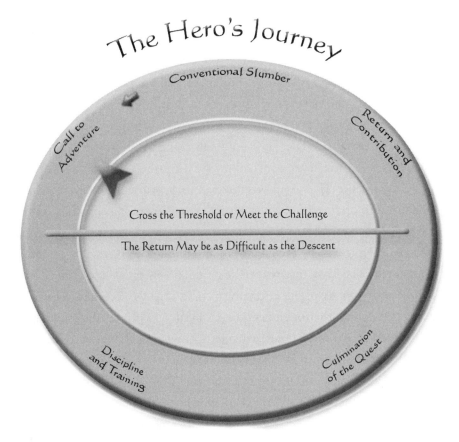

Fig. 5.2. The Call to Adventure

accepted into Honor Band or a negative one like going to juvenile hall for shoplifting. It can be a fairly everyday challenge like finding out you're failing three classes, moving to another school district, or getting picked on by a bully. It can be something more internal such as getting ready to speak in front of the whole school at an assembly or going out for the lead role in a school play. It might even be a single momentous event such as September 11th or the Columbine shootings. In short, the Call is about accepting the need to change.

The Threshold of Difficulty

The Threshold of Difficulty is not a stage in itself, but rather part of the experience of answering the Call to Adventure. It represents the specific challenges to be dealt with, the trials and ordeals that the boy will encounter in this endeavor that will test his resolve. The Threshold can present itself in any number of ways, from the simple fear of not making the football team to the fear of physical harm from a bully. These tests may occur unexpectedly: a boy might relapse when he is trying to quit drinking; another boy who wants to work might be turned down by numerous employers. (Tests can also be structured into an initiation, as we will see later.) The Threshold can come in waves or in separate incidents, so one is never really sure if he is finished with it.

Crossing the Threshold is supposed to be difficult: mentally, emotionally, and often physically. It tests the boy's persistence and belief in his Call. It is here that many Hero's Journey travelers stop or quit, for it's one thing to accept the challenge and another to have to work very hard for it. This dynamic repeats itself countless times in our lives and is reflected in many of our euphemisms and sayings, such as "When the going gets tough, the tough get going." Dealing with the challenges and difficulties becomes an inner struggle. Completing this inward journey helps the participant to be "reborn" into a new and better person.

Adolescent boys often get stuck at the Threshold of Difficulty, for without help they fail to work through the challenges set before them. While they may want to grow and be different, actually getting there may seem like too much work. Many teen boys have had few successes in life

Fig. 5.3. Threshold of Difficulty

or they lack family support, so they learn to give up easily. High-risk boys in particular often do not like to take risks, for their lack of self-confidence doesn't allow them to tolerate much more failure in their lives.

Discipline and Training

The third stage in the Hero's Journey, Discipline and Training, occurs after the boy has accepted the Call and faced the challenges of the Threshold. He may have already crossed the Threshold or might still be in the process of facing it.

This stage is about the boy accepting that he needs some kind of assistance to succeed. The boy realizes he doesn't know everything, and seeks out or accepts guidance from those who can help him. Discipline and Training often comes in the form of accepting teachers, mentors, or guidance from others, but it can come through other channels: books or stories, visions or dreams, or maybe entering college or vocational training.

If a boy who goes out for the basketball team does not make the squad because his shooting ability is not good enough, instead of spending the next year practicing his shots he might go to a basketball camp. The boy looking for a job could ask a neighbor who's a manager to help him practice interviewing or build a résumé. Maybe a boy needs to accept a tutor to get through algebra, or take karate lessons to learn self-defense. He may have to study rules and procedures to get into a certain club or organization. Teen boys commonly get stuck in this stage

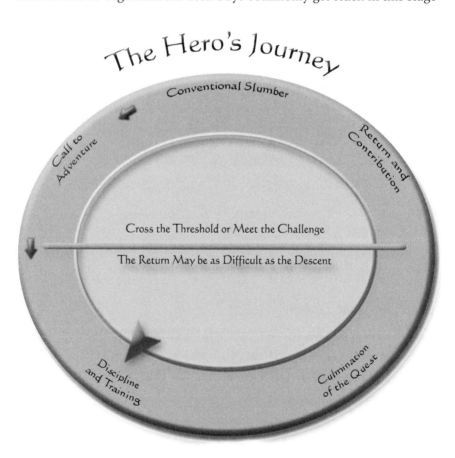

Fig. 5.4 Discipline and Training

because it often involves accepting feedback or input from their nemesis: parents and other adults.

When boys used to be formally initiated, they bonded with the older men involved in the ritual and easily accepted these elders as mentors. With today's generational split widening, boys now prefer to bond with their peers, from whom they get respect and acceptance. This creates an animosity with adult teachers of all kinds, and encourages the boy to listen to his peers' advice more so than that of the adults in his life. The loss of initiation and the institutionalizing of learning helped create the entire concept of peer pressure as we know it by pulling adults and elders away from boys and surrounding them with other young people.

Culmination of the Quest

The fourth stage in the Hero's Journey is the Culmination of the Quest, wherein the problem or challenge is successfully faced or completed. The boy finishes what he set out to do. Culmination might be graduating from high school, getting that black belt in karate, or winning the state football championship. It might be completing military boot camp or finally realizing he has kicked the cigarette habit.

In Western culture, quite often this is literally the end of the story. The hero saves the damsel or the day and rides off alone into the sunset. While we Americans are used to that motif, it is not universal. The Culmination is very important in that our boy heroes must, of course, have a chance at winning or completing their trials. But it's equally important that they answer these questions for themselves: What did I learn in my travels? What would I do differently next time? What advice would I give to the next boy on the Hero's Journey? How did it feel to do something out of the ordinary, or something I never thought I could do? What has changed in me?

As we'll see in a minute, in the Hero's Journey there's more that needs to be done.

One reservation I have about using the Twelve-Step process with adolescents concerns the fact that former users are always in recovery

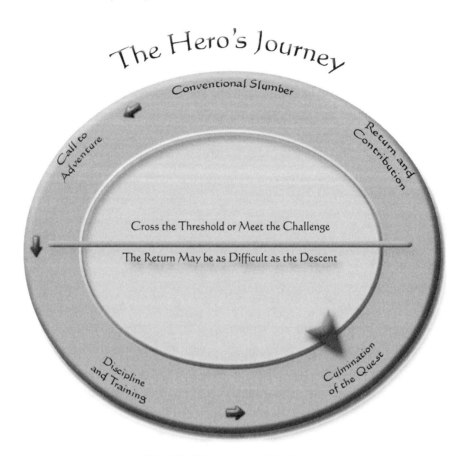

Fig. 5.5. Culmination of the Quest

but never recovered. I've always felt that there was no closure in this model. Being in continual recovery prohibits Culmination of the Quest, which stalls or even breaks the cycle.

Return and Contribution

The journey thus far has been an individual one. The boy was pulled or enticed out of his community to follow the Hero's Journey. Essentially a personal quest until the final Return and Contribution stage, the whole journey has been about "I" or "me." In the final stage, however, the focus changes to "we" and "us."

The final stage is about the boy returning with what he has learned or gained during the journey. The contribution may be in a tangible form or it may be an inner knowledge gained from testing himself, which then is reflected in his future actions and interactions. The key point is that this learning or acquisition must be brought back and shared with the community. This is where the student becomes the teacher, where the "I" becomes the "we." It is a return from a solitary inner journey to an outward present, and then a presentation of the hard-earned gift to the community.

Our basketball player might help the young boy down the block perfect his free throw or volunteer some time to a younger basketball team. The boy who got a job might help a friend create his own résumé. A boy who had struggled with a bully and took some self-defense lessons might help a younger boy down the block going through the same problem.

Fig. 5.6. Return and Contribution

A boy who benefited from algebra tutoring could help his best friend understand a difficult concept. Many of the youth workers I associate with are doing this very thing: they got some help somewhere in their lives that helped them make good decisions, and now they want to do the same for the next generation.

Many approaches to working with troubled adolescent boys fail because they do not create the opportunity for a boy to experience Return and Contribution. Most boys in placement are goal oriented. If they do certain things, they will be released to go home. In the youth care field, "community service" is too often about picking up cigarette butts at the beach or trash along the highway. We've made the process punitive, so the boys look at giving back as a chore, not as a good thing to do. If we encouraged them to share with younger kids how they quit smoking, or why they quit stealing, it would also reinforce what they have learned for themselves.

Group homes and other juvenile placements are notorious, though not due to any fault of their own, for sending boys home who have not learned to understand and give back what they learned. I say it is not the placement's fault because aftercare or follow-up with former teen placements is hardly ever funded. No organization I am familiar with will pay anyone to follow a boy after placement for six months to help him not only stay straight, but also find opportunities to give back and thus feel good about himself. I often ponder what a boy must feel when, after the adults spent so much time telling him he needs to get his act together, we take away all that support and expect him to hang on to this new way of being by himself. Without this follow-up by the grown-ups, we are failing in our Return and Contribution efforts and throwing a boy back into the Thresholds of Difficulty stage when he could be learning to contribute.

A couple of years ago we had some older teen group-home boys going into our middle school to talk to the younger kids. One boy, who for months had held fast to his gang involvement and affiliation, was telling the younger students about his experiences. He began telling them of a good friend, shot in a gang fight, who actually died in his arms. He was crying, remembering this awful event. The younger kids were silent and respectful. The message they heard, felt, and experienced from this older mentor was far and away more effective than all the "Just Say No" lectures they get. The boy seemed to enjoy speaking with the younger students and it seemed to be cathartic for him. He had given something back and felt good about it. He had benefited someone besides himself, and—an unusual experience for him—had liked it. Talk about a way to build empathy and lessen remorse.

Gangs, with their mind-set of reciprocal violence, are often stuck in the Hero's Journey at this stage. As we mentioned in the Rites of Passage chapter, gangs separate from their communities but don't return. The back-and-forth fighting and the get-even mentality prohibit them from moving through this stage of the Hero's Journey.

In my career with teens I am in a perpetual Hero's Journey cycle, and I revisit the Return and Contribution stage again and again. Once I learn how to do something valuable with teens, or gain a new understanding, then my challenge is how to teach and share that. Without consciously intending it, I have set myself up for perpetual growth—a good thing for an admitted "growth junkie."

During this final stage, familiar roles change. The boy comes back from the journey a man. The uneducated youth comes back enlightened. This final stage sets up the next journey, for after the Return has been completed, the next Hero's Journey can begin. It might start again for the boy, this time wrestling with the decision of whether or not to get married. Having finally accepted that commitment, our former boy might next find himself looking at the prospect of becoming a parent, and the journey starts over again for that issue. And so on, and so on.

The boy's Return may spark an adventure for someone else. For example, the father's role might shift when he sees that his son is now more responsible and less reliant on his parents. This becomes a new Call for the father because he now may start to explore what his life will be like when he is no longer so directly involved with the day-to-day responsibility of raising children.

Recrossing the Threshold

Somewhere after the Culmination of the Quest and during the attempt to Return and Contribute, the Threshold of Difficulty may rear its ugly head again. This time it may be some sort of impediment to physically returning home, or it could be a number of tests to challenge the initiate's new belief system.

Often, crossing the Threshold on the way home is the most difficult phase of the journey. A boy who has been clean and sober for his goal of sixty days may be tempted to relapse when he starts to miss the friends he used to drink with. Or, in his loneliness, he may shift his addictive nature to something else, perhaps becoming a "relationship addict."

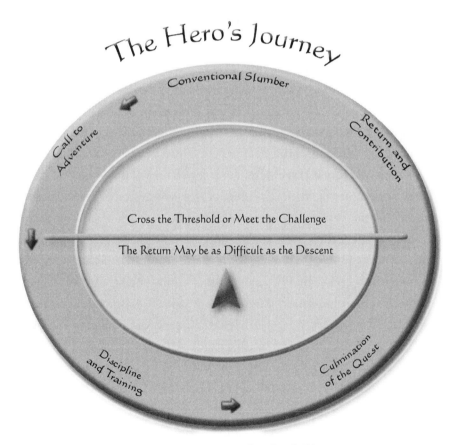

Fig. 5.7. Recrossing the Threshold

REFUSING THE CALL TO ADVENTURE

Action may not always bring happiness; but there is no happiness without action.

BENJAMIN DISRAELI

There is much that can get in the way of completing and/or accepting the Call to Adventure. Logic and rational thinking may tell us to be cautious, or that the smartest thing to do is look the other way. The Hero's Journey represents certain change, and thus comes up against resistance from those elements within us and outside of us that want to keep things as they are.

Sometimes the Call to Adventure is not some random event but instead something we create for ourselves. We may unconsciously create our own threshold to cross, our own trial to face. The unconscious, left to its own devices, quite often leads us to where we need to go. Resisting consciously does little good, because basically we get what we are supposed to get. We don't get to choose what will call us, the way we might choose a flavor of ice cream or a style of clothing.

Refusing the Call to Adventure may be costly, for most of us have learned the hard way that putting off something today only means we will have to deal with it later, when it will be more difficult. Typically, Refusing the Call doesn't really spare us, as the push toward growth often manifests itself in another, usually more troublesome way. Procrastination or indecision can come back to haunt us, often making what seemed difficult earlier the easier choice. The Hero's Journey cycle will continue to manifest throughout our lives, so we must get used to working with it. Refusing the Call sets a dangerous precedent for the rest of our lives.

For many teens, the Refusal is made by the adults around them. This can be parents who are too concerned about safety to let a boy take some chances. This can be the local community who believe that teen boys should be seen and not heard. This can be anyone who confines or protects the boy too tightly at the expense of inhibiting his growth.

We need to encourage boys to accept the Call and to understand the potential cost of refusing it. Boys who drop out of society, who isolate themselves from their community by refusing to grow up, often become perpetual victims. As they develop a habit of refusing challenges, they begin giving away their personal power to those who make decisions for them. They feel they are at the mercy of society, and this can lead to a sense of entitlement whereby they believe the world owes them something they haven't worked for. If this gets too ingrained, it will become a pattern throughout their lives.

The growing institutionalization of boys and men weakens their ability to follow the Hero's Journey because they fail to accept the challenges intended for them and allow others to make the final decisions, which they will have to deal with one way or another. Many of the boys I work with who are in some sort of placement against their wishes fall into this situation. They won't make good decisions for themselves, or they keep making bad decisions. Many boys are getting so used to being locked up that they fail to try and complete a program so they can go home. They get used to not having to make decisions, having food and shelter provided for them, and so on. There's a popular saying that reflects this dynamic: "Not to decide is to decide." By not choosing to do something, you choose the consequences of that inaction.

As modern society is bent on making day-to-day life as easy as possible, we keep avoiding potential Hero's Journeys as they relentlessly pursue us. Our Western minds are becoming quite adept at making things physically easier in life, but at what cost? I believe the confusion and negative attributes so associated with modern men are directly related to the waning of this archetypal process as a cultural model. Men keep refusing the responsibility and commitment that are so much a part of manhood and fatherhood. How can someone who has never started or completed the cycle be expected to teach others?

USING THE HERO'S JOURNEY WITH YOUR ADOLESCENT

As I studied older models of adolescence, I learned how the Hero's Journey can be woven into adolescence in many ways, from the inspiring stories we tell boys to the initiations that make them men. I began experimenting with showing and explaining the model with all of my boys. They liked it, and could easily see how it played out in life. I liked it because it was simple and I could pull it up anywhere. I could draw it on a napkin at a restaurant or in the sand at a beach. As I started weaving and overlaying the Hero's Journey model on the boys I was working with, I saw how it resonated with many of them. The mythological flavor of the terminology appeals to boys, and it doesn't sound like therapy.

Being curious creatures to begin with, the boys began asking me where I thought they fit on the model. I quickly found that when I began to discuss a particular boy's process in terms of the Hero's Journey, I had to give him a couple of different explanations. I realized that each boy is on a different stage of the journey with respect to the various issues he is dealing with. I wound up saying something like, "Bryan, when it comes to your drug problem [the central issue in his life], you are relatively asleep—the Conventional Slumber stage. But when I look at how you are now doing in school, I see you are currently at Discipline and Training because you are not fighting your teachers and your mentor says you are paying attention. And I know you've been helping Buddy with his guitar playing, which places you in Return and Contribution."

When I started sketching this out for each boy, I had to draw a Hero's Journey cycle for where the boy was overall in his life, but then I had to add a couple of other layers to describe more specific issues, as in the conversation with Bryan. The result was the 3-D model on page 121. When I put my counselor hat on, I realized that the Hero's Journey model, when used this way, actually "points" to where a boy is stuck in some aspect of his life. Since then I use this tool to help me focus on exactly where a boy needs attention without bouncing around all over the place trying to figure out what's going on with him. For example, I won't waste effort trying to get a boy to high school graduation (Culmination of the Quest) when he is actually stuck at an earlier stage like why he should be attending class on a day-to-day level (Call to Adventure). My efforts are targeted on one issue and one stage at a time.

Another benefit of using this model is that it helped me see how even "bad boys" usually have a good side that might be difficult to see otherwise. It gave me small positives to build on, a valuable asset in working with these boys.

I began experimenting with weaving the Hero's Journey model into more aspects of my work. I found it could be woven in directly, where everyone could see it and talk about it, or subtly—using the dynamics but not the overt model or terminology. Parents I was working with began using the model at home with their boys. Youth facilities I was involved with would alter the sequence of their program to better follow the Hero's Journey sequence. Following this universal model's sequence and dynamics made the work much easier—like swimming with the current rather than against it.

I suggest structuring any family behavioral-control effort or youth program to follow the Hero's Journey cycle. For example, suppose you are using a classic behavior contract with your son to get him to help with lawn maintenance. You can start by pointing out that he is in Conventional Slumber: he likes to work on his tan while lying on the lawn, yet he doesn't realize lawns do not water or mow themselves. His Call to Adventure is your request that he help water and mow regularly. He'll no doubt have some difficulty remembering to do this, or excuses why he can't (Thresholds of Difficulty) and you'll probably have to show him how to do it properly (Discipline and Training). With the threat of consequences (grounding, no use of the phone) over his head, he'll no doubt get the idea after a while and help create a nice lawn for naps (Culmination).

See if you can find a way to compliment him for something unique about his effort (he mows faster than you, figures out how to water the lawn in three sprinkler moves instead of your four). Ask him to show you or explain how he succeeded, show his younger brother how to do it, or simply ask him how he feels to have helped out the family and created a nice place to hang out (Return and Contribution). Allow him to enjoy the fruits of his labor before you try to get him to take on another chore (a new Hero's Journey cycle).

For those of you working with youth in schools or other programs, structure the goals or process to follow the cycle and it will help you see where problems or roadblocks show up. For example, I've been working with a charter school in Oregon that has adopted the Hero's Journey cycle as the core for the entire school's many programs, clubs, and fund-raising efforts. They claim it makes things easier and the kids are becoming adept at using the model to analyze problems. Older students greet new ones (Return and Contribution) and they've come up with a program of levels for promoting students that's based on the Hero's Journey. Each level follows the cycle, and before a student can move up to the next level, he or she must have completed all aspects of the earlier one, including Return.

THE HERO'S JOURNEY AS A TREATMENT MODEL

The Hero's Journey is an ideal tool for working with high-risk and adjudicated boys. I have repeatedly used it as a means for tracking the progress of individual boys and as a framework for structuring programs for them. I've found many boys are hesitant in, bored by, or downright hostile to closed-door therapy and what they consider psychobabble. The Hero's Journey is fairly simple to explain, and the boys almost always connect with how it works in stories and movies I use as examples.

I use the Hero's Journey in three distinct ways. First, I overlay it onto every boy I'm working with to see where he is in the cycle. Is he asleep to his problems and issues or is he truly aware of where he is in life at this moment? Has he accepted the Call to Adventure to "clean up his act" and face his responsibilities, or does he run away from or evade his issues? Is he Refusing the Call anywhere?

If he has truly awakened to what's necessary, and is accepting the challenges of his Call, is he amenable to parental input, counseling, mentoring, or other adult help? Most youth who are mired in behavioral problems tend to be stuck in one of the first three stages of the Hero's Journey. Many boys are certainly asleep to the problems in their life. Many boys are unwilling to accept the challenge to grow and have a healthier life. Many will accept challenges and risk but will not accept any input from grown-ups, thus bogging down in Discipline and Training. The beauty of the Hero's Journey is that it helps you focus on where they are stuck, and that is where you put your efforts.

The second way I use the Hero's Journey approach in my work with boys can be seen as a three-dimensional version of the model (see page 121). The graphic below shows my concept of how this three-dimensional model works. The top disk indicates what stage a boy is in on his overall Journey through life—how he is dealing with the most important issue he faces. I'm always looking for other, smaller areas in his life where he might be farther along in the cycle than he is on his overall journey. These are represented as additional disks underneath the top, primary one. In essence, I look for a part of a boy's life where he is experiencing success, and help give him an opportunity to transfer that small skill to get the bigger picture.

The intention here is for the boy to experience, recognize, and feel this successful stage on a micro level. The next step is to show him how it would work on a macro level—how he can apply his strengths and skills to the bigger issues on his life's journey.

For example, a sixteen-year-old boy in a local group home had a history of delinquent behavior and serious drug addiction issues, yet somehow along the way he had managed to become an Explorer Scout. His group home utilized a wilderness treatment model. As the newest youth in the program, Martin earned respect from the group when he was able to use his Explorer Scout training to help set up the tents and gather firewood the first time he went camping with them. At this micro level, he was already capable of Return and Contribution, which gave him some success at that far end of the Hero's Journey cycle that he was not experiencing in life overall. The Hero's Journey 3-D graphic shows how I used this model with Martin to depict his camping skills and other

The Hero's Journey 3-D Model

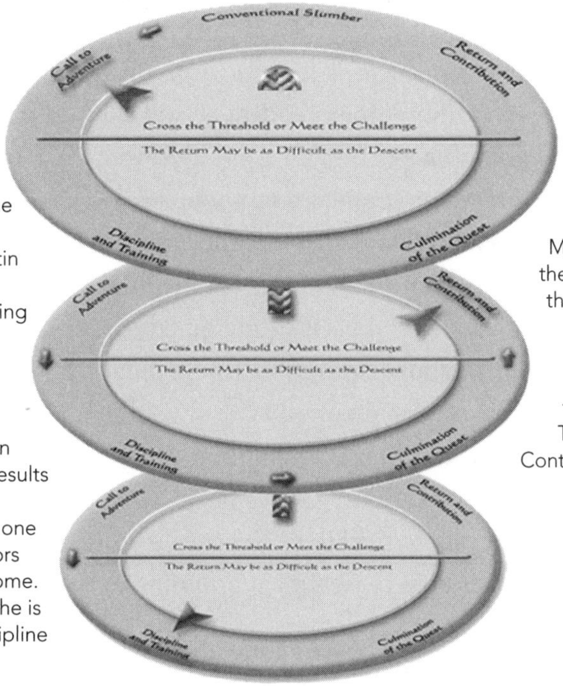

Stuck overall in denial about the severity of his problems, Martin keeps refusing the Call regarding drug use and delinquent behavior.

Martin has been getting good results from his school tutor, and likes one of the counselors in the group home. In these areas, he is accepting Discipline and Training.

Martin, although the newest boy in the group home, has camping experience he can share with the other boys. This Return and Contribution makes him feel good about himself.

Fig. 5.8. The Hero's Journey 3-D treatment model

aspects of his life at the time. Using the 3-D model, the goal then became to set him up as often as possible to teach what he knew, letting him experience success in this area again and again. I'm always on the look-out for ways that a young man might be able to teach or help others, giving him a taste of success and the completion of a stage of the cycle, even if it's only at a micro level. (By the way, I heard from Martin a few years later. He was clean and sober, and attending college in California.)

While teaching woodshop for some teenage boys a few years back, I kept an eye out for which boy might have a certain skill or process he could help others with. One of the projects I taught was how to create sandblasted signs and graphics. I had one student who had a great gift for this particular process. He became good enough to duplicate patterns he found on the Internet and CD covers, so I bought him a prepaid photocopy card at a local printing place so he could increase or shrink the images as needed. He learned to prep the wood by himself, and was very helpful aiding the less skilled boys.

He then worked a deal with a local chiropractor, trading a nice sandblasted graphic of the doctor's logo for free chiropractic adjustments. Even after the woodshop project ended, he still enjoyed the process and the praise he got from people. One day during a staff meeting, most of the counselors were complaining about how hyperactive this boy was, and how his attention deficit disorder was driving them crazy—he couldn't stay focused on anything for more than a few moments. It struck me that this boy had been sitting quietly for three or four hours working on a pile of about twelve different graphics. His ADD basically disappeared when he was involved with something he liked that challenged him. He wrote to me awhile back, reporting he was attending college and that all was well.

The third way to use the Hero's Journey is to weave it directly into a home or any other kind of treatment program, either openly or subtly, as I described earlier in the chapter.

When I get a new young client or a boy shows up as a placement in a program I work with, I have this Hero's Journey conversation with him in a casual way. This is usually easy because I use movie examples he can relate to in order to help him understand. If he has been continually grounded by parents or entered into a drug treatment program, for example, I assume, even though he might deny it, that he is still in Conventional Slumber or he wouldn't have made the mistake of getting in trouble or incarcerated again. I explain what I see as his Call to Adventure in this new setting and what challenges or thresholds of difficulty he could expect to encounter. I help him see what each successful stage might look like, and encourage him to get the information he needs to complete the challenge. I make sure to talk about including an appropriate Return and Contribution component, such as writing a letter of apology or donating time to a worthy cause.

We talk about how many boys, typical of adolescents in general, are resistant to input from grown-ups, and that one of his challenges is to accept the concept that he doesn't know everything. I suggest what

I expect his Culmination would be and ask him what he thinks might be an appropriate goal. We discuss the further difficulties he is likely to face later at home or wherever he goes when his treatment ends. Finally I try to help him see how he must Return and Contribute to complete the cycle, perhaps by talking to a class of students or writing an anonymous article for the school paper. Each time he understandably trips up along the way, we come back to the cycle to see where he is and why he is stuck.

If you ask a boy and his parents or the adults who work with him to outline in writing where each of them feels the boy is in terms of the Hero's Journey model, you'll learn a lot. You'll get a clear idea of how the youth sees himself, and discrepancies between his perception and those of the adults who work with him will help indicate where he is stuck or in denial. That's where you put your focus.

I even do this in my workshops. People entering the room to hear me are looking for more information, or are trying to become more awake to problems and possibilities in working with difficult teens. The audience's Call to Adventure is to sit through the presentation, or to survive the exercises I put them through. They may be tempted to leave or not participate, but the Call challenges them to hang in there.

There is often a difficult spot, or threshold to cross, in that they might not agree with all of my information or they may find it too challenging. The fact that they are listening and discussing the material shows they are in Discipline and Training, and often just pointing this out will make them feel more successful. They will usually complete the challenge or process at some point, and I help them see that now they will have to struggle to implement some new ideas into their work or families, and that further difficulties might arise in that process. Finally, I point out that while they have achieved culmination of their current quest, they are not finished with it. How will they share their newfound information? Whom will it help? As students a few moments ago, they now stand poised to go home and teach what they've learned. Only then do they actually complete the cycle.

THE HERO'S JOURNEY CONTINUES

Life is a storm, my young friend. You will bask in the sunlight one moment—be shattered on the rocks the next. What makes you a man is what you do when that storm comes. You must look into that storm and shout, as you did.

THE COUNT OF MONTE CRISTO
SPEAKING TO YOUNG ALBERT
ON HIS SIXTEENTH BIRTHDAY
(2002 MOVIE *The Count of Monte Cristo*)

As you can see, the Hero's Journey is so universal and archetypal that it applies to many of the mundane things we do every day. Try to be more aware of the model, and bring its dynamics into awareness around you. Set up the structure, and let the Hero's Journey guide and inform you and the young people you care about.

Following the Hero's Journey model through this chapter has, as it should, brought us back to a beginning of sorts. Will we adults and parents accept the Call to work and treat our youth a different way? Will we accept the guidance and mentoring of our elders, our older cultures, who found tried-and-true approaches to helping boys move forward? Will we find new criteria for Culmination of the Quest other than a large bank account, stock options, and a house in the suburbs? And most of all, will we take all that we have learned, both good and bad, and bring it back to Return and Contribute to the next generations of youth?

6
Modern Rules in an Ancient Game

World peace is good. Finding a stock at 5 that goes to 200 is better.

SLOGAN FOR SMALLCAPCENTER.COM

In this chapter we'll take a serious look at some of the current cultural and societal dynamics that have evolved in this country and how they have caused or exacerbated many of the problems we see in teenage boys. As evidenced by the slogan above, much of our modern cultural mind-set is consumer and profit driven, which pulls away our resources and efforts from programs and services for our youth. Most schools are operating on a shoestring budget, and most youth workers and teachers receive mediocre pay at best. This lack of support manifests in many caring people leaving teaching and social services to work in fields where they can make a better living. I've worked under countless grants that end every couple of years, not only putting me out of a job but also ending programs that were making a difference for kids.

There is also a serious lack of aftercare in youth programs. We have enough trouble getting money to actually pay for the programs, but no one ever wants to pay for services after a boy graduates from a program to ensure that he remains successful. Most states have an age limit after which they refuse to pay for youth services anymore, usually eighteen. This is called being "aged-out." I can't tell you how many times I've seen a boy put on a Greyhound bus on his eighteenth birthday because funding literally stops that day. It doesn't matter where he is in his addiction efforts, gang issues, and school progress, for example.

It is not my intent simply to culture-bash, but rather to bring to light aspects of our society that have become so familiar that we don't really examine them, nor do we see the particular impact they have had on the lives of adolescent males.

I believe the fact that we allow our policies on issues affecting adolescents to be skewed so much toward profit can be explained in part by what psychoanalyst Carl Jung termed "the shadow." In his words, the shadow is defined as "the thing a person has no wish to be." Shadow is composed of those parts of us humans we are not so proud of: greed, envy, cruelty, weakness, and so on. Jung determined that if you do not acknowledge your shadow qualities, you will project them onto the person you have an issue with.

Our country can be seen as having its own persona, with exemplary qualities as well as shadow qualities. And it is also capable of unconsciously projecting those undesirable qualities onto others—creating "cultural shadows." America, like many other countries and cultures, is more or less a patriarchy, which means that men hold most of the political and economic power. Our patriarchy is essentially made up of white, middle-to-upper-class men. If the shadow is that thing you least want to be, then what would constitute the patriarchal shadow? Well, the last thing most white middle-to-upper-class men interested in power would want to be is anyone who is not powerful or in charge. This would include women, people of color, Native Americans, gay people, homeless people, people on welfare, and old people.

This helps explain why, for example, 90 percent of homeless resources go toward homeless women, who are only 10 percent of the homeless population. Homeless men are caught in a shadow projection from the patriarchy, who, in their unconscious fear, withhold services.

I believe that in the twentieth century, the cultural perception of adolescents went from that of able, contributing family helpers to difficult, self-absorbed loafers—which places them squarely in the realm of shadow.

ADOLESCENCE AS A CULTURAL SHADOW

Ugly girl, ugly girl, do you hate her . . .
Pretty girl, pretty girl, do you hate her . . .
. . . Faggot, Faggot, do you hate him . . .
Oh Jew, oh Jew, do you hate him . . .
Cause he's pieces of you?

JEWEL, *PIECES OF YOU*

In the same way that aging and death stir up the control issues of the patriarchy, so does adolescence. We adults often project our jealousy and envy of youth directly onto them, urging them to "grow up" and "act your age." We envy their young bodies, their long future, and freedom from mundane adult responsibilities. I remember my own father coming home from a hard day's work to chastise me for just hanging around. Looking back, it makes sense that some part of him would be envious of my freedom from responsibility. The shadow aspect lies in the fact that we don't acknowledge the envy. We also struggle with our adolescents telling us that they do not want to be like us, which we do not want to accept.

As adolescence becomes more and more its own separate culture, it occupies more shadow territory in the adult psyche. The patriarchy is about control, and adolescence represents one of the least controlled processes. As more youth gravitate toward drugs, gangs, early pregnancy, violence, and dropping out of school, they become frightening to those who want to control them.

Children and teens react to their environment. If our kids are acting crazy, that is a reflection on our cultural parenting. Of course we always want the problem to be elsewhere, and it's hard for anyone, and the patriarchy in particular, to accept that kind of responsibility. I learned this the hard way when I would occasionally be asked to speak to a group of men like the Rotary Club about gangs or drug use. Inevitably at those gatherings, someone would ask me the crucial question: "What is the cure for gangs (or drugs)?" I would point to him, then myself, then all the other men in the room and say, "You, me, us!" The next thing I knew, most of the men in the audience would be angry, accusing, frustrated, and disappointed with my answer.

Shadow also plays a large part in the process of continuing to incarcerate boys and adults when all the evidence says that approach doesn't work. As I pointed out in chapter 4, about one in thirty-two black Americans is either incarcerated, on probation, or on parole. The freest country in the world has more rules and more rule breakers than any other country, as well as the most elaborate incarceration system. When kids turn to drugs to numb their family problems, join a gang to get a sense of family, or use guns to express their frustration and rage, that reflects on us as cultural parents. That, in turn, activates our fear of the shadow, for what do patriarchal parents least want to be? Ineffective parents. So we continue to try to sweep under the rug the evidence of our failure, by locking away the offending children.

I firmly believe that it's the shadow dimension of our national consciousness that allows us to consider economic growth and profit margins more important than taking care of our families, and enables us to do no more than wring our hands as unhealthy trends in our culture continue. Every time a father is laid off in a corporate downsizing or is replaced by a new machine, the shadow rears its ugly head, shielding us from the truth that these practices are encouraging the breakdown of families. The priorities and values we actually live by as a society are making the landscape of adolescence that much more difficult to navigate.

FATHERLESSNESS

The deepest tragedy of the Deadbeat Dad is not a loss of money. It is a loss of fatherhood.

DAVID BLANKENHORN, *FATHERLESS AMERICA*

We must instill in the next generation of fathers the
belief that fatherhood is a sacred trust, that it is their
non-negotiable responsibility to support their children
financially and emotionally, that children need and
deserve a father's love.

AL GORE

A multitude of studies indicate that the absence of a father in the first two years of a boy's life results in lower self-confidence, more-limited intellectual ability, fewer traditional male interests, and so on. These first two years are paramount for creating attachment and bonding abilities, and it is during this time that the child takes the first steps toward developing a conscience and the ability to empathize with others and show remorse. It therefore shouldn't surprise anyone that fatherless boys are often more violent, delinquent, and lazy than their counterparts with fathers. Consider these statistics: Sixty percent of rapists, 72 percent of adolescent murderers, and 70 percent of youngsters in state reform institutions are products of single-parent, fatherless homes. Eighty-five percent of male convicts are fatherless.

The incidence of fatherlessness in American families is without precedent, and things are not getting any better. The negative impact on boys raised without fathers is enormous, and not just a minor or inconvenient cultural dilemma. Mothers, try as they might, will never supplant the need and desire of boys for healthy interaction with their fathers. As various parts of this book point out, unhealthy masculinity is involved in many of our society's most devastating problems, and a boy growing up without a father must struggle even more than most to define himself as a man.

Research on fatherlessness began in the 1940s as experts tried to measure the impact on children of having their fathers away at war, or dead. We used to track negative behavior such as truancy, burglary, drug use and sales, and so on through socioeconomic data, which showed the differences in prevalence of these behaviors among people of different ethnicities or income. Historically, poor people of color have the most poverty and neighborhood crime. While this too often remains true, we're now seeing a strong correlation between crime and boys without fathers.

We often look at socioeconomic indicators as criteria for violent behavior, yet miss the common denominator of an absent or detached father. Eighty-five percent of men in prison are fatherless. The absence of fathers is arguably the number one problem in our country, yet it's treated as if it were a minor blip in an otherwise healthy system.

One reason so many fathers are distant or missing from their families is that men are taught not to seek help, even when the results of their inaction may mean the loss of family, the destruction of their children's future, and personal feelings of failure. Going for counseling or therapy is perceived as an inability to handle one's problems, and most men feel they must handle their problems alone. The mere act of going for help makes many men feel like they might get kicked out of the club. When will we make it all right for our men to ask for help in a direct way? The first thing I ever do when a father or any other man comes in for counseling is pat him on the back.

Simply put, eliminating fatherlessness comes down to prevention versus treatment. Rather than wondering what to do when so many dads are missing, rather than trying to get child support from deadbeat dads by putting their photos on milk cartons, we need to try and connect with these fathers earlier in their lives, before they are even fathers. We need to create parenting-skills classes for teen boys that don't turn boys off, but instead engage them in a fun and intriguing way. We need to meet teens and other boys on their own turf, so to speak, since they are so hesitant to come into counseling and therapy. We can weave educational models with sports or wilderness settings. We can add services for teen fathers as well as teen mothers. We can create for men initiation-style programs like the International Mankind Project that will help make the men healthier, more mature people. (I'll say a little more about this organization later in the chapter.)

America allocates huge resources to counterterrorism, with good reason. Treatment after the fact wouldn't work. The situation of our children in jeopardy of losing their fathers is similar. We claim that prevention is too expensive, but too often we seem to find the resources (although still meager) after the children have already fallen into the deep end. Allowing fatherhood to diminish further is damaging entire families, and particularly the boys, who absolutely need fathering.

Mark Bryan, writing in *The Prodigal Father,* is one of the few people today focusing on displaced fathers. Displaced fathers are fathers who left the family, perhaps after a divorce or maybe just ran out and never came back. Bryan was one of these teen fathers who panicked and took off, leaving a single teen mother to raise their son. When he finally matured enough to see his mistakes, he wanted to get back in relationship with his son but the son was too angry to let him. It took years of hard work and deep soul searching for Bryan to rebuild the relationship with his son, and his book is about those efforts and Bryan's subsequent work in helping other fathers get back into their families. His research zeroes in on our society's view that men are financial providers above all, and that we have let that become more important than fathering. As someone who specializes in fatherless boys, I am amazed at the lack of funding for doing work with fathers, which is where prevention should be addressed.

Bryan found that the number one condition on which displaced fathers are allowed to return home is if they can prove they have improved their financial situation. The failure to be financially successful should not be a criterion for being a good father. This backward approach continues to drive fathers away from boys, rather than working earnestly to bring them together. The shame of failing as a father is as bad as it gets.

More and more often in my reading, I come across research that seems too ridiculous to be true. In *Raising Cain: Protecting the Emotional Life of Boys,* for example, the authors point toward a number of studies that reflect the importance of men in a relationship, both as spouse and as father. The fact that we even have to research whether fathers have a purpose and value is one of the saddest commentaries on our culture that I can imagine. It's as though the underlying belief in our country is that fathers are expendable, except for the money they provide. As a man, and a father, I find this most insulting. Is it any wonder so many men don't recognize and fulfill their true responsibilities as fathers? Have we really digressed as cultural parents so far that we have to prove via empirical research that fathers indeed do have day-to-day value in the emotional upbringing of their children?

A hundred years ago I would have had a different job, as mine hadn't been invented yet. I basically make my living off fatherless boys, and as you can tell from this book, I put a lot of time, effort, and love into my job. However, my overall goal in this industry of "bad boys" is to unemploy myself. Fix the father issues in this culture, return to tested and proven models of initiating adolescents, and I'd suddenly find myself out of a job. That's a worthy goal, but I fear it won't happen in this lifetime.

ESL: EMOTION AS A SECOND LANGUAGE

Guns don't kill detectives, love does.

HUMPHREY BOGART AS
PHILIP MARLOWE, P.I.

Boys are raised to be tough throughout the world. In past times and distant places, the circumstances of men's lives made toughness a condition for survival. In some places, this may still be true. Yet in our culture, in less perilous times and with supposedly enlightened views about gender stereotypes, we still persist in teaching boys to be mentally and emotionally tough, to not show emotions, to show no weakness.

While it can be argued that it is important to make boys and men tough for the challenges that lie ahead, we have mistakenly equated emotion with weakness. The expression of emotions is one of the qualities that separate humans from so many other species. Yet, in our attempt to transcend our less civilized background, we came to believe that emotions, in and of themselves, represent weakness. So men are taught to suppress their emotions. It seems to me that now, when the most basic struggles for survival have been for the most part put behind us, would be a good time to express ourselves a little.

It is not just the expression of emotions that creates a dilemma for boys and men. Boys' fears of being too vulnerable have been programmed into us for millennia. For many of us guys, childhood was filled with coaches, fathers, and other male leaders telling us not to be sissies, not to cry, not to let anyone know when we were hurt. One of the components of their teaching was designating anything feminine as weak. So boys are taught that to be men, they must show none of the softer traits. The inability of men to express emotions derives from making this subtle distinction: Though you may not be sure how masculine you are, by being inexpressive you show the world that at least you are not feminine.

Because the criteria for entry into the "club" of men are so arbitrary, boys and men are forced to maintain their tough-guy routine throughout life—a veneer of manhood. Being strong does not mean not showing emotions. Feelings have been getting a bad rap for as long as I can remember, to the point where many boys and men cringe just at the sound of the modern "F word": Feelings. One of the major complaints from women about men is that they are incapable of showing or expressing any emotion other than anger.

Dan Kindlon and Michael Thompson's book *Raising Cain* aptly describes the problem as the "emotional miseducation of boys." They assert that we are teaching boys to be "emotionally illiterate." Anyone who has ever been a parent of or worked with little boys knows they are capable of a full range of feelings, until those feelings are culturally removed. Many of us working with high-risk adolescents have learned to translate the teen language of behavior into its hidden and unspoken counterpart, feelings.

I've been intrigued by a cultural phenomenon called X games, a competition involving a variety of athletic events that feature the "extreme"—always at the cutting edge of risk-taking, and of sanity, if you ask me. But I am always interested in how and why things appear in a society when they weren't there previously. It tells me there is a need, a void we are trying to fill. As the criteria for achieving manhood and masculinity in our culture continue to be nebulous, men and boys will have no choice but to continue working "the edge" to make sure they are on top of the male totem pole. With no set criteria, they will continue to pursue and pursue and pursue. Uninitiated boys and men crave the "rush" of extreme sports as the doorway to feeling, because feeling in other ways is prohibited to them.

In workshops I usually get a few chuckles at my play on words regarding Emotion as a Second Language (ESL), but seldom do my listeners argue about the concept. It's as if we are resigned to the fact that boys and men must be "emotionally challenged" to be accepted as men. Our unbending cultural approach of making our boys, and therefore men, emotionally illiterate is surely a strong factor in the rate of fatherlessness and crime, not to mention a 40 to 50 percent divorce rate.

If we really want to stop miseducating our boys, then we will need some tutors and mentors who are willing to go against the grain of traditional male training. Healthy men will need to model how to express feelings while remaining masculine.

A great example of how this can work is the International Mankind Project. After scores of men went through its New Warrior training, and made great strides in becoming healthier and happier men, they noticed something important. The men now felt, as healthily initiated men, that they needed to give back (Return and Contribution). So they've created a fascinating mentoring group called Boys to Men in which the stronger men work with needy boys and help point them toward a better vision of manhood.

EDUCATION OR ISOLATION?

The development of general ability for independent thinking and judgment should always be placed foremost, not the acquisition of special knowledge . . .

ALBERT EINSTEIN

Our school system as we know it is about a hundred years old. On the one hand, that's a blink of an eye in human history. On the other hand, many see the public school system as a dinosaur that has reached its peak and is declining. Schools have made a strong impact on American youth, in good ways and bad. For boys, school has created a number of problems that can offset its positive aspects.

For a fascinating look at the history of education in America and its impact on teens, I highly recommend Thomas Hine's book *The Rise and Fall of the American Teenager*. Hine paints a clear picture of the events and changes that have occurred in our educational philosophies, systems, and beliefs. I also recommend John Taylor Gatto's powerful *Dumbing Us Down,* which includes strong views gleaned from a career of teaching inner-city kids. Gatto was named New York City Teacher of the Year three times and received a similar designation from New York State, only to resign immediately afterward. His explanation for that move was that once everyone saw his techniques and theories on teaching, they'd probably have to fire him for his alternative approaches. His book is a fascinating look at the educational system from someone who had spectacular results with very difficult populations of kids.

As an advocate for education and learning in general, it is not my intention to denigrate education, but instead to point out that many aspects of our educational systems do not work or are indeed backfiring from their original intentions. My own career has been filled with teens who don't fit into the traditional public school system very well, and I've been looking at that model for many years now. Many of the teens I've worked with have been made to feel like failures for their performance in school, particularly those boys who are headed toward work in a trade, rather than to college.

I've come to understand that the goal of "standardized" education is improbable if not impossible. Standardization is at odds with our diverse culture, and the standardized testing that the educational system adheres to continues to show us our cultural differences in spite of our efforts to get everyone to the same place at the same time. By forcing our youth to interact primarily with kids of the same age, we take away their access to diversity. Older boys won't mentor younger boys, and younger boys won't see the modeling of older youth. And this approach completely disregards the individual boy's developmental stage.

Schooling Then and Now

America's evolution into compulsory education goes back to our earliest years as settlers. Most of us are familiar with stories of the schoolhouse where all ages were engaged in one room, arguably the best school model around. Kids were taught basic skills on which they could build throughout their lives as needed or desired. This setting allowed for mentoring and rising to one's personal best without having to wait for other students to catch up.

Education actually had a difficult time getting a foothold in America. The problem was that teens were actually considered irreplaceable at home or work, the result of a long history of contributing to society and the family. While some younger boys and many girls could attend school, for a long time teen boys were needed elsewhere and for them school was seen as a frivolous diversion. As I've pointed out elsewhere in this book, having healthy, able bodies meant that teens were always involved in either working to help support the household or at least contributing to chores. The role of teens in our society has gone from being indispensable for their contribution to the family's daily existence to being irresponsible and out of place. Or, as Hine claims, "The principal reason high schools now enroll nearly all teenagers is that we can't imagine what else they might do."

During the Depression, jobs were scarce, and when the New Deal was implemented, it prioritized who got to work. Fathers with multiple children got the first shot at employment, and fathers who had fewer or one child were next on the list. They were followed by men with wives and finally single men, with male teens holding the last place for employment. Adults quickly learned that something now needed to be done with these newly independent and uninvolved teens, so school was a convenient holding place for them. The separation of teen boys from mainstream work left them open to create their own culture, which we are all too familiar with today.

World War II sent older teens off to fight. The manpower shortage created the need for younger teens and women to work more than they had previously. But once the dads and other men came back from the war, they took their place at the top of the employment list, and once again teens found themselves removed from actively participating in the world of employment.

All-day school became the norm, and many changes were made to school systems and curricula that reflected a new focus on technology, an outgrowth of the war.

Soon after World War II, our Western trend toward developing technology and the burgeoning of white-collar jobs prompted the belief that to succeed in life kids would need more education than ever. Hine quotes from an article written way back in 1934, in which the National Education Association asked, "What are we to do with our youth up to the age of eighteen or twenty when our best technical engineers and industrial experts are agreed that they cannot be used in the industry or agriculture of the future?" Suddenly, blue-collar work, so long the backbone of America, was considered old-fashioned in an increasingly technological society. Today that trend continues as we create devices and tools for doing blue-collar work, often costing thousands of workers their jobs.

We do vocational testing with my high-risk teens. What we have found year after year is that they will probably grow up to be trade people such as mechanics, carpenters, sheet-rock layers, bricklayers, truck drivers, and so on. What really bothers me is that they are usually taught in the educational system that this is not good enough. Teens are encouraged and cajoled to finish high school, then to go to college and get a white-collar job that pays more and is easier on the body. While that may be good advice for many kids, blue-collar jobs are still the backbone of this culture, and I take offense that so many kids feel like failures because they are unable or unwilling to attend college. I don't know about you, but it makes little difference to me if the person who tunes up my car went to college, or if the guy fixing my roof or putting in new carpet completed college, or even high school for that matter—as long as he is good at what he does.

SCHOOL AS PARENT

As parents and as teachers, we teach who we are, not just what we think or what we give children to do.

MARY LEUE, ALBANY FREE SCHOOL

School was never designed to replace parents, but in effect that is what has happened. In the past, whether the parents were farmers, hunter/gatherers, or shopkeepers, their children were with them throughout the workday. There was no childcare available other than the extended family, and most able-bodied people contributed to daily production in one form or another, so there was no one sitting around just to watch the kids.

Mandatory schooling and the trend for both parents to work out of the home have cast school in the role of a baby-sitter of sorts. This is unfortunate, for it prevents children from observing and learning from the world of work, and from identifying with adult role models in that context. It also eliminates many of the opportunities parents used to have to teach and model their values to their kids in an authentic setting. And, last but not least, grouping children of the same age for most of the day fosters the development of a peer culture that is resistant to other social influences.

Being near parents who worked gave children a very real look at daily life. They saw firsthand that effort equals results, and that hard work and cunning put food on the table. They slowly learned the skills and nuances of their parents' work. Present-day children see their parents go off to work and come home, occasionally with this piece of paper called a paycheck that represents their efforts. Children in modern culture seldom see their parents working, and have little grasp of what all that work stuff is really about. It's far easier for a father to model good work ethics in person than just to lecture about it at home. Allowing children to see the actions and results of work moves them out of the abstraction of principles passed along in school and into the reality of actual experience.

When I was a kid, one of the coolest things I did was to go to work with my father occasionally. When he was a bread delivery driver, sometimes my brother and I would tag along. We'd help out, get some pastry treats, and feel grown up. For a time, my dad was a night security guard at a new high school that hadn't opened yet. My brother and I sometimes went there to keep him company. We got to play on the switchboard, have the run of the building, and make his rounds with him, which was kind of scary. But I had a good sense of what he did when he said he was going to work.

In my classic blue-collar neighborhood, I picked up little bits and pieces of the work puzzle from the other dads. We had the milkman down the block, the roofer across the street, the carpenter next to him, the truck driver at the other end of the block, and the butcher next door. We boys hung around anyone with tools, played on the roof while it was being repaired, and checked out the truck driver's big rig. We saw what our dads did, and wanted to be like them.

A critical offshoot of this dynamic is that having children tag along throughout daily work efforts keeps them under the family's learning umbrella. Family values and ethics are constantly reinforced, while a modern child in public school is actually removed from his or her parents for a minimum of six hours a day, five days a week, for twelve years. Typically, once all family members return home at the end of the day, most available time is taken up with homework, dinner and dishes, baths, chores, and so on. Modern parents strive to create "quality time" with their children, partly because they are removed from the family for such large blocks of time. The average American father spends only twenty minutes per day talking with his children. Is it any wonder, then, that family values and parenting abilities have diminished?

As children now often spend more of their awake time at school than at home, it's not surprising that parents face an uphill battle trying to instill their own values in their children. Keith Jackson, with the San Diego Gang Suppression Unit, provided the following information from a study regarding the changing influences around children in this rapidly progressing society:

Greatest Influences in a Child's Life

1963	1993
1. Family	1. TV/Other Media
2. Church	2. Peers
3. School	3. School
4. Peers	4. Parents
5. TV/Other Media	5. Church

As you can see, the influences have basically reversed themselves in just one generation. This is a critical shift, in that it opens the doors for other problems to manifest. A century ago, teens were not separated off into their own section of society, but this is precisely what has evolved as a result of compulsory schooling. According to renowned sociologist S. N. Eisenstadt, this is not the path adolescents naturally take. As Hine explains:

> Eisenstadt argued that age groups are not universal, but that they have been found in many different times and places where either of two conditions exist. The first of these is that the power of the family must be diminished. . . .
>
> Eisenstadt's second condition for the formation of youth groups is the unwillingness or inability of the older generation to pass on wealth and power to the young.

I believe that a high divorce rate and removing children from their families five days a week for schooling have certainly created a "diminished family" system. And rather than parents passing along vital information and modeling about work and life, we now expect school to do so. Having deferred this great responsibility to our under-equipped and overburdened schools, it should surprise no one that so many of our teens seem to be aimless and disdainful of adult life.

Perhaps no one can speak more knowledgeably or eloquently on the subject of kids and school than John Taylor Gatto. He spent much of his illustrious, award-winning career deprogramming kids from the daily school ritual. Gatto contends,

> Young people are indifferent to the adult world and to the future, indifferent to almost everything except the diversion of toys and violence. Rich or poor, school children who face the twenty-first century cannot concentrate on anything for very long; they have a poor sense of time past and time to come. They are mistrustful of intimacy like the children of divorce they really are (for we have divorced them from significant parental attention): they hate solitude, are cruel, materialistic, dependent, passive, violent, timid in the face of the unexpected, addicted to distraction.

So what can be done? Gatto concludes:

> [School] needs to stop being a parasite on the working community. . . . only our tortured country has warehoused children and asked nothing of them in service of the general good. For a while, I think we need to make community service a required part of schooling. Besides the experience in acting unselfishly that it will teach, it is the quickest way to give children real responsibility in the mainstream of life.

Whether or not he was aware of it, Gatto's suggestion falls right into the realm of the final stage of the classic Hero's Journey: Return and Contribution. An education should not be free, or like many free things, its value will seem diminished. Children should learn to pass along and give back what they have learned, accruing responsibility and confidence as they do.

School should not just be for college preparation if only one in five people gets a degree. Schools should not promote kids who are not learning or achieving. Doing so creates false self-esteem, but perhaps even worse than that, it sets them up for potential failure in our adult world.

TELEVISION AS PARENT, TEACHER, DRUG

The heading for this section might sound like a bit of a stretch to some readers. But TV is so thoroughly enmeshed in children's everyday lives that its influence cannot be overstated.

Parents today often use television as a distraction and baby-sitter, which on the one hand makes a lot of sense in a culture in which both parents usually work and half the marriages fail. But although some programming is educational and beneficial, it also reinforces kids' perception that TV is a teacher, conditioning them to trust and believe what they see on the screen. And because television is littered with commercials, it molds children's desires and creates in them a consumer consciousness.

By the time a child graduates from high school, he will have witnessed eighteen thousand murders and seen 350,000 commercials on television. He will also have spent more time watching television than he spent in school. There are also a number of studies that directly link obesity in children to television.[*]

Before 1960 you could hardly even find child obesity statistics, because children were more active before the sedentary viewing began. Today 14 percent of children ages six to nine are classified as obese or overweight—three times more than when I was a kid. The child or teen "couch potato" is largely a product of the second half of the twentieth century. Ironically, TV sets are now manufactured at the same rate as children are born in America, about a quarter of a million per day.[†]

Too much TV viewing is a constant complaint of teachers and

---

[*]http://www.kidsource.com/kidsource/content2/obesity.html
[†]*Connoisseur Magazine*, 1990

schools. Many teachers tell me they can distinguish between the kids who don't watch TV and those who do. The ones who don't watch have a better attention span, greater creativity, and more initiative. There also seems to be a correlation between how much time a child spends zoned out with television and how uninterested he is with the rest of life.

Teen boys are especially susceptible to the lure of television. They are caught between a rock and a hard place: no longer allowed to be children, but not allowed access to the adult world. Television has become one of their favorite drugs to escape this dilemma. In the three years I worked at Rite of Passage, or ROP, a boot-camp-type residential treatment program in Nevada for very troubled boys, it struck me that the safest time of the week was when the boys were watching the Sunday movie. I don't remember a single restraint being necessary during a movie period. The drug effect was evident.

Adults contribute to this problem by separating teens off from most adult activities and using television to keep children busy. Many people blame teens for being too lazy, but people, and particularly adolescents, seem to have this propensity for following the path of least resistance. Once again, the symptoms of the problem are being confused with the cause. Give teens nothing to do, and they will do nothing.

We now have grandparents who grew up with television, so nostalgia for what life was like before television is disappearing. For more and more people, television has always been there. They have no frame of reference for life without it.

SHIFTING LIFE STAGES

If you break down the typical human lifespan, there are some basic stages almost all of us go through. For most of human history, the sequence has been unchanged—only the age span for each stage would change over time. But the twentieth century saw a change in this sequence.

Below is a graphic representation of the major developmental stages of a typical human life as they have played out for millennia.

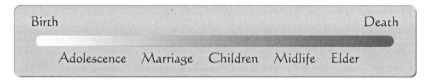

Fig. 6.1. Typical Developmental Stages of Life

In the mid-twentieth century the divorce rate began to soar. With 40 to 50 percent of marriages now ending in divorce, I think we have to look differently at the middle stages, perhaps adding a Divorce component after Marriage.

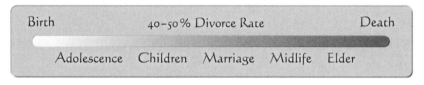

Fig. 6.2. Modern Developmental Stages

Also, since one-third of all children today in America are born to unwed mothers, for many people we will now have to put Children before Marriage as a developmental stage to go through. Here is yet another example of how we have been prepped and trained for millennia to follow one spectrum, yet are now living enmeshed in another.

7
Nuts-and-Bolts Approaches

Rebels been rebels since I don't know when . . .
DON HENLEY, *ALL SHE WANTS TO DO IS DANCE*

"Why does he do it?" This has to be the single question I am most often asked by parents. We've discussed how the interaction between teens and grown-ups is like a dance; it really takes two to tango. The answer to the question "Why does he do it" could easily be "Because he is supposed to." While I'm not advocating, and never will, that negative behavior is acceptable, I have learned that much of the angst we grown-ups suffer with our teenagers we tend to bring upon ourselves. Adolescent behavior is often inconvenient, certainly, but that doesn't make it wrong.

Controlling adolescent boys to the general satisfaction of most parents and teachers would give them little opportunity to grow. Simply getting kids to do what you want is missing so much of the whole picture and process.

Many of my workshop participants come to hear the teen guy tell them how to control and eliminate their boy's bad behavior. I've learned, though, that giving the tools too early just gives parents the skills to better handle and control their teens, without understanding the problems driving the behavior any more than they did before they met me. I have found that unless parents really learn to look at and deal with their boys in a different way, just giving them more ammunition will often compound the problem rather than fix it.

So, when I do many of my workshops, the material basically follows the flow of this book. First I discuss what a teen anywhere in the world or in history might be like. Then I try to show what a modern teen is like. Then I explain how boys used to be crafted into healthy men and members of their community. Late into the process is when I finally start discussing the control pieces so many parents and other adults come to me for.

In this chapter I will give you many tips and techniques for eliciting better behavior from your teen boys based on current behavioral theory. In the next chapter I will present what I call transpersonal approaches— more spiritually based, ceremonial, creative tricks to add to your parenting tool belt. While the nuts-and-bolts approaches are important, I consistently find the transpersonal approaches get better results, and have a deeper effect on kids. A blend of the two gives you a lot of options.

A number of the examples I use in my explanations of these nuts-and-bolts approaches involve the troubled, adjudicated boys I've spent so many years working with. But rest assured, the principle being illustrated is equally true for any other adolescent. Whether you work in a counseling agency or treatment program or you're a parent trying to get your son to clean his room or do the dishes, these techniques can work for you.

Ultimately, the best way to get teens to do what I want or need them to do is by being patient, prepared, and tricky. I treat the baddest of boys with respect and no judgment, and that in turn gains me their respect and trust. To accomplish this, we adults first have to readjust our own attitudes.

THE BRICK WALL

Living and working with adolescents often feels like running into a brick wall. Adult logic seems to have little value in working with teens. Indeed, one of the best skills I've developed is to let go of my adult logic when working with them. It will drive you crazy if you keep trying to filter their behavior and beliefs through your adult system of logic.

The image of a brick wall is very useful for me in dealing with teens, for whenever I find myself butting my head against it again, I ask how else I might get to the other side where my goal is. There are actually lots of ways. You can go over the wall or under it. You could go around the wall, which takes time, or find a way to forge a gate or opening in the wall. The important part is to be creative and flexible, willing to try different things or even adapt your goal if necessary. Too many people, when working with teens or any other population, become overly attached to a goal, even when it's apparent that it simply is not going to happen. We also get attached to behavioral strategies that worked when our boys were children. But since your adolescent boy is probably not playing by the same rules as he was a couple of years ago, you must play by different rules also.

A good example played itself out one week at the treatment center for troubled youth that I worked at in Nevada. We had always had a few boys who claimed to be devil worshippers ("D.W.'s," we called them), but they seldom took their behavior to any extremes. Most of the time I found it humorous and reasonably harmless. Many of the younger, smaller boys claimed to be D.W.'s because it kept the other larger, stronger boys off guard. One morning, a group of ten to fifteen kids from Central Camp came out for roll call with their eyebrows shaved and satanic slogans and pentagrams written and carved into their bodies. Somehow they had managed to get a razor blade.

They soon became unruly and noncompliant, and were removed from the main camp to a separate area of the complex known as Specials. Being a D.W. became quite in vogue that weekend, and populations varied from fifteen to twenty kids. The average in Specials was typically three to six boys, and because everyone there was noncompliant to some degree, this particular incident required almost half of all available staff for supervision and control, leaving the other half to monitor about one hundred kids in three camps. The intent of the D.W.'s was to disrupt camp, and for almost four days and nights they continued their antics. They often tried to run away, attempting to split up staff, in what we called a starburst: A few more boys than we had staff would head off in all directions of the desert. As a staff person got near a running boy, the boy would stop running and peacefully surrender. Their goal was to get one or more of the boys to succeed in running away by outnumbering us. They caused fights, refused to cooperate at all, and kept staff involved in dozens and dozens of physical restraints.*

As exhaustion and frustration settled in for us staff, we feared someone would soon get seriously hurt. Many of us were running on no sleep, while the kids were working in shifts, so to speak, in their attempts to wear us down. A couple of us realized that we needed a different plan than physically breaking down their "rebellion." The point was no longer to win in the game of them versus us, but to end the stalemate and move on. Traditional attempts at behavior management simply were not working, and being bigger and stronger was not getting us what we wanted.

In our exhausted minds, we decided to fight fire with fire. Around 3 AM of the fourth day, we found some lumber by a construction site and built a twenty-foot-high, twelve-foot-wide cross. We dragged it to Specials about four in the morning. We dug a deep hole and sunk it in the ground on the top of a nearby sand dune. Two of us sat there for the next few hours, waiting for the sun to come up and the boys to wake. Soon we heard the first morning mumblings coming from the sleeping hut, and heard the boys talking about what antics they would pull today. They had a routine down. They would be compliant for the first hour of the day or so, so they would get a hot breakfast and possibly a shower. Then, as if by some unspoken command, they'd all get crazy and the game would continue. Boys are very adept at using the system's loopholes to their advantage.

---

*Out-of-control boys were physically restrained to calm them down and keep them from hurting themselves or others. The technique we were trained to use for conducting safe restraints is described in more detail in chapter 9.

This particular morning, we watched the boys stumble from the hut, rubbing their eyes and looking around at the new morning. Suddenly, they noticed the giant cross on top of the sand dune, and they stood there stunned. After a few moments of silence, one of them finally laughed and said, "That's f—ed up, man." They all seemed to find some humor in it, and I realized that while it had made sense in my delirium to fashion a cross to battle devil worshippers, I really didn't know what it was supposed to do. What it did do, though, was to break or move the stuck energy of the situation, and suddenly the war was over. The boys didn't seem to know what to do.

The lesson was clear for me. For too long we were attached to not losing, not letting the boys get the better of us. As they had the same mind-set, we were at an impasse that lasted a very long four days and nights. Allowing ourselves to ponder a different picture of success and different path toward that success was the starting point in shifting the situation. It's not as simple as us getting what we want versus them getting what they want.

If you have hit an impasse at home with your son, remember this incident. You need to get the focus off you winning or him winning, and find a way to bring a new perspective and a different kind of energy to the issue. Take a deep breath and try something new and unexpected.

One woman told me how she did this with her eighteen-year-old son, who was refusing to get up one morning after she had repeatedly reminded him that he needed to get up early to do his chores before heading to school. Frustrated, with few consequence options at her disposal and unwilling to physically force him out of bed, she returned to the kitchen and busied herself with getting breakfast ready, steaming all the while. Looking out the window at what was already a lovely spring day, she was reminded of a song about spring from a musical. Remembering how she'd always found a particular singer's rendition of the song rather annoying, she suddenly thought it would be really funny to go back to her son's room and sing that song annoyingly at the top of her lungs. Just thinking about it made her laugh, and she decided she had nothing to lose by doing this. So she returned to her son's room and sang with maddening enthusiasm. Her son first covered his head with his pillow and then complained and told her to stop. But she kept it up until finally he couldn't help laughing, and grudgingly got out of bed. The battle of wills was sidestepped, and they could move forward with their day.

Here's an analogy that illustrates this point. While rafting a river, you might need or desire to pull over at a certain stretch of beach, but the current is making that difficult or impossible. You can flail about and burn large amounts of energy, determined to get to that particular spot, and you'll either make it or you won't. Once you accept the fact that this direction might not work so well, you can ponder other ones. Perhaps you just have to go a little farther downstream and then walk or wade back to where you originally wanted to go; and there is always the possibility that this new spot is actually better than the one you originally thought you wanted. This new direction could seem like more work, until you factor in all the expended energy of fighting the current. That kind of openness to changing strategies midstream is necessary if you find yourself beating your head against the brick wall. If you can get over your attachment to the way you want to get to your destination, you'll be pleased to find that you can get there from a different direction.

REDEFINING SUCCESS

I've seen too many people get caught up in discovering their teen doing something wrong. This is a very common dynamic in group homes and at other residential facilities for youth. New staff continually come to me with lists of things they have caught the boys doing wrong. Heck, I tell them playfully, these are adjudicated, addicted boys. Catching them doing something wrong is a given.

Rather than always looking for what a boy is doing wrong, there is much to be gained by keeping track of what he is doing right. What makes this difficult is that the negative behaviors of teens can really push our buttons, making us very reactive instead of proactive in our responses. At facilities that deal with troubled boys, we had to teach staff not to take things personally, and that when a boy inevitably messed up, not to take pleasure in doling out the requisite consequences. Many teen boys have a history of making bad or wrong decisions. Expecting them to cross over to the functional side right away is unrealistic.

I can't tell you how many times I've seen adults become more concerned with winning the argument or controlling the kid than with helping him make good decisions. It's as though our competitive training surfaces and suddenly it's more important to be right than to be effective. The best people I've seen working with teens keep their ego in check. Being vindictive has no place in this work, and it is not about getting even after a youth has said or done something to hurt you. Particularly with adolescents who have a history of making bad choices and decisions, the finesse to the work is to help them make better decisions.

For example, there was a boy I worked with who had the destructive habit of telling some staff member once a day to "f— yourself." At Rite of Passage, this was considered disrespecting staff and the boy subsequently "lost his day," meaning he had to stay in the program one more full twenty-four-hour day because of that one remark. As Terry lost his temper almost every day, it looked like he would never get out of placement. It became a sad joke among staff as to who would take Terry's day this time, and the belief was that the behavior-change model of receiving negative consequences would eventually make him stop. While waiting for Terry and so many of the other boys to actually change according to this hopeful behavior model, it seemed to me we needed to find some different interventions that might work faster or more simply. After all, our program was by the behavioral book, so why were so many boys still resisting us?

I talked with Terry about his recurring behavior a number of times. He had a rebellious streak that just would not allow him to become completely subservient, which is how he viewed compliance. He also was bipolar, or manic-depressive, and his mood swings were dramatic and unpredictable. He could be laughing at a joke and a moment later he'd be crying. The fact that his verbal disrespect was costing him dearly was lost in his denial, his magical thinking, and his pride. (Magical thinking is an unrealistic belief, or magical hope, that reality will not manifest somehow. Teens do this all the time; it is a carryover from an earlier developmental stage.)

One day I suggested that he try substituting the word *fine* when he was angry, while knowing in his heart it really meant "f— you." He could even say it with some malice or negativity, I suggested; it would still be a more appropriate response. One day, a staff member instructed Terry to do some chore, and I could see the conditioned response coming. He looked at me, then at the other staff, and said slowly with lots of sarcasm, "Fine!" The staff member knew very well, I believe, how Terry felt, but had no grounds to "take his day." The moment passed and Terry still owned his day.

He had the beginnings of a new skill—self-discipline—and a tool that, while a compromise, gave him some degree of control in his dealings with authority figures. He continued to earn his days pretty regularly after that, although his self-destructive patterns often manifested in other areas. Rather than just being content to not let him get away with anything, I learned a lesson in how to succeed by looking for different options, working with a boy's abilities and disabilities, and not being overly attached to familiar approaches.

Awhile back a group-home boy was given a drug test, which is common. Although staff felt he might be using something, he denied it, but his history of lying had placed him in the realm of the boy who cried wolf; no one believed anything he said anymore. His drug test came up negative, meaning nothing was showing up and he was clean. Most of the staff then assumed he had tampered with the test, which he had no history of doing. My point is that they already had an attachment to a particular outcome, and were determined to make the results fit their expectations, even if the boy was innocent. Many teen boys tell me they feel that adults treat them as if guilty until proven innocent. This group of staff had no desire for the boy to succeed, and seemed bent only on proving how bad he was.

COMMUNICATION STRATEGIES

Before we head into the specifics of dealing with teen behavior, I want to take a look at communication skills. Having knowledge of behavioral strategies doesn't guarantee success if your communication—your delivery system—antagonizes or challenges a boy.

Of course we grown-ups are older, more experienced, and supposedly wiser than our young people; simply relying on using our power and authority, however, will not work. Getting children to do things "because we say so" may have worked well when they were younger, but it only antagonizes adolescents, and makes them put up defenses and attitudes. Communication with adolescents must make them feel like they have an equal right to express themselves. Though we parents and authority figures will forever be trying to determine what is in their best interest, we need to try and do so in a positive and productive way.

When speaking to teenagers, adults have the tendency to talk down to them as if they were second-class citizens or, at best, large children. This is particularly true with boys labeled as delinquents, who often remark about how disrespectfully and dismissively adults speak to them. For instance, a seventeen-year-old group-home boy had earned some free time, which takes quite an effort. He chose to hang out at Starbucks and drink coffee. He had an hour-long conversation with a man and woman, talking about politics, schools, and a number of other subjects. When the group-home van, which is recognizable in our town, arrived to pick him up, the adult couple quickly got uncomfortable and slipped away. He was terribly hurt by this stereotyping, particularly since he had impressed them as a decent young man for an hour.

The next eight sections of this chapter offer a variety of communication strategies that will build mutual trust and respect and help avoid the classic impasses and painful arguments that so commonly occur between teenagers and parents or other adults. These techniques are appropriate for teenagers in any setting.

Horizontal Communication

Horizontal communication is a term I use to describe to parents and other adults how discussion *with* teens should be straightforward, direct, and respectful. In contrast to this horizontal mode of communication, many adults talk condescendingly or "vertically" down *at* teens. If you want a boy to act like an adult, talk to him like he is an adult. I don't want boys to accept what I say because I'm an older adult or parent. I want them to make up their own minds about what I'm saying. As a counselor, there are many times I know what I want a boy to realize or say, but it is infinitely more effective if he tells me rather than I tell him. Thus, my goal, which remains malleable, is to help the youth see the issue for himself.

The best way to explain how horizontal communication works is through examples. The following stories illustrate adults using disrespectful, vertical communication toward teens as well as horizontal, and the results of each.

Terry, the boy I mentioned a little earlier, was referred to us by social services, not the courts. He didn't have a criminal history or mind-set, but his behavior was considered too disruptive for placement in a foster family or group home, and he was headed for a psych ward. (His first day at ROP, he had so much Lithium in his system, he was barely able to talk and could not complete one push-up.)

A couple of months after I started working with him, I received word from ROP's clinical director that Terry was to be pulled as a program failure. The clinical director, or CD, had decided that Terry was inappropriate for ROP because of his lack of progress for a number of months. Although Terry had a pile of behavioral problems, he didn't do drugs, steal, or fight. Being pulled meant he was most likely headed for a rubber room somewhere.

I asked the CD how he could ethically make that decision if he had never met or even seen Terry. He told me he got his information from Terry's file. That was interesting, I said, since half of what went into his file was written by me and was not that derogatory. I demanded he at least talk to Terry in person before making such a decision.

Terry requested that I be present, and the CD agreed. Nearly eighteen with an IQ of nearly 140, Terry was quite bright and seemed very confident. We went to an isolated picnic table, and the CD began his interview. Terry interrupted him and asked if he was going to take notes. The CD asked in a condescending and patronizing tone if this was "important" to Terry, who replied that if it hadn't been important, he wouldn't have brought it up. The CD then asked in that stereotypic tone if it was important to Terry that notes be taken. Again with perfect logic, Terry said if he hadn't wanted it, he wouldn't have asked. Next, the CD asked if Terry would feel better if the CD actually took notes. I don't know about Terry, but I was about to slap the guy. Terry replied with a totally logical answer again, then broadened his reply. He told the CD he knew he was being pulled based on what was in his folder, thus it was important for Terry that what went in there during this meeting was accurate. Terry also pointed out that he had been dealing with shrinks most of his life, and note taking was part of the process.

And rather than just taking out a legal pad and getting to work, the CD came back one more time saying, "Fine, if it is that important to you, I will take out a notepad and take notes." Anything else, he asked? "Yeah," said Terry, "now you can take that notepad and shove it up your f—ing ass!" Although I knew he had just cemented his fate, I also realized that Terry believed he had no chance in this meeting, that the CD hadn't even intended taking notes, which implied he probably already had his decision made. Terry had decided that he would go out on his own terms with pride. The CD was totally caught off balance, canceled the meeting, looked at me, and said he had told me so. I thought he had just missed a great counseling opportunity, and also that he had treated Terry like an object, not a person. Terry and I had a good laugh afterward, but I couldn't help crying when they took him away. I never heard his outcome in the real world.

In 1994 and 1995, I was fortunate enough to be involved in helping create and staff the first ever Youth Conferences for the International Transpersonal Association's Annual Conferences in Ireland and Santa Clara, California. They were the brainchild of Cathy Coleman, Ph.D., then dean of students at the California Institute of Integral Studies. Cathy had been to numerous conferences that offered no child care, or at best offered baby-sitting. She wondered why children were so often kept out of the life-learning situations. It was her dream to provide a full and rich conference for the children within the framework and concept of the main conference. My role was to structure the teen component and handle the adolescents, as well as help design the overall program.

The first conference in Ireland had the Youth Conference relegated to background events, but the phenomenal success of the program and responses from the children and their parents helped us get a few child presentations in Santa Clara listed on the main conference agenda. As a person specializing in adolescents, my job was to work with anyone past twelve years old. In Ireland, we had provided field trips to local castles and lakes, created rock sculptures on the beach, built and played drums, walked labyrinths, and did dreamwork and a variety of guided visualizations. Main presenters such as Angeles Arrien and Rupert Sheldrake put on private workshops for the kids.

Sadly, Santa Clara did not attract as many people with children as Ireland had, and with only a week or so until the conference, I still had no teens registered. We decided to bring six teen boys from a Lake Tahoe group home I was familiar with. Rather than supervising the highly functional children of presenters, professors, and psychologists as I had in Ireland, I showed up with six drug-addicted, adjudicated teens. As they waltzed through the convention center, I felt my career jeopardized as they made catcalls to women and talked about what they were going to steal. This was to be my biggest test in trusting transpersonal approaches with high-risk teens.

One of the Youth Conference presentations was a forum called Men and Boys. My intention had been to moderate a discussion about masculinity and manhood between the six teens and three male presenters who had volunteered to participate. Stephen Larsen, a psychologist from the East Coast, Stanley Krippner, an expert in personal mythologies and dreamwork, and Keith Thompson, editor of the men's movement book *To Be a Man* were my grown-up panel members. Prior to this workshop, as in Ireland, the boys had been doing dreamwork, Holotropic Breath-work, drumming, guided imageries, and working with the younger chil-dren as part of my experiment.

From the time I first mentioned the forum to the boys, they were negative about the project. No matter how hard I tried, they simply would not believe these three "rich authority dudes" were not going to mess with them. As we prepared to go to the workshop, I could see and feel the boys shutting down, getting defensive, and putting on their "armor." They walked into the room with chips on their shoulders, ready for battle with the enemy: grown-ups. Even as the boys and men sat down together at the front of the room, the boys failed to interact, speak, or even be polite with the three men. As the room was filling with intrigued attendees, I sensed my career was about to go out the window.

One of the boys, a large, heavy-set young man named Nate, sat wearing his sunglasses and a frown, and had his arms folded across his chest. Just as I was about to kick off the discussion, a woman in the front row spoke condescendingly at Nate. "Would you take off those silly dark glasses?" she demanded. Nate just stared at her for a long couple of moments, then said simply, "Nope."

My stomach lurched as she continued: "I'm finding it very difficult to see your eyes, young man. Would you take off those glasses so I might see your face with no distractions?" Another few moments of deafening silence. "Nope," Nate said, hunkering down for a bigger argument to come.

The woman countered with, "Well, I can't see why you have to be so rude about it. All I've done is to ask you to take off those glasses so I can see your eyes when you talk. I don't know what's so hard about it all!"

I knew Nate was finished with his simple one-word responses and was about to let her have it in this now crowded room. Suddenly Stephen Larsen spoke up, and simply told the woman: "Leave him alone. He can wear his glasses any way he wants. Quit telling him to do things that have nothing to do with what he is going to say here."

The tension was thick, and the woman's face reddened as she

responded. "I did not tell him what to do, I asked him to take off his glasses."

"No," replied Larsen, "you told him what to do in the form of a question, and if you had 'asked' me to do so in the same way, I'd have refused also."

As I stood there wondering what other fields of work I might pursue as a new career, Nate looked at Stephen Larsen, who was sitting next to him. A smile crossed Nate's face, and he said simply "Cool!" Nate then put his arm around Stephen's shoulders, and suddenly they were a team. Nate had an advocate, someone who had stuck up for him just being himself, with no judgment. For Nate, it was no longer about kids versus panel members; it was panel members against the audience. I breathed a deep sigh of relief, and we all had a great time with the forum.

Nate and many of his teen peers live in a world of them against us. Halfway through the conference, I was asked to address the audience and give an update on the Youth Conference. As I tried to share what the youth, particularly the teens, had been up to, I found the audience barely paying attention. I raised my voice to get their attention, and proceeded to tell them how disappointed I was with their apathy.

I explained that the group-home boys were not even volunteers, but guinea pigs in my quest to find alternative approaches to working with high-risk boys. I made it known that the group home was camping half an hour away, and the boys were embarrassed by their appearance. They were coming in the back exits of the conference center to use isolated bathrooms in an attempt to clean themselves up. They were eating institutional peanut butter and jelly sandwiches on plain white bread each day. They hadn't had a shower since arriving. I further pointed out how proud I was of their behavior, that they had responded to the transpersonal approaches and were doing fascinating personal work. I pointed out that the boys had noticed how we adults got our custom lunch boxes each day, sat outside in a garden, and were being entertained daily by local magic and theatrical groups. Finally, I told the audience how proud I was of the boys, particularly in light of their logistical problems.

Once again, Stephen Larsen rose to the occasion. He got up from his seat, walked over to where the boys, who were apparently highly embarrassed by my vehemence on stage, were standing. He handed his hotel room key to the boys and said "The next shower is on me." He also handed over some of his food tickets, and suddenly an outpouring of compassion from the adults in general solved all the problems. More room keys and food tickets were offered. Soon, the boys were part of the conference, enjoying the same amenities as the rest of us. They sat and mingled as if they were part of the adult conference. I'll never forget one boy talking addiction strategies for an hour with addiction expert Christina Grof. And when two boys were asked to offer a few words at the closing ceremony, they spoke from the heart, bringing down the house with a standing ovation from a thousand people and not a dry eye to be seen.

One of the two boys had his parents in the room. This, he said, was no small feat. They had been bitterly separated for years and had been unable to hold any civil conversations at all, he claimed. They had come to the conference all week to see what their son was doing, and in doing so had put aside some of their differences. They watched him rise to the challenge of addressing a thousand professional people who cried at his words and gave him a standing ovation, and he got to see his parents holding hands, a healing experience if ever I witnessed one.

I was feeling completely fulfilled when yet another wonderful thing happened. One of the six boys, Matt, had refused to participate in almost everything except our didgeridoo-building workshop. We had wrestled for the first day or two, until I convinced him to leave us alone if I'd leave him alone. Even back then, I knew you couldn't reach every teen with the same approach.

As we were loading up the final morning to drive home, I was saying good-bye to the group-home boys. Matt pulled me aside and quietly said so that no one else could hear him, "I just want you to know that I wish I had participated more. I think I missed out on some cool stuff." Well, I thought, how do I improve on that? Probably can't; it's perfection all on its own.

Until more people are able to speak and act with teens on a horizontal level such as Stephen Larsen did, kids will continue to stereotype all of us as we tend to stereotype all of them and the battle of them against us will continue. Even bad boys will often forget to be bad if we don't dump shame, blame, guilt, and judgment on them.

Whatever!

Few single words teens use on parents are more irritating than "Whatever!" It effectively cuts off the communication with no closure or collaboration. It's very similar to the "talk to the hand, 'cause the head isn't listening" bit popularized in the media some years ago. But after thinking about this polarizing word for a while, and with some input from my teens, I now see it in a different light.

If your teen answers you with "Whatever," this means that he feels he has no hope of being heard, no hope of getting his point across. This is not to imply that what he is ranting and raving about is something you have to agree with. He may be completely wrong. But resorting to "Whatever" effectively closes off the discussion or argument, because he has quit participating. It struck me that when a teen told me, "Yeah, Bret, whatever!" I had left him no avenue to be heard, to at least have his say. I've learned to go back to a kid who says this and ask him what I did to make him feel he had no hope of getting through to me. Typically I find I was being judgmental or critical, or didn't seem interested.

So I have learned to come back after I hear "Whatever" and essentially try again. This doesn't mean I'm going to change my mind, but I will desperately try to let the boy know he has a voice, that I honor his opinion, and that I will hear him out. Since learning this, I hear "Whatever" less and less often in my dealings with teens.

Metaphors

Using metaphors is one of the best tools you can develop for communicating with teenage boys. A *metaphor* is a way of explaining or describing something by calling it something else. For example, one angry teen once told me that life in his family was like being in a blender. Now, I already had information about his family's chaos but when I tried to discuss it, he typically lapsed into family loyalty and denied everything. By giving me his metaphor of the blender, I got a graphic description of how he felt. Remember, adolescent boys are notorious for not being able to express their emotions very well, so a metaphor like the one above helps them convey to you quite vividly what they are feeling.

Metaphors can also be a vehicle for you to reframe their position, which is often stuck. With the boy I just described, I latched on to his metaphor—the blender was a great image to work with. I had him visualize a blender with about ten buttons, and he remarked that the far right one was stuck in the *on* position. I helped him work on "going home" into the chaos, visualizing his blender stuck on "frappe" or "liquefy." Then I had him imagine pushing a button for a lower, slower speed. After a few sessions he was toning his button down to the lowest setting, which was symbolic of the fact that he was essentially refusing to engage in the family's dysfunctional dynamics. His goal after that was to be able to exchange the blender for a less threatening metaphor.

Metaphors are one of the reasons I use guided imagery so much with teens. The imagery process helps a youth give you a "picture" of what he is feeling. If I waited for every teen boy to tell me how he was feeling in words, I'd die of boredom in the silence.

The teen's metaphor is always better than any image that might occur to me. It's very important to reiterate back to a boy what he told you, in his words, rather than words of your choosing. If you are not careful, your words may turn him off, be inaccurate, or even backfire. I learned this the hard way. One boy told me how his father behaved in the evenings. Oh, I said, your father is an alcoholic. The boy yelled back at me that he didn't say his father was an alcoholic; he said his father was a jerk with a drinking problem. Since then, I use just the words I hear from the boy.

If you can use an actual object as the metaphor, this gives boys something tangible they can work on or cling to. Down in Arizona is the Trail of Tears, the trail Geronimo's people were forced to walk after their eventual surrender. The Trail of Tears took them to the reservation our government had dictated was their new home. Along the way, many died as the soldiers ignored their exhaustion and hunger. There's a particular stone that is common along the trail, a kind of black obsidian pebble that rock hounds call Apache tears.

One day in private counseling, a boy painted me a disturbing picture of his home life. It struck me that he had been dealt a bad hand of cards, that he had been given a difficult path to walk in this life. I gave him an Apache tear and told him the story. It was easy to see how he empathized with the Apaches, forced into a difficult situation outside of their control. I pointed out to him that while he was indeed walking a difficult road in this life, he was not alone, and that many others had walked such a road and survived. He said that made him feel less lonely and relieved some of the stress. This taps into the labyrinth metaphor of walking a path that has been successfully traveled by others before. Since then I have used Apache tears a number of times, usually with the same result.

I've learned to keep all kinds of strange things around for these moments. I've given some boys feathers: owl feathers for wisdom, hawk feathers for courage, blue jay feathers for beauty, and sometimes a feather just for lightness in his life. It never fails to amaze me how willingly the "bad" boys embrace these images.

Playing Chess

As I've mentioned a number of times, if you ask or tell a boy to do something, particularly something he doesn't want to do, chances are he will argue and try to get out of it. One thing I always remember is that if I were in his position, I'd probably do the same thing. If you know he will most likely argue or refuse, then when that actually happens it should come as no surprise. This is where the chess game comes in. The skill in chess is to anticipate as many of your opponent's moves and strategies as you can. In chess, you always need to be at least three moves ahead, with contingency plans in case your opponent goes in a direction you didn't foresee.

Dealing with adolescent boys requires the same foresight. *Expect* them to say no. *Expect* them to argue, change the subject, shift blame, and any number of other communication tricks they have at their disposal. Catching them off guard with your already-thought-out replies, you are no longer reacting to the boy but instead making him react to you.

For example, you want to ask your son to help with washing dishes now that you are working longer hours. Of course he is going to try and get out of it, that is his job. Knowing this, try to plan for his negative replies so they do not catch you by surprise and prompt an emotional response. In your head, practice replies such as "I know none of your friends has to do dishes, but if you want to continue eating warm, cooked meals, you will be expected to help." Or, "Yes, I know your schedule is overbooked and you can't squeeze in one more thing—so maybe you'll need to cut down the time you spend on the phone with your friends." This will also alleviate a lot of your stress, for being prepared helps you remain calm with all the teen turmoil going on.

Ask Me, Don't Tell Me

The other day, a sixteen-year-old from a group home was complaining to me about how unqualified and untrained the staff were. This is so common that I just nodded my head, waiting for the next issue to unfold.

"They're so stupid," he said sarcastically. "Don't they know if they *tell* me to do something, that as a defiant teenager I've got to challenge it?" I asked him what they should do instead. "They should try asking me once in a while. I still might not do it, but they'd have a better chance."

Teens constantly complain to me that no one asks them to do things, that most often they are told, and not in the most polite ways. I know some of what they report is embellished, but much of it is true. One fourteen-year-old boy, who was really a nice kid, was complaining that his mother kept telling him to clean the house and watch his younger brother until she got home. In working with them, I helped him explain to her that he did not mind doing these things; he knew they had to be done in a single-parent family. What had been irritating him, that he had trouble putting into words, was that all he wanted her to do was ask, not tell him. "Oh yeah," he added once the tension had been broken, "maybe you could say thanks more often." Good point!

Threats

No one likes a threatening teen, especially one now big enough to back up his threats. Some kids will go so far as to physically intimidate parents to get what they want. Others will threaten us with something out of character like blowing their grades or quitting band or their favorite sport, and then there is the old standby—saying they will run away. Whatever the threat may be, one of the best ways to defuse it is to agree with it. This trick comes from suicide-prevention training.

When studying how to work with suicidal people, one of the main tips you learn is first to agree with the fact they can indeed pull the trigger or leap off the bridge. This is necessary to build rapport and trust. Initially disagreeing with a potential suicidal person can create a perceived threat to stop him, and you may actually incite him to progress forward. By first acknowledging he has the power to do as he threatens, you have actually agreed on something, and a relationship is being created.

In my attempt to get a teen boy to make a good decision when he threatens some negative behavior, I agree that is indeed a possibility. Since he does not feel threatened, he relaxes a little. I then say that I agree he has the ability to carry out his threat, but if he would give me a couple of moments, I could give him a few options to ponder. After that, he is free to do what he wishes. When boys are at the threatening level, they feel they have no options left, and they are stuck in black-and-white thinking, but at some level they are often anxious to hear other, less destructive options.

I learned another good point in my suicide training. When someone is threatening to end his life, you basically get to throw out the rules. You do just about anything to help him find a way out of self-destruction. Many of the boys I work with are slowly killing themselves in a variety of ways, including drugs, gangs, violence, unprotected sex, and so on. One day it struck me: Why should I wait for a teenage boy to get to the point of wanting to kill himself before I did whatever I needed to do to help him? I decided that I would now treat every teen like he was suicidal.

There are very few things I won't do to help a kid. There are a number of grown-ups around who might argue with my methods, but my clientele are teen boys, not adults. I do what I do because it works for me and, more important, it works for my boys. That is my prime directive. If you make it your primary goal not to win a power struggle but to really help your boy when you hit a difficult impasse, you'll be surprised at the creative solutions you'll be able to envision.

Getting Sidetracked

One of the major tricks teens use in trying to get their way is to get you sidetracked, to get you to stray from the topic or issue at hand. Teens are the masters of this tactic. You are trying to talk to them about their failing grades and they have you in a discussion about anything else but. There are three words I've found that will help you stay on task and remain detached enough to keep your wits about you. The words *however, regardless,* and *nonetheless* are wonderful tools for bringing the topic back to what you want to discuss.

For example, if you are trying to talk about school attendance and your teen seems stuck on going other places in the conversation, a statement like, "Well, regardless of the fact that you've never been to Hawaii, I need you to . . ." Or, you might try something like: "I understand you feel the need to get a job; however, I'm concerned about you missing too many classes." Just keep using those three words to come back to the topic, and your boy will have trouble confusing you or distracting you.

A HEALTHY DOSE OF HUMOR

I can't tell you how valuable a sense of humor is when dealing with adolescent boys. You have to laugh with them, not at them. Humor regarding their inappropriate behavior often makes them more open to feedback about that behavior. One of my favorite lines after a boy tries to pull something on me is simply "Nice try! Didn't work!" The boy almost always smiles as if caught in a private joke or something. It defuses the situation and makes it difficult for him to overreact. This quip reflects the principle of the dance we do with teens—that their job is to get one over on me and my job is not to let them. This is a symbiotic relationship, which is much more workable than a challenging or threatening relationship.

WHAT REALLY CHANGES BEHAVIOR?

Everything I ever really let go of had claw marks all over it.

ANONYMOUS

It's evident from the literature on working with adolescents, as well as from the comments I get from so many parents, that behavior management is a primary concern for anyone who deals with teenagers, whether at home, in school, or in treatment. Becoming familiar with behavioral models can help adults make sense of teens' behavior and determine which approaches and consequences are appropriate.

Although it's helpful to know some tricks and techniques for working with teens, it's important to recognize the limitations of focusing on behavior modification. We always have to look at the dynamics leading our teens and us into areas of concern. The most effective behavior management tool is to remove the cause of inappropriate behavior or, perhaps more accurately, eliminate the need to act inappropriately. All the behavior modification in the world will not be effective if the overall causes for misbehavior are not reframed somehow.

Behind any behavior is a belief or attitude about the behavior. It's essential, then, to work directly on the belief system in question, trusting that a change in attitude will bring about new behavior. Your son may be failing in school and you want to improve his grades. You may be able to leverage him with only a behavioral approach, such as grounding him if the grades do not improve. But you also have to work on *why* he thinks school is not valuable. Similarly, we might get a teen to stop shoplifting by using behavioral approaches, but we need to work with him on why he believes it is all right to take things that do not belong to him. Maybe he thinks all teens shoplift, or that it's all right to steal from big stores but not individuals (like I did). Or that because his family does not have enough money, he has a right to do so. Finding out what beliefs or thoughts are driving the behavior gives you a better chance of changing that behavior, and doing so permanently.

People, both young and old, do not change their belief systems or paradigms overnight. There are relapses and failures, semi-successes and brilliant openings. It takes time for a boy to reframe his old belief system into a new one. It's not as hard to learn new things as it is to unlearn old things. So be patient, and when necessary rely on some behavior-modification tools to keep things under control while this process unfolds.

I've tried to synthesize most of this information to some basics that anyone can remember. One of the pitfalls with behavioral work is that when circumstances are tense or scary—your thirteen-year-old son is threatening to move in with your ex, or a seventeen-year-old adjudicated boy is telling you all the terrible things he intends to do to you—it can be difficult to keep your head and remain calm. Keeping the approach and understanding simple is the key to thinking clearly in difficult situations.

So let's look at what motivates behavior, both positive and negative.

Changing Behavior Using Rewards

According to established psychological theory, there are basically three ways to change another person's behavior: rewarding it, punishing it, and ignoring it. Rewarding or reinforcing good behavior immediately after it occurs is the best of the three ways. This is how we train every creature, from toddlers to dolphins, that is capable of understanding the principle "If I do this, I get that reward," and concluding, "I think I'll do this some more!" In fig. 7.1, you can see how a behavior is occurring at some steady level. When the rewards start showing up, the behavior increases.

We are all familiar with rewarding good behavior. But what do you do with a teen whose behavior seems to be consistently negative? A particularly valuable skill for working with such difficult teens is what is called, in behavior-management jargon, "successive approximations." Let go of that cumbersome term, but remember what it

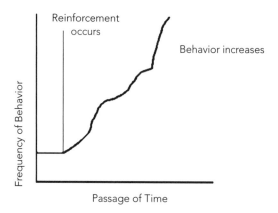

Fig. 7.1. Reinforcement (Positive Rewards)
Any positive reinforcement or reward following a behavior will increase that behavior. Reinforcement works on both positive and negative behavior.

means. Sometimes you have a boy who just doesn't seem to be doing anything right, which obviously makes it hard to reward him for good behavior. Rather than lapsing into the punitive side, look for something that he is doing wrong less often.

Here's how it works. If you pay attention, you'll notice him *not* doing something wrong that he normally does frequently. Perhaps he hasn't used profanity in a record ten minutes, or hasn't intimidated his younger brother for an hour. When you give him strokes for not teasing little Johnny in the past hour, watch the expression of surprise come over his face. When you reward him for not swearing for ten whole minutes, it may at first confuse him, but eventually he will enjoy getting this positive attention. This is a very powerful tool, because it relates back to really wanting him to succeed as opposed to focusing on failure. We are programmed to prefer rewards to punishment, but with some people's behavior you have to be creative to see what they are doing right or, at least, doing wrong less often.

It often occurs to me that if everyone knows that the best way to change someone's behavior is to reward the positive behavior, then why as a culture do we put so much emphasis on punishing people and locking them up? We'll see in a minute why punishment doesn't work, but first I need to make a very important point.

Rewards or positive reinforcements work on *both positive and negative behavior.* If your son does something good and he gets a reward for it, he will be likely to do that in the future. However, if your son does something negative but gets a positive reward, or a reward that he perceives as positive, then expect the negative behavior to increase. The lack of a consequence when one would be expected—in essence, getting away with something—is perceived as a reward, and reinforces the negative behavior. So be wary of inadvertently rewarding undesirable behavior.

It's very easy to slip into this dilemma. Let's say your son is supposed to clean the car, and he does a mediocre job. If you tell him to just skip it, you'll have Dad do it when he gets home because he always does it right, then junior just got a reward for negative behavior. Dad, by the way, received negative consequences because of his positive behavior. In essence, Dad is being punished for being good at washing cars. Teens are very adept at setting you up for this.

Changing Behavior Using Punishment

The second way to change behavior is through punishment or negative reinforcement. This model is the basis for the use of consequences, but as we will see shortly, there is a big difference between punishment and consequences.

Punishment has the reverse effect of the rewards just described. When a behavior (again positive or negative) is followed by a punishment, that behavior will supposedly decrease. Let's say, just for argument's sake, that every time your son was late to dinner you slapped his face. This might very well make him think twice about being late to dinner. However, history continues to show us punishment works only in the short term. This is because the person receiving the punishment develops a tolerance for it.

Humans, as well as many animals, have an incredible amount of endurance and tolerance for pain. Prisoners of war get accustomed to daily torture. Most boys, when describing the abuse they receive, tell me they were at first afraid to get hurt, then got used to it to the point of not caring. Even a boy I worked with whose father used to hit him on the head with a hammer and throw beer bottles at him somehow got used to it.

Figure 7.2 shows how punishment affects behavior. As you can see, once again the behavior is cruising along at a certain level when suddenly a punishment shows up. The punishment stops or decreases the behavior, but only until the person gets used to the discomfort or inconvenience; then the behavior tends to increase. This is the inherent flaw in our prison system.

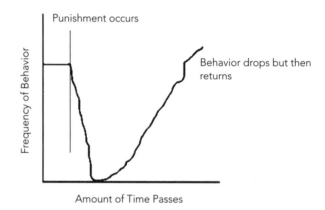

Fig. 7.2. Negative Reinforcement (Punishment)
A behavior that is followed by a punishment will typically decrease dramatically, but tends to reappear as the person adapts and gets used to the punishment.

One of the ways many older cultures survived for thousands of years without a need for incarceration was that they focused more on rewarding the behavior they wanted than on punishing the behavior they didn't like. Some societies continue this tradition. Below is an excerpt from the *Peace Pilgrim Journal,* the fascinating story of a woman who walked the globe from 1953 to 1981 to spread the message of peace. It explains how one African tribe, the Babemba, deal with negative behavior.

In the Babemba tribe of South Africa, when a person acts irresponsibly or unjustly, he is placed in the center of the village, alone and unfettered. All work ceases, and every man, woman and child in the village gathers in a large circle around the accused individual. Then each person in the tribe, regardless of age, begins to talk out loud to the accused, one at a time, about all the good things the person in the center of the circle has done in his or her lifetime.

Every incident, every experience that can be recalled with any detail and accuracy is recounted. All his positive attributes, good deeds, strengths and kindnesses are recited carefully and at length. No one is permitted to fabricate, exaggerate or be facetious about his accomplishments or the positive aspects of his personality. The tribal ceremony often lasts several days and does not cease until everyone is drained of every positive comment he can muster about the person in question. At the end, the tribal circle is broken, a joyous celebration takes place, and the person is symbolically and literally welcomed back into the tribe.

Isn't that inspiring? The entire community realizes the risk of losing a person to the dark side, and sets aside everything to prevent this. Can you imagine, in our day and age of efficiency and profit margins, stopping everything to help one member of the community get back on track? This kind of commitment to the well-being of the whole community is what used to prevent the need for control and incarceration. Focusing on the positive rather than dwelling on the negative can be a very powerful act.

Changing Behavior by Ignoring It

The third way to change behavior involves neither reward nor punishment. This is neutral, or no, reinforcement, sometimes called extinction. Basically, you ignore the behavior you want to discourage. Most parents have been in situations with their children in which the best thing to do is to simply ignore the behavior or comment, knowing that if they give it any interest or energy, it will get out of hand. This response is particularly appropriate (but also difficult to manage) when you know your teen is doing something he knows will irritate you.

As in the previous graphs, we see that if you ignore the behavior, something will shift. What happens when no reinforcement is received, either positive or negative, is that the behavior actually tends to increase for a while as the boy tries to get you to reengage with him. If he doesn't get some response, the behavior typically starts to decline.

This is the classic defense against bullies. Ignore them long enough, and they will be forced to look elsewhere for their inappropriate rewards. This also is the dynamic behind the stereotypic scenario of parents who work too much, or for other reasons do not engage with their kids. For a while things seem all right, but slowly a boy's behavior starts to deteriorate due to lack of attention. A boy who came to Rite of Passage was stuck in this dynamic. His previously attentive father had become too involved in work. The boy tried harder through positive efforts like better grades, accomplishments in school, and so on to get Dad's attention, but when his father kept ignoring him, slowly his behavior deteriorated until he was arrested for stealing cars and Dad had to become involved. The boy eventually learned to provide his own internal, inherent rewards since he wasn't getting any external strokes. Too many boys don't have the wherewithal or confidence to pull this off.

We all know boys who use negative behavior to attract attention. Humans are social creatures, and one of the most difficult things for them to endure is isolation. This is what breaks down prisoners even more than punishment. People, including wild teen boys, need interaction and attention from others. If a boy does not get any positive attention for what he is doing right, and he will not accept the limbo of neutral reinforcement, you can bet money he will act out negatively to get some sort of attention. A boy will stand in front of the TV until he gets yelled at to get out of the way. A boy will flunk a class you know he can pass because people stopped giving strokes for his better grades. The behavior of some teens can be expressed in these simple but stark terms: Kiss me or kick me, but don't ignore me.

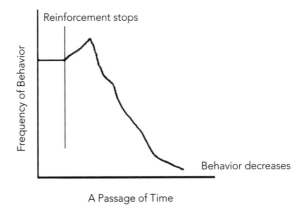

Fig. 7.3. Neutral Reinforcement (Extinction)
When you withhold a reinforcement, the behavior will temporarily increase as the
person tries to regain your attention, but it will then diminish.

If your boy's attitude or performance is declining, you can bet the reason can be explained in terms of one of these three behavior models. Learn to look for what rewards your son might be receiving that are not so direct or obvious. Look for how his negative behavior could be getting reinforced due to a lack of consequences. Many parents mistakenly operate out of a sense of guilt that they should be able to give their children more than they have. This belief often leads to enabling or minimizing the consequences of bad behavior. Letting your son get away with behavior you know is inappropriate may seem like the caring thing to do at the moment. But think about the rules to real, everyday life and ask yourself if what you are teaching your son will serve him in the future or actually harm him. And remember that if you are not paying enough attention to a boy who is behaving normally, you risk seeing his behavior change, and not for the better.

THE IMPORTANCE OF CONSEQUENCES

The use of consequences is a basic component in any behavioral program. It's important to understand that there is a marked difference between consequences and punishment. From my perspective, the major distinction is that punishment is personal and vindictive—strongly attached to the deliverer's emotions. Punishment is too often about getting even. Consequences do not have that punitive aspect. And if the need arises, they can usually be taken back, so to speak.

For example, if an adolescent does something wrong like coming home after curfew, you have a couple of options. If you call him a name, say other derogatory things, or hit him in any way, you can never take that back when you find out your child was indeed telling the truth about the car breaking down. With a punishment, the damage is done and is usually irreversible. But as a consequence, you could take his phone, ground him, or make the curfew earlier. There is nothing personal involved to complicate the matter. Indeed, the more objective you are, the better. And, should you discover that your son was actually telling the truth about having car problems, you can give back your consequences in a number of ways.

You can give your child a "Get Out of Jail Free" card, for instance, that can be redeemed the next time he or she does something that would usually mean getting grounded. Or you can give him extra phone privileges. See the difference? A good consequence is not personal, and can be given back if necessary in some related form.

Appropriate, effective consequences have four basic characteristics, each one equally important. First, the consequences need to be *fair*. In other words, the consequences must fit the offense. Kids need to learn that the consequences are related to the severity of the behavior.

Second, consequences must be administered *reasonably*. If you are vindictive and punitive, they won't work as well. Keep your cool, and don't make the incident larger than it already is.

Third, consequences must be *clear*. Be specific and precise in your directions and expectations. Kids need to know what they are risking, and knowing the rules and the consequences for breaking them beforehand helps them make better decisions. For example, don't tell them to be home by dark, as darkness is relative and therefore arguable. Give them a time, and, if possible, let them know exactly what will happen if they fail to comply. If curfew is at 9 PM, for example, consequences begin applying at 9:01 PM if they are not home.

Fourth, and probably the determining factor in whether or not you achieve success, is *consistency.* Follow-through is essential. What you say you will do you *must* do, each and every time. Without consistency, the other components are worthless.

Never make a threat or promise you can't or won't keep. Never impose your toughest consequence first, as then there is no room for adding to the consequence as your teen argues or rebels against the first one. Structure your consequences in levels of three, each level being more serious than the previous one. Once a kid gets to the third and worst consequence, you've done about all you can hope to do productively at this point.

CHOICES AND CONTROL

"You want me to give my out-of-control teenager choices and control?" At the core of adolescence is the need for boundaries, and then to test those boundaries. One of the most difficult lines to walk in parenting is to maintain control over teens while allowing them to expand, experiment, and rebel a little. Parents are usually dubious when I suggest allowing the kids, who seem out of control already, to be able to make choices and have control over some things. Adolescents need to make decisions and choices even if their previous efforts have fallen short. If parents simply make all the decisions for a boy, how will he learn to do it right?

If the need to rebel, to test limits and boundaries, is a fundamental dynamic of adolescence, we have to help structure those boundaries and ensure that our kids stay within acceptable limits. The goal here is to give teens enough room to do what they need to do without alienating them from their parents. Quite simply, if you as parents or we as adults do not help sculpt the choices and control issues, the teen will make his own.

Providing choices and control for teens is not much different from the old peas versus carrots scenario we enacted when our kids were toddlers. We learned quickly not to ask if they wanted vegetables, because then they'd just say no. We parents learned to structure the question around whether the child wanted peas or carrots. You use the same tactic with teens. While you really want them to eat vegetables or wash the dishes, do you really care if they eat peas or carrots or wash the dishes before or after their favorite TV show? Allowing them to make many of those smaller decisions will help keep them from rebelling at the big ones. You are happy and they are reasonably happy. Of course they will probably not want to eat vegetables, but that is the family boundary and there are consequences for that. Try to let them have as much leeway between your healthy boundaries as you can, and that will make them feel like they have some control. If they feel they have no options at all, expect them to go the way you don't want them to.

Let's return to the boxing-ring analogy we used in chapter 1. Your goal as the parent is to hold that ring size at fifteen feet, while your teen's job is to push against the ropes. If your son comes home half an hour late, for example, and receives no real consequences, your boundaries have been stretched to fifteen feet, three inches. It doesn't seem like a lot, but this now becomes the standard boundary in your teen's mind. He now learns to believe that 10 PM really means 10:30, and you'll have to work twice as hard to get your boundary back to fifteen feet.

When parents bring me an out-of-control kid, what I always find is that the current boundaries are about eighty feet. Getting your personal boundaries back to normal with an out-of-control youth is difficult, if not impossible. It's like trying to lose weight. How long would it take you to put on an extra thirty pounds compared to how long and how much effort to remove those thirty pounds? Once again, prevention is the key.

One of my favorite cartoons has two boys talking on a playground. One boy says to the other, "Hey, isn't that your mom calling you home?" "Yeah," the second boy replies, "but it's only the second time." Each time she called him home with no results and no consequences, her boundaries got stretched.

It is critical to understand here that this is not in the best interest of your son. Imagine a boy living in an eighty-foot boundary. While to some degree that must be heaven for a boy pursuing independence, part of the boy knows he is on dangerous ground. To use another sports analogy, he is now like a bicyclist going down a very steep hill with no brakes. Exhilarating, yes, but wild and wobbly on the other hand, with disaster but a moment away.

Often when I work with a family that has an out-of-control boy, I have to wonder how the parents let the child get so far out of bounds. Why didn't they call me when he was thirty feet, fifty feet, even seventy-five feet out of control? What I've come to learn going through that process so many times is that often a youth will cry out for boundaries and help through his actions, not through his words. When he was just forty feet out of control, for example, and no one stepped in to stop or help him, quite often what happened next was a test to see if or when someone would stop him from self-destruction. Many kids with drug problems have secretly told me they are happy to be on probation and required to be tested for drugs, because now they have an excuse not to use with their friends. They still need us to set limits and provide structure in their lives, even when they are vehemently claiming the opposite.

I want to end this section with one more point. There's a phenomenon with teens I call "the ooze." Let's say your teen has been abusing his phone privileges, and you set up a behavioral consequence system to get that in check. Suddenly, while the phone issue is seemingly cured, you notice he won't clean up his room, and you work to fix that. Next a pattern of breaking curfew appears. This is the dance, and it helps explain some of the limitations to behavior-management models.

Because teens have to test boundaries, just because we stop one inappropriate behavior doesn't mean they will never try again. Thus, the testing oozes into different areas. That is the process, whether we like it or not. Adolescence is like the common cold. There is no cure, no real prevention, and once you get a cold, if you resist it, quite often it gets worse. If you relax into the cold, do what you need to do even if it is inconvenient, it will pass more quickly and benignly.

SOME RULES ABOUT MAKING RULES

With a solid understanding of what your teenager needs and of how principles of behavior modification operate, you can formulate the rules that will support his growth, as well as your sanity. You do not have to be a therapist or trained professional to use these concepts successfully with your teen boy. It is not always easy but it is and should be relatively simple.

Below is a short list of basics to remember when devising your behavioral approaches. Use them wisely, and always look for what is causing an undesirable behavior.

To be of maximum value and effectiveness, your rules should be:

- ► Designed to achieve a specific purpose. Try not to use a broad, sweeping approach like "You need to get your act together, young man!" or "You need to show more responsibility."
- ► Simply stated and not overly wordy or legalistic. Put them in terms your boy will understand.
- ► Clear about your expectations and the consequence for not meeting them. There should be nothing that can be misinterpreted. "Your responsibility is to do the dishes each night before eight. If you fail to do this, then you will not be allowed to use the car for one week."
- ► Reasonable and realistic guidelines for your teen to follow. Make them unreasonable or too tedious to accomplish and he'll just ignore or defy them.
- ► Fair, involving consequences but not punishment. Don't even use the term *punishment* in your conversations. Make sure your consequences are neither unusually harsh nor too mild. If you are not sure, just ask a bunch of parents what they would do and see what the middle ground is.
- ► Few! Cover the most important issues, and often the small ones will get figured out. Remember, for example, that hair grows back and piercing can close up, but tattoos are permanent. If you have to compromise, think like that.

Make sure that you can live with the consequences you designate. When I was a kid, often a seven-day grounding turned into a two- to three-day grounding, because my brother and I made it miserable for our mom until she kicked us outside.

FOR BEHAVIORAL PROFESSIONALS

I often enlist the help of my group-home boys for all kinds of projects, much to the amazement of many adults. The boys have helped me and most of my friends move, build or tear down fences, stack firewood, shovel snow, and just about anything else we can think of. My wife manages two multimillion-dollar beach houses in Lake Tahoe, and the boys have worked there remodeling, cleaning windows, gardening, fixing boat docks, and so on. In all the years I have done this, we have never had a single negative incident. The boys tell me they appreciate being treated like adults with respect.

I always tell the boys before we begin to work that I will start with trust and respect, and adapt if necessary. As a person who likes things out in the open, I usually just ask the boys if they are up to turning off their negative behavior for a while. If they won't be delinquents, I won't be a controlling disciplinarian. Almost without fail, they agree and just become boys rather than bad boys. They tell me how much they enjoy not being in trouble, not being looked down on and talked down to, and not being expected to screw up.

A group home was struggling with the amount of profanity its boys used in the house and, even worse, out in public. The staff seemed concerned, and were convinced that the boys had no ability to control this swearing without serious consequences. I quietly remarked that a couple of months before, I had hired and worked with three boys from the same group home for two very long and hard days moving from one house to another. I had a lot of my friends helping, as well as my then seven-year-old daughter and some of her friends. I had asked the boys before we started if they were willing to curtail their swearing, and the rest of their defiant behavior. They agreed, and for two full days they never said anything inappropriate. On the third day two of them stacked my winter firewood, and once again, even when I took them to the river for a swim with my daughter and myself, they were completely appropriate. One boy slipped once and swore moderately, caught himself, and apologized.

What makes this even more significant for me is that a month before I was to move, for the first time in five years, I was concerned about involving the group-home boys in this kind of off-site activity—this particular group was exceptionally unruly, so adamantly opposed to anything adult. So, as is my style, I told them what my fears were.

The boys responded that they would present me no problem, that their animosity was directed at staff and other adults who didn't treat them with respect. I was still concerned, and left the plan tentative. When I saw them a week later, they told me the six boys had held a meeting. They acknowledged that I had always been there for them, held their confidentiality, and advocated for them with staff, and they were bothered that I didn't trust them. They had agreed unanimously to help me with no pay, to prove their worthiness. I had to honor this mature decision, so I settled on three helpers.

The boys worked diligently, and I was very proud of them. None of the people who helped me knew they were group-home boys, which was a rare treat for the boys. My therapeutic moment came when, while eating a picnic lunch of pizza and drinks, the toughest boy looked around and said, "Wow, this is like a real family thing, isn't it?" "Yes," I replied, "this is how you can live if you choose to let go of the dark side."

The point is that if you treat a teen boy with disrespect, he'll meet you with equal or greater vigor. Treat him with respect, set him up to succeed, and he usually will.

That's all I want to say on conventional approaches to behavior change. If you want to learn more, the self-help section of your bookstore is full of books on this topic. For my money, the best approach is to take away the need for teens to act as they sometimes do. They need to be cared about and listened to, and not just controlled. Children, particularly teens, have a voice and an opinion for a reason. Carefully nurtured, they need not end up in placements like Rite of Passage, removed from their families and communities.

All the behavior modification in the world cannot override a boy's inherent belief systems. If it did, prisons and other lock-down facilities would have more impact and success than they do. Our misguided belief that incarceration will scare teens out of negative behavior will continue to fail, for boys have been conditioned for millennia to face fears and risks and will continue to see this avenue as a challenge to be faced. *Healthy* challenges are what they need.

8
A Transpersonal Approach

Why is there never enough time to do it right, but always enough time to do it over again?

ANONYMOUS

When I began following the concept of creating a healthy body, mind, and spirit, I started to understand the limitations of using behavioral models with teens. I came to believe that some people's histories make it almost impossible to elicit a change in them solely by using behavioral approaches. Many boys and girls have been wounded at a spiritual or soul level—behavioral or social treatment models often won't work with these damaged kids. The abuses they have endured make them impervious to threats and pain. How could I expect consequences like push-ups, calisthenics, and this abstract thing called a day loss to override the sexual and physical abuse they had tolerated already? Punishment has never been an effective behavior-change model because, although it works in the short term, people have an amazing tolerance for pain and abuse and often they simply adapt. Therefore, my work took a shift in the transpersonal direction.

Transpersonal, according to the dictionary, means "transcending or reaching beyond the personal or individual." That means you

182

can work with someone and look beyond his "personal psychology" —his story, the drama, and baggage that is helping create negative situations. Focusing on those details is a one-dimensional, linear look at what might be bothering someone, while the transpersonal approach is more three-dimensional and acknowledges the whole person. Inherent in transpersonal psychology is a foundation in Eastern philosophy, and a belief in the value of native cultures and wisdom and the inclusion of Spirit. According to John Davis, Ph.D., at Naropa University, "Transpersonal psychology integrates psychological concepts, theories, and methods with the subject matter and practices of the spiritual disciplines."

Because it embraces many psychological methods, the transpersonal model allows me to be eclectic in my work, but with structure. That may seem paradoxical, but that's exactly why this approach works so well with adolescents. The practices described in this chapter are not exclusively transpersonal ones, but that label is my frame of reference for them. They are creative and experiential, appeal to the person on many levels, and are appropriate for boys in a home setting or in a teen program. Another good reason I've gravitated to these approaches is that they are cross-cultural, as in not just for white kids. They work just as well with girls, Asians, fourteen-year-olds, nineteen-year-olds, and even adults. Because they are archetypal and have been used by many cultures over many centuries, they are time-tested. This model has helped me work more successfully with boys than has any other system I've tried.

You can see how much the transpersonal model has permeated my work through my stories thus far. In this chapter I want to paint a picture of how to use transpersonal approaches with all adolescent boys. If you are interested in creating depth and meaning for your boy and creating contemporary initiations and rites of passage, then these approaches will suit you. Weaving in the concepts of transpersonal psychology with native components, ceremony and ritual, a bit of magic, and Spirit creates a very powerful and healthy way to work with adolescent boys. I'm sure your imagination will come up with plenty of variations.

On that note, with few exceptions (sweat lodge, vision quest, and existing native rituals), feel free to adapt all of the ideas that follow to your needs, surroundings, and capabilities. Many blend well with each other so you can mix and match, so to speak. Some of the activities described in this chapter would add interesting dynamics to a birthday celebration to make it more memorable, especially significant birthdays like thirteen, sixteen, and eighteen. Many are great for transitions such as moving from sixth to seventh grade. You may want to integrate some of these ideas into your existing holiday celebrations—for example, making masks every Easter. Some of the transpersonal approaches, like making prayer ties or an intention box, are more of a process than an event. They are about visioning and manifesting one's goals and dreams.

For an initiation, you can orchestrate a transformative and memorable event by combining many elements into a multiday process, perhaps in a wilderness setting. Rather than simply having a sixteenth birthday with cake and such things, you could create a deeper and much more meaningful celebration, or yearly ritual, by utilizing a number of transpersonal approaches. With the Hero's Journey to help guide your sequence, these can add up to a powerful experience certain to have an impact on a boy. I'll elaborate on this as I explain each approach.

And, of course, be alert for unplanned but nonetheless significant events that can be experienced more deeply by using these ideas. In the last chapter I'll tell the story of a boy who had given up his gang but was disappointed that this had not been honored and celebrated as vigorously as his entering the gang. Don't just quietly approve when your son makes a decision to relinquish a bad choice—celebrate it. For example, it's relatively common for a boy to want to remove an inappropriate tattoo, and I strongly support that. But don't just let it be an insignificant medical procedure. Embellish it with ceremony and ritual, using some of the approaches in this chapter: making a mask so he can use art to express his process, or making a power shield to symbolize his new strength, or participating in a sweat lodge to purify him for his next chapter in life. Make his positive decision a memorable one, not a disappointing one.

Many people consider my approaches to be alternative to traditional methods. However, as I pointed out earlier, our traditional approaches are barely one hundred years old whereas the "alternative" approaches have thousands of years of history behind them. I don't use these because they are cool or impress my boys. I use them because they work.

SETTING THE STAGE

Remember the developmental issues we discussed in the first chapter? It is very common for teens to rebel against just about anything their parents stand for, including religion. But, and this is very important, just because your son tells you there is no God, or that the religion you've raised him in is irrelevant, it doesn't mean he still doesn't have a need and a desire for Spirit, ceremony, and ritual. He actually needs them more now than ever. If we adults just label these things as wrong and shut them out of our lives, boys will get that fix elsewhere. Ever wonder why alcohol is called "spirits"? Drugs and alcohol often substitute for the empty feeling we experience in the absence of meaningful rites of passage.

Of course, you can expect some resistance for anything new or out of the ordinary. That's why you have to set the stage for introducing ceremony and ritual into your home or program.

Words of Power

I've found that teen boys love the mythic. Look at half the video games they play, or Dungeons and Dragons, and you'll see mythical flavor everywhere. Rather than just let our boys get their fix from the media and shoot-'em-up games, I'd rather fill this need with something healthier.

One of the things I like to do to stir up this healthy energy is to use vocabulary that is archetypal and mythical. Begin by weaving some new words into your house or program. They don't have to be fancy. Just don't make a mockery of them or the boy will also. I've listed a few of my favorites below. The first sentence after each word is simply a dictionary definition, sometimes followed by my own interpretation of these concepts.

Hero: In mythology and legend, a boy or man who is endowed with great courage and strength, celebrated for his bold exploits, and favored by the gods. A person noted for feats of courage or nobility of purpose.

Intention: A course of action that one intends to follow. An aim that guides action, an objective. Having the mind and will focused on a specific purpose. This is prayer, hope, an attempt to manifest something in your life.

Journey: The act of traveling from one place to another; a passage. Rather than taking a "hike," I'd reframe it into a journey, which sounds more adventurous and challenging.

Mystic: Inspiring a sense of mystery and wonder. Kids who are bored, or show disdain for real adult life, could use a dose of "mystery and wonder."

Pilgrimage: A long journey or search, especially one of exalted purpose or moral significance.

Council: A meeting to decide or discuss something. Give your family meetings or school projects the feel of a more ancient setting.

Sacred: Dedicated or devoted exclusively to a single use, purpose, or person.

I don't know why some of these words threaten so many people, but they commonly do. Why wouldn't we want our children to experience sacred ideas and moments? Isn't that what many people dream and hope for, a connection to something bigger than themselves?

You can begin by referring to the school year as a "journey" or use the word *intention* as your boy begins searching for a college or a good job. If you use the Hero's Journey (HJ), overlay a project or time period with the HJ cycle and use its terminology. Conventional Slumber could refer to being new to middle school and having to wake up to this year's expectations. The Call to Adventure could be maintaining good grades. Thresholds of Difficulty might be balancing homework and after-school activities, or dealing with shifts and realignments in his familiar social circles. Working weekly with a tutor could be defined as Discipline and

Training, and being named to the Honor Roll might be Culmination of the Quest. And how to Return and Contribute after a successful journey through the school year? Maybe helping a younger sibling with math, or offering to stack the tutor's firewood as thanks for her assistance.

Sacred Sites

The experience of meaning in rituals is enhanced when they are held in a special place reserved for this purpose. A sacred site should be located somewhere near the home or program if possible, and should be private and secluded enough for emotional safety. I would treat and refer to a sacred site as just that: sacred. A good way to facilitate Return and Contribution for a boy is to have him maintain and manage the site. This should be viewed as a great privilege and responsibility. Remember, we're trying to overcome a century of irresponsibility.

If necessary, the sacred site could be an indoor area. The important thing is to treat it reverently so the boys will also be inclined to do so.

It might seem to many of you that there is no way your boy, or the one(s) you are working with, would ever be open to this spiritual stuff. I've found that a little reverse psychology goes a long way. Typically, the first time I set up a boy or boys for something out of the ordinary, I don't ask them to participate. Make them participate and, true to their nature, they will resist. Instead, I arrive at group late, or come in telling everyone what a cool time I had doing this weird stuff. Sure enough, if you withhold it from them, they'll ask for it. This is how I've gotten delinquent boys from every walk of life to participate successfully in everything I mention here.

The Sacred Fire Pit

Fire is and always has been an integral part of ceremonies and rituals worldwide, so it seems obvious that it should be included in the design for sacred space. The fire pit can be used for bonfires for storytelling and celebrations, burning of Intentions or Give-Aways (see page 220), and a place of vigil or meditation and contemplation. I've never met a kid who didn't like sitting around a fire. This is where what I call ETV—Elder

Television—originally happened. People have been sitting around fires telling stories for thousands of years. A fire is calming and purifying, and can be incorporated into a number of the activities described in this chapter.

The Altar

We've spoken at length about the need for Spirit, ceremony, and ritual in a boy's life. One of the ways I like to invite these dynamics into a home or program is by setting up a place where a boy can put special things and express sacred intention—an altar or shrine of sorts. A desktop, dresser, or small table will do nicely.

An altar should be nonreligious, and I strongly suggest allowing the boy to structure it to his liking. This is a place to put prayer ties, lyrics, tarot cards, letters from loved ones, pictures, masks, feathers, crystals, and so on. Many of the following approaches involve making or using items that can be placed on the altar.

Try not to judge what a boy puts on his altar, and never place something on it without permission. Instead, ask permission once in a while to put something of yours on the altar, saying you'd like his energy and magic to help you with something you are struggling with or trying to manifest.

I have never, ever seen a boy defile an altar. We've put them in group homes and private homes. There is always one at a sweat lodge, and at many other ceremonial events. My wife has one, I have one, and my eleven-year-old daughter has a sacred space just for her. Make this offer to your boy, and it will probably work well, unless you try to control and judge it.

Magic

Never underestimate the power of magic, or at least creative suggestion. In a few minutes you'll read about how I used "story crystals" with a group of boys setting out on a hike. It's a great example of using mystical components to get a modern solution.

I once had a ten- or eleven-year-old client who was brought to me because he had developed a fear of showering alone. He was afraid some monster was going to come up through the drain and drag him down into oblivion. I originally tried behavioral approaches with his mother, who tried to wean him slowly from having to have her in the bathroom when he showered. This was distracting and time consuming for her, and humiliating for the boy. She could slowly get to the door with no problems, then the boy would lose his courage.

As I was in a counseling agency, I had a lot of feedback and input from my colleagues. We tried cognitive reframing with him, to no avail. We tried Neuro Linguistic Programming (NLP), a type of retraining of the mind, with no success. Everything we tried failed to rid this young boy of his monster worries. One day as he sat in my office, I felt I had let him down. Since I had hit a brick wall, it was time to get out of the box and get creative.

An inspiration came to me to fight magic with magic, so to speak. I reached over to my desk and picked up a small amethyst. I told him I should have given this to him much earlier, but it was the last one I had and I didn't know where to get any more. He excitedly asked me what it was. I told him it was an "Anti-Monster Amethyst." He was to take it home, put it on the windowsill in his shower, and wait. I told him to ask the monster to show itself.

"Are you kidding!" he exclaimed. "You want me to invite the monster to show itself?"

Yes, I said, as I continued to make this up as I went. Not only did I want him to ask the monster to show, I wanted him to *demand* the monster show. Why was this necessary? he wanted to know. Because, I said, when the monster finally shows his ugly head in the drain, watch what happens when the Anti-Monster Amethyst goes to work. It is the coolest, grossest thing you'll ever see. He begged me for more information, but I wanted him to step up and handle his own fears, so that's all I would tell him.

I saw him only one more time after that. He was very disappointed, he told me, because the amethyst didn't work as promised. He did everything I told him, including begging and demanding that the monster show, but it never did. Without realizing it, he had solved his own problem with a little magic, a little imagination, and some courage. Success comes in many disguises.

Now that the stage is set, you can begin to implement rite-of-passage dynamics that will help your boy experience meaningful initiation. While most of these approaches are not full initiation experiences individually, you can blend the ones that seem appropriate to address a particular issue or transition.

OUTDOOR RITUALS

Labyrinths

One of the metaphors I used early in this book was that of the labyrinth. As I pointed out, a labyrinth is a clear, easy-to-follow, meandering path leading to a central area and back out again, which mirrors the model of adolescent guidance many older cultures subscribed to. Labyrinths are typically tile paths or dirt paths with boundaries of rocks. Some may be defined by hedges. They can even be painted onto blacktop. There are now hundreds appearing around the world as this ancient tool gains popularity. An Internet search will show you if any are located nearby. San Francisco's Grace Cathedral Web site lists over sixteen hundred labyrinths in the United States alone on its Labyrinth Locator. This can help you find one that may be near a place you'll be visiting, so you can add ceremony to an otherwise ordinary trip. If you want to build a labyrinth locally as a community project, there are instruction packets and models available online for that purpose, and there are even portable ones you can buy or rent to set up wherever you choose.

The center of a labyrinth is a great place for sitting, praying, meditating, or any other reasonably quiet exercise. Parents can walk the labyrinth with their boys, comparing notes afterward. This would be an ideal activity on a birthday, particularly one of the more noteworthy adolescent birthdays like thirteen, sixteen, and eighteen. Your son could walk the labyrinth by himself, and the adults involved in the ceremony

(Community Acceptance) could walk separately, praying or creating intention for your son's future. You might share with him any insights or feelings (pride, concern, for example) that manifested during your walk, and ask him to process his journey through the labyrinth.

You may want to keep a journal of experiences you both have within the labyrinth to share later, or to use in connection with other activities in this chapter. A symbolic object such as a bundle or mask (discussed on pages 214 and 222, respectively) could be carried into the center of the labyrinth and left for a period of time. The heart of the labyrinth is a natural altar setting where you will often find crystals, flowers, poems, and other items left by walkers who felt the need to commemorate their experience.

Perhaps your son would just like some private time to be by himself— this is a healthy, safe place for that. Often, simply walking the labyrinth will calm a boy, or open him up for conversation afterward.

Counselors and therapists can use the labyrinth's center for group or private sessions. Dreamwork and guided imageries always work best, I have found, when done in a sacred area like a labyrinth rather than a classroom or other sterile setting. There's something about the energy of such places that helps set the kids up to participate. Have the boys walk into the center of the labyrinth, and do your guided imagery or storytelling there, while they are affected by the labyrinth's energy. Ask them to ponder or create intention for growth as they exit the labyrinth and close out the process.

The labyrinth can help create metaphors and images and elicit from a boy other comments or information that I can use when I put my counselor hat back on. It's common for a boy to mention after walking the labyrinth that he feels more "balanced" or says something like "I'm walking into my future." Walking the labyrinth and/or doing prayer or meditation within one works just as well for parents. Sometimes when I've had a difficult trip or flight into Reno, a city I travel through frequently, I walk one of its public labyrinths to get focused or let go of my travels.

At the International Transpersonal Association Youth Conference in Ireland, one of our rituals was to have all our kids walk a real labyrinth each morning. We'd do a quick meditation to get everyone calm, let them walk into the center, and then we'd really go to work. All the kids would lie down with their heads in the center and feet pointing out like a big star-burst. We'd do drumming, native chanting, singing, and other exercises to help them tap into their intuition, feelings, and dreams. The information they brought back from these "journeys" was simply amazing. There will be more on guided imagery (see page 199) and drumming (page 224).

At the core of my teen group were five American boys. The first time they walked the labyrinth, they tried to run quickly through it. (Refer back to the labyrinth image on page 37 if you need to.) It seemed the desire to win was largely an American trait, as all the other kids were happy to take their time as instructed. Going so fast, they often acci-dentally ended up on another path, got confused, and had to start over. One time they huddled for a moment, which made all my "Caution!" instincts kick in. They walked more carefully for a couple of minutes, then as they noticed the path they were on paralleled the path closest to the center, they cheated and switched paths.

What they failed to realize was that the labyrinth, like the Hero's Journey, occasionally took them near the center and back out again. The new path they chose actually led them out of the labyrinth. It was a classic moment, for the typically aggressive, cheat-the-rules, impulsive behavior so common with our teens backfired on them while the slower walkers all completed their journey. It was a lot like the archetypal story of the tortoise and the hare. This was a very symbolic moment for me to see how ill-prepared our kids are to walk the labyrinth of life compared to many of their counterparts in other cultures.

If you want to try a fun experiment, have your boy walk a maze first (assuming you can find access to one) to get the confusing and challeng-ing feelings going. Then have him walk a labyrinth, and help explain how this might work in life.

Sweat Lodge

You've heard me mention sweat lodges a number of times now. The sweat lodge experience is a powerful and healthy one for boys when it's done right. The ceremonial purpose of the sweat lodge is to purify the body and the spirit. Typically, a lodge is built of bent willow branches covered with blankets, tarps, or, as in the old days, animal hides. It is similar in appearance to a dome tent. The lodge is completely covered to make it totally dark, except for an entry section typically facing east, but there are exceptions. In the middle of the lodge is a hole or small pit.

Outside is a sacred fire area. A large ceremonial fire is constructed honoring the seven directions, ancestors, and animals or elements of nature (trees and rocks, for example). In the fire are numerous rocks (often a hundred or more), preferably lava rocks, that are heated until red-hot. There is often a dedicated fire tender, and much ritual is followed. Depending on which tribe's tradition you are following, there will be strict protocols for how to walk or talk around the fire. The path from the fire into the lodge cannot be walked on, so cedar boughs are laid down to create a protective barrier between the feet and the sacred path. Tobacco or cornmeal may be offered to Mother Earth with prayers, or participants may be "smudged" by having burning sage smoke waved around their body. The variations are endless, and by subscribing to them you bring the power of ritual to the process. The fire tender or lodge leader usually performs these duties.

Once the participants are inside the lodge, often after a sage blessing or purifying, rocks are brought in by the fire tender and placed in the center pit. When all the required rocks have been placed, the opening to the lodge is closed and water is added or tossed on the rocks, creating steam. Essentially this is a ceremonial steam bath, which purifies the body.

Prayers are offered to the steaming rocks so that the prayers may float out with the steam and smoke to wherever they need to go to be fulfilled or completed. This is the spiritual purification. Usually there are four rounds of prayers and rocks, each round with a different intention. The four rounds I am most familiar with are: first, prayers for yourself to get that out of the way; then prayers for family; then prayers for others; and the fourth is commonly a celebration round with singing, chanting, and drumming. Again, there are many variations in how this is done in different cultures.

It is common for lodge participants to experience a shift in consciousness, an altered state. This may be due to the heat and smell of burning herbs, or from the intensity of prayers. Fasting is common in these rituals because it makes the cleansing and the shift of consciousness happen more easily. I've even seen eating-machine teens fast for a day or two to prepare for one.

It is usually frowned upon to pay the lodge leader in money. Gifts are exchanged, or food is brought for the ceremony afterward. One group of adjudicated, probation-mandated group-home boys made food for twenty people in advance. Many even made presents for the lodge leaders with whatever they could find around the group home. Sometimes a group of boys will cut and prepare wood for a sweat lodge. This kind of participation enables the boys to give something back and to be invested in the process. I continually find boys to be calm, tired, and anything but bad after a sweat lodge.

If true Native teachers and lodge leaders are involved, the process is even more powerful. The stories they tell, backed by the rituals and ceremonial pieces, seem to fill a deep need in boys. The purification aspect of a sweat lodge makes it an ideal experience for a boy about to begin a quest such as entry into middle or high school. Birthdays and other milestones such as graduation are also good times to participate in or construct a sweat lodge. I also like to use them to mark the start and the completion of something—before and following a solo hike, for example, or at the beginning and end of a vacation. Two lodges used this way create a sort of "bookend" dynamic, enclosing the experience or situation between two powerful components. If parents and boys are at odds and fighting a lot, a lodge for the whole family may help bring harmony back into the family. It lets a boy know how serious you are about this process and that you do not see the current bickering as being only his problem.

As a side note, sweat lodges are very good for girls (and boys too) who have been sexually abused. One of the lingering effects of sexual abuse is the feeling of being dirty. Well, what better way to fix that than with a purification ceremony? Imagine if you created a sweat lodge just for that purpose, and how honored the girl or boy would feel. Also, because lodges are so dark, there is a great deal of anonymity, so kids feel safe—a new feeling for survivors of sexual abuse. Finally, exiting the lodge is symbolic of leaving the womb, so it is very common to connect it with the concept of rebirthing yourself, or birthing a new part of you.

After one lodge that I led personally, a boy gave me an interesting gift. He had tied an elaborate necklace with hemp twine, a favorite of pot smokers. But attached to the weaving was the skull of a barn rat. While that sounds a bit bizarre now, this skull was a memento from his rural hometown, which I had actually visited. Because I was familiar with his small town, and many of my boy stories were similar to his, he felt I would appreciate such a weird gift. He treasured this little skull, managing to keep it safe through juvenile hall and a number of months in the group home.

I asked him about the meaning behind the creation. He told me the skull was special for the reason mentioned above. Dangling from the bottom of the necklace was a uniquely folded dollar bill, which was 20 percent of one week's allowance from the group home for him. He said he knew we adolescent workers made terrible money, and the dollar was to represent my financial success in this field. It was quite a poignant moment that he created all on his own, and I was very touched. I will always honor his gift and his efforts.

Vision Quest

A vision quest is one of the most powerful experiences you can set up for a boy. Many Native American tribes traditionally provided this rite of passage for their boys, and some still do. Similar approaches are also found in other cultures. In its simplest form, a vision quest is a period of isolation for a boy that allows him to get a vision of his future. Because the vision quest was so difficult and potentially dangerous, it also served as an initiation.

Typically a boy used to go away from his tribe for anywhere from three to five days and nights. He had to do this alone, usually with no food or water, with only a blanket and maybe a knife. During this isolation period the boy would not eat or drink, which helped bring on nonordinary states of consciousness. Exhaustion and fear added to the equation, and although he mostly just sat there, he was at the mercy of the elements and wild animals, and in his exhausted condition, might have fallen or made some other costly error.

This short but powerful experience addressed many developmental needs all at once. Often, the boy would receive a vision not only of his new role within the community and world, but also of his new adult or spiritual name, thus aiding his search for identity. Having survived his vision quest, he got to join the realm of initiated men, and was then treated as a man. Having faced nature alone, his confidence soared. Many such approaches helped end adolescence quickly by enabling developmental challenges to be completed over a short time as compared to our modern, extended adolescence.

Today's vision quests for boys have been toned down due to liability issues, like so many other rite-of-passage attempts. Nowadays, we cannot let our youth get hurt or be mistreated, so current vision quests require the boy be checked a couple of times a day, and that he be given water or juice and sometimes nominal amounts of food. This certainly minimizes the power and effect of the vision quest when safety is guaranteed. However, since so many boys in modern society are unaccustomed to dealing with nature, it is still a powerful test for them. Isolation and a good imagination can take a boy to his personal fear edge, where growth can occur.

A critical component for the success of a modern vision quest is arranging for how community acceptance comes in. As I have stated a number of times, if a boy goes through all of this and has no one at home to really embrace the process, its effect will be minimized or even neutralized. Ideally, the family or community is nearby at the vision quest during the boy's efforts. I've been at vision quests for other people who say they really appreciated knowing someone was thinking of them and praying for them when the quest got difficult. Supporters will obviously get a better sense of the boy's experience by being present and sleeping by the fire for a few days rather than waiting at home for him to return.

The energy you put into a boy's ceremony will largely determine the strength of the outcome you get.

Wilderness Initiation

Blending the flavor of wilderness treatment models with transpersonal psychology is one of the best recipes I've found for working with teen boys, and it is equally appropriate and effective for boys who are not in treatment. The wilderness component, whether rock climbing, river rafting, or backpacking, helps create an element of risk and puts the boy in an uncomfortable spot. As we've seen, these are common dynamics found in initiations and rites of passage.

One group home with a strong wilderness component was planning its yearly 120-mile hike of the John Muir Trail through California's eastern Sierras. There were seven twelve-thousand-foot passes, and the trek took three weeks of walking. The final day culminated in an ascent of Mt. Whitney, at over fourteen thousand feet the highest point in the continental United States.

We decided to reframe the hike to have more of an initiatory component. I helped provide guided imageries to be done at each summit, with coming-of-age stories and cultural riddles for nighttime conversations. This is how you add ritual, ceremony, and Spirit to a hike or a backpacking trip.

There is no single source for such stories and imageries that I can recommend. The bibliography and recommended reading sections at the end of this book list a number of titles that include folktales and mythological stories, such as those by Robert Bly, Michael Meade, and Joseph Campbell. You may want to do an Internet search for folktales of your particular heritage. If you do a similar Internet search for male coming-of-age stories, you'll hit a wealth of resources you can tap in to.

Guided imageries are something of an art; there is a finesse to delivering them effectively. One way to get a feel for how to structure and deliver a guided imagery exercise is to get David Oldfield's *The Journey* guided imagery tapes (see page 200). I offer workshops for people or communities on how to design and deliver guided imageries with teens.

For more information, contact me at my Web site, which is listed at the back of this book.

Right before the boys were to leave, I got an idea. I showed up at the group home with some small, inexpensive crystals. As I plopped them down on the coffee table, the boys did what I expected them to do; they quickly snatched them up off the table.

"Oh no," I said. " Why did you do that?"

They all replied with something like "What's the problem?"

"These are 'story' crystals," I told them, "but now I can't remember which crystal goes to which story."

"What do we do now?" was the typical response.

"Well," I began, "each crystal has a story, but now that I can't tell them apart, we'll have to wait until the crystal tells the story." At this point I noticed a couple of the boys holding the crystals to their ears, shaking them, trying to make them "work." "No, they won't use regular sounds or words to tell you the story, they'll use magic somehow. Take them on your trip. Put them in your pocket and take them out once in a while. When the time is right, you'll hear the story." (By the way, these boys ranged in age from fifteen to seventeen. I've found older boys are not necessarily averse to these kinds of approaches. You just have to find a way to engage and intrigue them.)

So off on the hike they went. When they returned three weeks later, all but one had gotten some sort of story from their crystal. One young man, an disadvantaged teen from the Bay Area, told me that he was the very first person to reach the peak of Mt. Whitney that day. He even beat the daily hikers, and had several pristine minutes of solitude at that great height. He said that while he was alone up there, he was holding his story crystal. It suddenly occurred to him that he had been looking at his life from a very small perspective. The hike, and the hard ascent, had taught him that he needed a "higher vision" for himself. Thus, he left his crystal hidden in the rocks to act as his higher vision from here on out.

A couple of months later, when I was teaching woodshop, one of the boys came up to me with a closed fist. He opened his hand and there was the story crystal. "Remember this?" he asked rather dejectedly.

"Wow," I said, "I forgot about that."

I was totally amazed he still had it this long after the hike. He told me that he had been carrying it around every day, waiting for his story. Last night, he told me, it struck him that perhaps the magic and the story were not for him. He told me he thought of his mother, and felt bad for his previous behavior. Maybe, he said, the story wasn't for him. His mom had not had a very good life, and he had not been a very good son, and he realized that his mother could use some magic in her life. He asked me if it was all right for him to give it to her, and I was thrilled.

This boy had been typically egocentric and selfish. This incident was the first time I ever saw him put someone else's feelings before his. A twenty-five-cent crystal with a dash of imagination made for a very powerful tool.

TAPPING UNCONSCIOUS IMAGERY

The following approaches are set up to tap in to a boy's unconscious thoughts, which manifest in symbols and images. Most inappropriate and repeating behavior comes from the unconscious and is usually driven by a person's bottom-line belief system. Ever know someone who makes the same mistake over and over again—for example, repeatedly getting involved in unhealthy relationships? Although a man's brain may know that this woman is all wrong for him, the unconscious belief that "I am not worthy" will override the conscious understanding of her faults. Likewise, your boy or boys may be habitually engaging in unhealthy or unproductive behavior rooted in unconscious beliefs. The symbols and images that are evoked by the following techniques can tell you volumes about a boy's unconscious beliefs and motivation.

Guided Imagery

Guided imagery is one of my most useful and valued tools. Doing guided imagery with teen boys is a blast, and leads to some of the most fruitful therapeutic moments I've seen.

A guided imagery is like half a story. You narrate just enough material and suggestions to incite the imagination of your listener, allowing his unconscious to fill in the rest. A boy's unconscious symbolic "comments" will give you much information and insight about him, and provide rich material to discuss with him later.

Guided imageries work best in quiet surroundings but can be done almost anywhere (except while driving). They usually begin with a calming introduction, or induction, during which the narrator speaks of calming scenes like sunsets, clouds, and meadows. Participants are often led through some breathing exercises to calm their bodies and minds. Once they are calm and in a light trance, the narration shifts to lead the listeners through a story and/or provide prompts to generate images. The prompts may be vague and general, such as "See if there is something here that can help you in your future." Listeners might be asked to do specific things: for example, an imagery for a teen boy might ask him to notice if there is a message for his graduation. As in hypnosis, the recipient is talked into a light trance state, and when the imagery "journey" is over, the narration brings him back to full consciousness by refocusing his attention on his surroundings.

It is a little difficult finding good imagery to use with teens. That's why I often make my own. David Oldfield's *The Journey* is the best I've found. An Internet search will lead you to others, such as Fern Fujimoto's E-Motion series and Eileen Curran's *Guided Imagery for Healing Children and Teens*. In addition to gaining insight from the imagery process, teens will also benefit from the quiet, relaxing time. Many will come out of the experience refreshed and in a better mood than before the imagery.

I like to make my imageries teen-friendly. Teenage boys like action, mythology, technology, and off-the-wall things, so I try to incorporate these elements. Many prepackaged imageries use calming music, soothing narration, gentle messages, and the like, which put off most teen boys. Teens really seem to resonate with imagery that calls for them to walk through a graveyard or down a dark basement hallway, or asks them to watch aspects of their lives on an imaginary DVD. I bring in dragons or other mythological challenges, like a dark knight, to prompt their imaginations.

The content and focus will vary based on what I am looking for. For example, sometimes I have little information on a boy, so I will use the imagery exercise to explore or go fishing for insights. Other times I have an idea of what I want to work on, such as anger, drug abuse, or depression, and I point the imagery in a more specific direction. Delivering guided imageries takes some practice because you've got to learn timing, patience, and reading the energy of the boy or boys.

Guided imageries feed into a boy's need for non-ordinary states of consciousness: he gets a brief high or escape from everyday life. If nothing else, this can be cathartic or healing in itself. This is what stories used to do for youth: give them an imagination "fix" without having to do drugs.

Some people call guided imageries visualizations, but I shy away from that term because, like many people, I am not very visual in my mind. I used to stress out in guided imageries and hypnosis, because so much of the process seemed to rely on "seeing" things. I've learned that giving nonvisual people permission to get the message another way has been helpful for me and encouraging for them.

Boys love movies and videos, so I utilize them in the two imageries I use most. In one, I have each boy imagine a movie theater of his design. He can sit anywhere he wants, and can have any seating arrangement he wants. He might sit all alone against the back wall, or have only two seats in the whole theater, his and one to put his feet on! I point out that this theater is special because there are three screens rather than just one. As this point I casually mention that the curtain on the left screen is opening up, and it is about to show a movie about his past. I could mention a time period or I might let him choose it himself. I might suggest he remember a good time or a bad time, depending on what I'm chasing.

For example, I could ask him to focus on a time when he felt safe, healthy, and happy. Many of the boys I work with have few of these, but they usually find something. I ask them to feel this feeling, remember it, taste it, embrace it. I suggest they find a way to remember or hold on to this good feeling, for there could come a time in the future when they need it. I often suggest they put it in a hidden pocket, wear it around their neck, or just keep it safe in their heart. Then I have the curtain on the movie from the past begin to close.

Next, I explain that the right screen is now showing a movie from some part of their future. If I had them get a good feeling from the past, now I take them to a difficult time in their future, a time of fear, frustration, or danger. I let them sit in this feeling a few moments, then suggest they pull out that good feeling and see if it is of use in this more trying situation. Almost invariably, boys tell me they were able to draw on their private, positive feeling. I suggest they find a way to keep this feeling permanently, for they could have further need of it in the future.

I then have the right curtain close, and, of course, the middle one now begins to open. This is a movie of their present, not necessarily this precise moment but this point in their lives. Here I want to tie it all together, so I ask if there is something from the "good" past they can use now and something in their "bad" future they can prevent right now. You'd be amazed how well even the most hardened boys are able to see the connection, and the important part again is that they find it within themselves rather than having a therapist or other adult try to give it to them.

There was a boy awhile back who was typically in denial about his addictions. Because he only drank alcohol and smoked pot, he felt somehow less affected than the kids using methamphetamines, heroin, and other hard drugs. In processing his response to the movie imagery, he told me his happy time was the first time he got high, his future hard time was being in rehab, and his present was being in a group home because he was supposed to have some silly addiction. I asked him how he kept his good feeling from the past. He said he rolled the good feeling into "a great big blunt"—a marijuana joint. He told me he stuck the blunt behind his ear like he used to do with a cigarette.

Then he was silent for a few moments. Finally he said, "Y'know, each one of those three movies had me and pot in them. Maybe I need to look at that a little bit." No kidding! I knew that and the group-home staff knew that, but up until this moment he hadn't known it. Once again, a boy finds his own path to the problem with a little creative help. (Notice how the sequence of the guided imagery follows the Hero's Journey, with the final "present" piece a Return and Contribution moment of teaching himself something. He went into the imageries stuck at either Conventional Slumber, being asleep to the problem he had with marijuana, or at the Call to Adventure, knowing he had a problem but not ready to face up to it yet. If he accepts this challenge to clean up his drug usage, he will most likely face Thresholds of Difficulty in his efforts to quit.)

I love to combine approaches, to see how many proverbial birds I can kill with that one stone. For example, I often use guided imagery to spark the design for mask making. Perhaps I'll do an imagery activity while drumming softly, which really seems to amplify the process. Sometimes an idea for imagery will come from something I hear, as in the situation I described earlier of hearing a boy say he felt like he was in a blender. Immediately I could ask him to close his eyes and imagine that blender. Then I might suggest he lower the setting, pull the plug, or throw the sucker out the imaginary window. The point is to empower the boy to fix his own problem, to slay his own dragon.

One Halloween, a group home staff member wanted to help change the energy at the home. To most boys in group homes Halloween means partying and drugs, so the staff typically will try to downplay these party holidays if they can, and the boys can get angry and depressed. This staff member wanted to bring in the mystery of Halloween but not with anything too immature or hokey. So we came up with a Halloween-themed guided-imagery exercise with a related artwork activity afterward.

After an induction, the imagery had each boy walk through a graveyard late on a stormy night. In the distance was a house, which, although it didn't seem haunted, didn't look too inviting. As I had the boys walk through the dark graveyard, I suggested that on one particular headstone, they would see a message left only for them. Then I had them go into the house, and go into three different rooms. In one room, they looked for a symbol that would represent who they used to be. In the second room they were to look for something symbolic of who they will become one day. And if you haven't already guessed, the third room had something inside that stood for who they were now.

Then back outside and back through the graveyard. But wait, there is one more message on a headstone. What does this last message contain? Once again the boys all learned something about themselves. Also, once again I hope you can see where most of the Hero's Journey stages get touched, including giving a message back to themselves. I try to have boys, particularly troubled ones, give themselves something because often their self-image is so low. The symbols and images, as well as the pictures they draw afterward, help us grown-ups gain insight into the boys' beliefs and feelings and offer innumerable therapeutic openings. They're also really fun for everyone involved.

The Journey

I've referred to David Oldfield a number of times. Based in Washington, D.C., he is one of the great thinkers in the field of rites of passage for adolescents. A long time ago, when David was a student at Yale Divinity School, he worked as an intern at a mental hospital. He tried to apply what he had learned in his studies as he worked with adolescent boys locked up in a juvenile psych ward. When that approach didn't work very well, he began retelling Greek myths—which the "wild" boys absolutely ate up. In using these stories for teaching, he found the boys much more willing to engage with him.

After looking a little more deeply into the topic of mythological stories, he ran into Joseph Campbell's work and the Hero's Journey model. Based on the fact that the actual critical initiation takes place internally, David felt he could create a process for generating internal rites of passage for his clients. He created the Journey, a five-part, mythologically influenced guided imagery that walks a boy through the five stages of the Hero's Journey. Rather than fighting archetypal processes, he went with them, incorporating mythical images such as magic boxes, hidden places, and a labyrinth. I have found teen boys love this approach.*

Here's a good example of how this tool works. A few years ago I was guiding a middle school class on The Journey. In the third stage, the "traveler" is instructed to go into the labyrinth of life and deal with whatever awaits him there. This is where a boy can "slay his dragon"— kill his anger, overcome his addiction, and so on. After the students had completed their journeys and we began to process what they had experienced, one boy apologized to me for cheating.

I asked him how a person cheats in a guided imagery. He said he was walking through the labyrinth in his mind, as instructed, when he came to a large, deep hole that he couldn't get across. He fell into the hole and couldn't get out. That's when he cheated, he said. As I pressed him for details, he pointed out that while in the hole, he tried everything he could to get out. He tried climbing and jumping. He screamed for assistance, but nothing worked.

At this point he got a little embarrassed. He looked around the classroom until it seemed all right to say what he was going to say next. He sheepishly told me he had a guardian angel that followed him everywhere. When all other attempts to escape the hole failed, he asked her to assist him. She gently lifted him up and put him down on the other side of the hole where he could continue his journey.

The reality of his life, reflected in this journey, was that he typically tried normal approaches to solve a problem, and they failed him. On the journey, he found within himself some sort of higher power or guiding intuition, call it what you want, to help him. He taught himself to be creative and solved his own problem. Therapeutically, this was perfection, because rather than me telling him he had this ability, he learned it for himself. Trust me when I say that new insight sticks with boys a lot better and longer when they find it rather than when you give it to them.

---

*David Oldfield's material can be found at www.midwaycenter.com. You may choose to play his cassettes or read the imageries aloud as I do, to control the timing and adapt where necessary.

WRITING POETRY AND LYRICS

I wrote earlier about doing process groups with boys and their favorite lyrics. Although they may tend to hide it, many boys love to write poetry and song lyrics. Don't underestimate how poignant and deep boys can be in their written expression. Even if a boy's song is terrible, it will give you great insight into his belief system. Having you listen to his lyrics is a risk for him, so honor that risk and don't judge, blame, or shame.

Teen poetry is anything but boring. Yes, it is often dark or troubled. Teens can be moody on a good day, and their songs and poetry often reflect troubles or turmoil they are experiencing. This does not necessarily mean your son is in psychological trouble, just that he is going through the ups and downs of adolescence. (However, continued dark and troubling content may indeed be an indicator of deeper problems, which might indicate it is time to get some professional help.) Rather than trying to deny how teens feel or, worse, trying to make *them* deny how they feel, I encourage expression of those feelings and see what can be learned in the process. If a boy is writing dark poetry or lyrics, remember—he could be out doing so many other, more dangerous things.

Here's a poem from a boy in a group home who got his act together and is now living successfully in this difficult adult world.

GO

Go away
"come back, stay"
is what they tell me
this is what I say
"make up your mind"
do a lot of thinkin'
search inside your brain
and what you will find
you won't believe
the stuff you see
you can't conceive

I've led a life of crime,
beatings, drugs
and now I'm doin' time
people . . . right away they judge me
cause of the way I lived
I've lied cheated and fled
away from my problems
now I have no rights
they were stripped off me
but long I didn't realize
didn't even see
my life is wasting away
my brain go away
come back and forever
you will stay ....

BY J

Many teens wouldn't dream of writing poetry, but I believe we all have a little poetry in us somewhere. One way to get boys to express it is to place a set of magnetic poetry pieces on a refrigerator or other metal surface. You can get these kits at most bookstores. Buy a couple of sets that include a lot of feeling or emotive words, put them on the fridge, and walk away. Boys can then arrange them into poems or statements that will give you information about how they feel or what they believe. I recommend writing them down before they get scrambled, and they can then be placed in a bundle, Intention Box, or Clue Box (see pages 214–221); read at a ceremony; or given to someone who can use that message.

Many boys write with little or no encouragement from adults. Some, inspired by rap music, have become quite adept at creating rhyming lines.

You can make the writing of lyrics or poetry a more ceremonial affair by playing tribal music in the background or by lighting candles for a different feel to the room. Often, I'll tell the boys a story or guide them through an imagery exercise before they are to write, to help get their imagination going. For sharing their poetry or lyrics, consider a "talking stick," a sacred stick of some sort that allows only the person holding it to speak. All others must be silent. I also find that writing outdoors in nature can be inspiring for teens.

STORYTELLING

Everyone loves stories, and I have found that it is one of the best therapeutic tools at my disposal. Storytelling was the original form of entertainment. In our media-centered society, it still is—through the modern delivery systems of radio, TV, DVD, VHS, VCR, e-books, and the like. Many cultures use stories for teaching. In the Sufi tradition, for example, a desired standard of behavior is not taught through lecture but instead vividly communicated in the moral of a story. Other cultures use specific stories for specific tasks. There are coming-of-age stories, stories to help break a boy from attachment to his mother, stories to test values and ethics, and stories for specific topics or problems such as anger.

This is different storytelling from what we did with our kids when they were younger. These stories compel the listener to examine his values and beliefs, and often require him to complete the tale. Of course, you want to catch your teen in a receptive mood, which can be challenging. I seldom hold storytelling sessions with teens without combining this activity with another, such as a sweat lodge or mask making.

It helps to connect the story to some kind of theme, to establish a purpose and focus for the listener. Play on his curiosity by saying something like, "You know how Native Americans used to handle anger problems with their boys instead of giving boring lectures?" (This would be a great way to introduce the story "Grandfather," which starts on page 209.)

The suggested reading list at the end of the book includes some sources for stories, and Internet searches have made this easy for almost anyone. Try search criteria like "Sufi stories," "folktales for teens," and "coming-of-age stories."

Cultural riddles are stories that have no correct answer, thus forcing a boy to think abstractly, which is one of the basic developmental tasks of adolescence.

For example, here is a Native American story that works the issue of anger. This story strikes a deep chord in most boys who hear it, and is much more effective than teaching dry anger-management models.

Grandfather

There once was a grandfather. His little grandson often came in the evenings to sit at his knee and ask the many questions that children ask. One day the grandson came to his grandfather with a look of anger on his face.

Grandfather said, "Come, sit, tell me what has happened today." The child sat and leaned his chin on his grandfather's knee. Looking up into the wrinkled, nut-brown face and the kind dark eyes, the child's anger turned to quiet tears. The boy said, "I went to the town today with my father, to trade the furs he has collected over the past several months. I was happy to go, because Father said that since I had helped him with the trapping, I could get something for me. Something that I wanted. I was so excited to be in the trading post; I have not been there before. I looked at many things and finally found a metal knife! It was small, but a good size for me, so Father got it for me."

Here the boy laid his head against his grandfather's knee and became silent. The grandfather softly placed his hand on the boy's raven hair and said, "And then what happened?" Without lifting his head, the boy said, "I went outside to wait for Father, and to admire my new knife in the sunlight. Some town boys came by and saw me. They got all around me and starting saying bad things.

"They called me dirty and stupid and said that I should not have such a fine knife. The largest of these boys pushed me back and I fell over one of the other boys. I dropped my knife and one of them snatched it up and they all ran away, laughing." Here the boy's anger returned: "I hate them, I hate them all!"

The grandfather, with eyes that have seen too much, lifted his grandson's face so his eyes looked into the boy's. Grandfather said, "Let me tell you a story. I too, at times, have felt a great hate for those that have taken so much, with no sorrow for what they do.

"But hate wears you down, and does not hurt your enemy. It is like taking poison and wishing your enemy would die. I have struggled with these feelings many times. It is as if there are two wolves inside me, one is white and one is black. The White Wolf is good and does no harm. He lives in harmony with all around him and does not take offense when no offense was intended. It will only fight when it is right to do so, and in the right way.

"But the Black Wolf is full of anger. The littlest thing will set him into a fit of temper. He fights everyone, all the time, for no reason. He cannot think because his anger and hate are so great. It is helpless anger, for his anger will change nothing. Sometimes it is hard to live with these two wolves inside me, for both of them seek to dominate my spirit."

The boy looked intently into his grandfather's eyes and asked, "Which one wins, Grandfather?" The grandfather smiled and said, "The one I feed."

This simple tale affirms how important and wise our elders are, and empowers boys to look at and deal with their anger in a different way. This story works wonderfully in a group of boys and will stir a lot of discussion.

Here's another favorite of mine. This one addresses many different themes, but mostly values. Because it has two endings, it helps with abstracting skills. It's also a cultural riddle that doesn't have a set ending, but rather calls upon the listener to create the ending. Thus, with a number of boys, you will get a number of answers, generating a lively conversation:

The King and the Thief

Once there was a great king, loved and admired in his kingdom. He had a beautiful daughter, and his country was prosperous. But for quite some time now, there had been many reports by people that a thief had broken into their homes. In each of these homes, the thief had only taken only the one item of greatest value. He never caused any damage and never took more than one item. But interestingly enough, somehow, each time, the thief took the family's most prized possession.

This fact had long intrigued the king, and until recently had not seemed a great problem, as most thieves usually took many things from the homes they robbed. But the people of the kingdom were growing increasingly irritated by the thief's success, and the king's inability to stop him. The king decided to increase his efforts, and put word out that the thief was to be caught at all costs. But even with all the resources of the kingdom, the thief continued to steal, each time taking only the most precious possession.

Frustrated, the king devised a plan to catch the thief himself. He decided to disguise himself as a thief, and hoped to find him that way. So each night, the king would change his clothes and prowl the streets. Many nights went by with no success, and yet the thief still made off nightly with someone's greatest possession. Becoming more concerned all the time, the king began to enter people's homes at night to steal things, hoping to run into the thief.

One night, after searching the house while the occupants slept, the king chose a beautiful vase. Suddenly, a voice behind him remarked that although the vase was an excellent choice, it was not the most prized possession in this family. As the king turned around, he saw in the shadows a dark figure he assumed was the thief. He told the thief he had heard of him, and that somehow he had the ability to always choose the best piece. The thief smiled, and asked the king if he would like to learn how to do it himself.

Hoping to get close to the thief, the king quickly agreed. The thief said to meet him the next night.

For the next few weeks, each night they would go into a house, and somehow the thief would always find the greatest prize. But he would never tell the king how he did it. One night, after breaking into a house, the thief asked if the king wanted to go home with him and have some food. Eagerly, the king agreed. As they walked down a dark and abandoned street, suddenly, right in front of him, the thief vanished. The king looked everywhere, but could not see the thief. He heard him laughing, though, and as he peered intently into a dark shadow, he noticed a crack in the ground just big enough for a man to slip through.

As the king dropped through the crack and below the surface, he realized he was staring at perhaps the greatest treasure ever collected. The king had never realized that when all of the greatest possessions from every family were put into one place, they would make a sight so spectacular it seemed unreal. Although the king knew all the items were stolen, he was still greatly impressed with what he saw.

The thief appeared, saying he would go change clothes and his servant would bring some soup and wine. When the servant appeared, he quickly whispered to the king. He said the thief had lured him to the chamber to kill him because the thief knew he was the king. Dazzled by the great wealth and beauty before him, and not sure whether to believe the servant, the king pondered what to do next. But the servant was insistent, saying the king must hurry or he would surely be killed.

Reluctantly, the king slipped back up through the crack in the street and returned to the palace. He immediately gathered his special guards and returned to the opening of the thief's hideout. The thief was arrested, as was the servant, and all of the special possessions were taken to the castle. The next day was to be the trial, and although everyone was sure the thief would be hanged, no one was sure about the servant who had supposedly saved the king's life.

All of the valuable possessions were on display, and when the king began the proceedings, suddenly his daughter ran forward crying and screaming. She claimed to have been in love with the thief and he with her. They had been meeting in secret for a long time, and had hoped to be married. If the thief was hanged, she claimed she would kill herself and curse her father for eternity.

When the story has been told, this question is asked of the listeners: *Who is guilty of what and how would you solve the dilemma?*

This story brings up a wealth of possibilities for discussion. Boys, especially those who have had brushes with the law, are intrigued by the fact that the king actually began breaking into houses and stealing. Many listeners assume that the king's daughter is his most prized possession, and that the thief "stole" her and may not really love her. As the boy or boys try to figure out what to do with the thief and his helper, you and they will learn a great deal about their belief systems.

I mentioned there are two endings. After we have discussed the story, I then read the last few paragraphs again, and in the final paragraph change a few words, as shown in italic below:

All of the valuable possessions were on display, and when the king began the proceedings, suddenly *a peasant girl* ran forward crying and screaming. She claimed to have been in love with the thief and he with her. They had been meeting in secret for a long time, and had hoped to be married. If the thief was hanged, she claimed she would kill herself and curse *the king* for eternity.

The shift from king's daughter to an ordinary peasant girl drastically changes the dynamics. Interestingly, even boys from the lowest of socioeconomic levels often treat the king's daughter differently than just a simple peasant girl. Punishments for the thief change, and you've got a whole new conversation going on, with the boys often finding themselves in a double bind between conflicting ethics and values.

BUNDLES AND BOXES

I use the concept of a "container" to help a boy visualize his strengths, weaknesses, and the possibilities that are open to him. This idea is related to the popular notion of "thinking outside the box." I explain to boys that their "box" is their set of values and beliefs, skills, feelings, attitudes, strengths, and other aspects that make each of them unique on the planet. I tell them that the Hero's Journey essentially asks us to make our box larger as we meet the challenges we face in life. Refusing the Call to Adventure or failing to follow the Hero's Journey placed before you means you keep your box, and your growth, limited to a small size.

Using real objects as metaphors, a boy can see how much is in his personal container, as well as how big his container is. A larger box is needed to accommodate the learning and understanding that he gains as he confronts challenges. Expanding his container allows him to think bigger thoughts, dream bigger dreams. I've seen this model work well as a frame of reference for boys to visualize how they can grow even if they are not fans of school. When a boy gets a new insight, such as recognizing that gay people are not threatening to him, you can help him understand this change as well as integrate it by adding the new understanding to his container. Having him draw an expanding container, or what his box looked like before the learning and after, is a good way to weave transpersonal components together.

To work this dynamic I use two kinds of literal "containers": bundles and boxes.

Graduation Bundle

A graduation bundle is a collection of objects assembled over a period of time to celebrate a boy's accomplishments. The boy may collect or hold on to them, or an adult in his life can have that responsibility. If you assemble or hold the bundle for your boy, approach this as an important and even sacred task you are performing for him.

A bundle is something like a scrapbook, but with a twist, as you'll see in a moment. You could start a bundle at the beginning of middle or high school, ending at the completion of the year or of each trimester.

You could begin a bundle for your boy's band efforts, or to hold awards, concert programs, newspaper articles, and so on. It might contain drawings he made after guided imagery, or a personal metaphor he discovered in a story.

Parents or adults help collect the parts and pieces while the boy is working toward his goal, wrapping these objects in a special cloth such as a sheepskin, leather, silk, or deer or rabbit fur. The boy can help decide what goes into the bundle, based on what is important for him.

The bundle should be kept on an altar or in another sacred area. The boy should be ultimately responsible for the bundle, but he may allow others to add to it or watch it for him.

Here's where the twist comes in: After the boy has completed his task, project, placement, or whatever his goal, it is time to release the bundle. One way I like to do this is with a sacred fire. The boy can say some prayers or express intentions about what he wants from the items in the bundle, then offer them to the fire. These prayers or intentions could be wishes for a successful high school experience, thanks for having had a good childhood, hope of making the honor band, or a promise of some kind. The concept is that the smoke from the fire will take the prayers or intentions to where they need to go.

I've seen youth release their drawings, poetry, an article from a magazine that had an impact on them, or something they made. A boy might release his childhood baseball glove or first woodshop project. This is a good lesson in letting go of attachment. Things come and go in life, and this process will help a boy see how something he may have thought he could not part with, like a state championship patch, can be relinquished and he will not be diminished by it. It is a good way to symbolically let go of childhood, or adolescence.

Another way to release the bundle's contents is in water, letting the bundle drift out to sea or down a river's current. We need to be responsible when putting things into a river or a lake, for obvious reasons. I believe that most natural fabrics or paper will break down rather quickly and efficiently, but you would not want to break any litter laws or put in the water non-biodegradable products that could harm the water or living things. Following the same commonsense criteria, another way to release such a container is to bury it.

Your son may not think much of religion right now, but this ceremony keeps him in touch with his basic spirituality. And release of the bundle helps support the notion of not being attached to material things, a good antidote for too much consumerism.

Liberation Bundle

This is just the opposite of the graduation bundle, with the emphasis this time on releasing negative things. Collect objects that express these negative aspects of himself that he wants to let go of: an association with a gang, an addiction, a difficult relationship. The bundle might include a pack of cigarettes to represent his smoking habit, or a photo of a girl with whom he had a trying experience. Relevant art pieces, poems, or whatever he may have created in connection with negative feelings can also be included in the bundle. These items can be collected by him or by you, if he allows outside input.

The process for releasing this bundle is the same as for the graduation bundle. Burn it in a sacred fire, let the ocean or river carry it away, if appropriate, or bury it. Once again have the boy, and adults if he allows it, say prayers or express intentions for these negative influences in his life to go away. The point is to release them, to not remain attached to negativity and victimhood. Powerful liberation ceremonies I have witnessed included making and burning a drawing of the boy's old self-image, parting with a mask a boy made that reflected a dark period in his life, and writing a promise never to steal again.

Prayer Ties

In the Native American tradition, prayer ties are small colored squares of simple fabric, two inches square, holding a pinch of tobacco and tied up into small bundles, all connected into one long string. The tobacco is included as a natural element, and reflects giving something back to Mother Earth. If tobacco is not considered appropriate, use cornmeal, lavender, sage, cedar, or some other herb.

Each color used for the prayer ties has a specific association. For example, in the table below, yellow represents the east and sunrise, the place of new beginnings. A boy's prayer to the east might be for courage in the upcoming school year or to be successful in trying out for football or band. The colors and meanings vary among different tribes and traditions. Your seven colors can reflect anything you want or need to pray about: family, personal growth, health, fear, forgiveness, guilt, and so on. It doesn't really matter what color prayer ties you designate for each dynamic; just be consistent and somewhat logical about it. This table offers one possible interpretation.

Color	Direction	Association
Yellow	East	New Beginnings
Red	South	Compassion
Black	West	Introspection or Dreams
White	North	Wisdom
Green	Down (Mother Earth)	Nurture and Support
Blue	Up (Father Sky)	Overseeing, Protection
Purple	Inside, within (Spirit)	All Things Possible, Big Dreams

Boys can make the prayer ties all at one sitting, perhaps before a sweat lodge or other ceremony, or they can work on them over a longer period, like an entire school year. Each prayer tie represents a specific prayer or intention that will be released minutes, hours, days, or even months from now.

A boy holds the fabric in the palm of his hand, places a pinch of tobacco in it, makes a suitable prayer based on that color, pulls up the edges to form a small pouch with the tobacco hidden inside, and ties it to his long string. He repeats this process over and over, dozens or even hundreds of times, using random colors or creating a pattern, like ten red ties, ten blue, et cetera. If you are not following a particular tribe's rules, you can do it any way you like.

Each new prayer is tied about two inches from the last one on one long continual ball of string—kite string is fine. When all the prayer ties have been attached, you have what looks like a long string of colored pennants.

The prayers are sent into the world by "releasing" the prayer ties. Prayer ties can be burned ceremonially, releasing the prayers into the smoke to travel where they need to go to fulfill the prayers. Or they can be set afloat in a stream or river.

Prayer ties can also be used to mark a sacred space. When my daughter was born and we held her birth ceremony, the prayer ties were left dangling on the trees so they would slowly release the prayers as they decomposed. For a couple of years I was able to go to her sacred spot and see remnants of her prayer ties, reminding me of prayers and promises I made to her as a father.

One day, six teen boys were working on their prayer ties prior to participating in a sweat lodge. One particular boy came from a very dysfunctional family, but he was fiercely loyal and in denial about their level of problems. Repeated attempts through individual counseling and groups to get him to see his family situation for what it was fell on deaf ears. As the group prepared their prayer ties, I overheard this particular boy ask of his peers, "Hey, what color is family? My family's pretty messed up and need all the prayers they can get." Since the color associations we were using did not include a specific one for family, his prayers for his family went in many different directions: new beginnings for his family, dreams for his family, compassion and wisdom for his family. This was a therapeutic breakthrough for this boy; afterward he was open, for the first time, to discussing what was really happening in his family. Boys, even the hardened ones, like to pray if it is safe to do so. I firmly believe that spirituality, as distinguished from religion, needs to be woven into any approach dealing with youth.

If you have any Native populations near where you live or work, I strongly suggest trying to tap into them. They can teach you and your boys some wonderful things, and no one is as good at ceremony and ritual as Native people are.

The major distinction between bundles and boxes is that bundles hold things and boxes hold non-things—such as prayers, wishes, and dreams—in physical form. To give form to a "non-thing" like a dream, just write or illustrate the dream on a piece of paper and put the paper in the box. Whenever something is added to the box, say a prayer or express some other form of intention.

You can use any kind of box for this purpose. I've used cardboard and shoe boxes, as well as exotic wood boxes I made myself. Perhaps a boy can make his own box in woodshop at school or you can go to a nice gift store and purchase one. It doesn't have to be made of wood—a wicker or metal box will work just as well. This makes a great gift to present to him at the beginning of school, or as he starts a project, or even for his birthday or a religious holiday.

With both bundles and boxes, you should always have a system for the boy to put things in anonymously that you never see. This gives him the control he needs and safety to risk and grow, and builds mutual respect as you don't interfere or micromanage everything he does.

Intention Box

As with bundles, boxes can be used to process both positive and negative aspects of your boy's experience. Intention Boxes are for containing his positive thoughts, feelings, and wishes.

Make sure that what goes into it is private and not for public viewing. If necessary, get a box with some kind of lock. Teens need a few secrets and private space for themselves. Every once in a while, or on a more ritualistic schedule (monthly, full moon, perhaps) get rid of the contents in a ceremonial way as described earlier, such as burning or burying them. Maybe on every full moon, build a fire and let him slowly feed in his intentions to release them. Or at the end of each school trimester, take a walk and bury them in some outdoor setting that has meaning or power for him.

Although I am a fan of ceremonially releasing all of these hopes, dreams, prayers, and other intentions, there is nothing wrong with collecting them and holding on to them. One of the reasons I like these types of approaches is because they are so malleable and adjustable to our needs. If you or your boy thinks it would be more fitting for some reason to keep them, by all means do so. This important collection would be a great legacy for your son to pass along to his son or daughter later on.

Give-Away Box

As you guessed, the things that go in a give-away box represent the negative things a boy wants to give away. They could be anger, addiction, depression, overuse of profanity, or any other issue he has. Dark stories, bad dreams, and negative energy of any kind can be disposed of in this healthy way. Have your boy write these things down and put them in the box, or add photos or drawings if appropriate. One boy might draw a picture of a marijuana pipe with an international "no" symbol signifying his intention not to smoke pot anymore. Another might write the name of someone he hates with the intention to have less animosity toward that person. The possibilities are endless.

Clue Box

A clue box is used by a boy to collect what strikes him as life's truths, or expressions of what is important to him. "Clues" in this sense are typically in print—quotes he's been drawn to, a poignant line from a movie, his favorite lyrics, and so on.

The first clue box I saw twenty-five years or so ago was just a shoebox holding dozens of quotes and other important words of wisdom that a friend at college found personally significant. The majority of clues were quotes from famous people, but there were also a number of handwritten notes that recorded a great line in a movie, or something poignant a friend had said.

A number of clue boxes manifested all over the country as many of us shared the idea in our travels and with our friends. My own clue box is an exotic wood box I built just for this purpose. Many of the quotes used in this book came from my clue box.

Unlike the bundles and boxes mentioned above, a clue box is meant to be kept and added to indefinitely and shared publicly. I have hundreds of clues covering two decades of my life. It will be one of my favorite legacies for my daughter, for after I am gone it will show her a lifetime of what appealed to her daddy, what values I held dear, and what I was passionate about. Many boys I've worked with have embraced this simple but powerful process. Often they will put their poetry in their clue boxes, or lyrics they have printed out. For boys who participate, I will sometimes pass along some of my favorites as a gift and to support the process.

I've often brought along my clue box to a group of boys, had one of them pull a quote, and off we go exploring what it means for them. Like storytelling, you never know where a clue will lead. But a boy's clues will give you a good glimpse into his belief system as he interprets them and explains what they mean to him.

CREATING TANGIBLE SYMBOLS

Boys are kinesthetic and like to touch and make things. Boys would rather "do" than "be." A number of transpersonal therapeutic approaches have to do with creating something in physical form. Creating these tangible, long-lasting objects serves to anchor and integrate a boy's experience. These approaches come from a wide variety of sources and traditions. They may help serve as a reminder of what he has learned, or of what he still has to work on.

Rock Cairns

A rock cairn is a pile of stones that is slowly built up over time as a sort of shrine. Many indigenous cultures have used rock cairns to preserve food stores for traveling or as a way to signify a sacred or important spot. You may want to build one at a sacred site or the ceremonial fire area. The boy or boys pick a stone, put some sort of prayer or intention into it, then place it with all of the previous stones. The pile can be constructed in a random form or slowly sculpted into some design such as a spiral, wall, or container. The sight of all the stones left by others can create a timeless sense of community and of shared hopes and goals. In addition, the ageless strength of rocks conveys a safe and stable energy for youths to experience.

Masks

Mask making is one of the best tools to use in working out adolescent identity issues. I often use a "before and after" dynamic with masks. For example, as a group of boys prepared to go on a multi-week hike, I had each of them build a mask before he left showing who he thought he was. Then when they returned, they would build another mask to show how they perceived themselves after this experience. The similarities and differences provide plenty of information to ponder and discuss with them.

Often, many of us wish we were someone else—someone who is more popular, confident, brave, or funny, or maybe just someone taller or more handsome or less pimpled. Masks are a powerful tool to really work with identity issues. For example, you can have half of a group of boys walk in a small circle and the other half of the boys walk in a larger circle in the other direction, with all the boys holding their masks to their faces. Have them look at each other, and ask each boy to see if there is a "face" he'd rather have. After a few moments, suggest the boys swap their masks. (Some boys will not want to part with "themselves.") Now have them walk around in the same way, this time wearing some-body else's "face." Ask if it makes them feel like they'd hoped, or if it feels unnatural. Then have them put their own mask back on. Often boys who don't necessarily like themselves seem to appreciate having their own persona back, and once again, you will have tons of material to talk about.

Even the process of decorating a mask is fascinating. Many times boys will discover metaphors about the process itself that they can share. One boy had a distinctly two-sided mask. He pointed out to us that he realized he had two sides to his personality, one good and one bad, both in a constant struggle with each other. This was the first time he had really owned up to his darker side, and again it was infinitely more powerful that he discovered it rather than just having me tell him. I think it gave him an acceptable image of himself to work on, and I could hardly wait to see what manifested in his next mask. As you can imagine, a sequence of masks over months, or even years, gives you a revealing graphic record of a boy's growth and the changes he has been through.

To make a mask I use fast-setting plaster, which molds very precisely to the face and is reasonably hard. Six-inch-wide rolls of this plaster can be found online through almost any orthopedic medical supply store.

Making plaster masks is a messy activity, so I make "aprons" out of large trash bags by cutting holes for the arms and head. The teens can wear these like ponchos. You'll want to spread some sort of tarp or newspapers over the floor or carpet.

Before applying the plaster, vaseline is smeared liberally over the face, particularly on the eyebrows, mustache, and so on. This keeps the plaster from sticking to the skin or hair. Before you start, cut a number of strips from the roll of plaster in various widths from half an inch to two inches. You end up with a number of six-inch strips of varying widths.

The strips are dipped one at a time in a bowl of lukewarm water and laid carefully over the face. With wet fingertips you can make the plaster mold perfectly to the contours of the face. I typically start by framing the face with four strips. Run the first strip across the forehead just below the hairline. Then run strips down both the left and right sides of the face from the temple down below the jawline. Run the last strip just below the chin, connecting the two strips coming down from the temples.

Next, run a thin strip up from the top lip, over the nose and up between the eyes to the forehead, then another from the nose down under the chin. Now run one thin strip across the face from each of the initial side strips at the ear, meeting over the nose. You now have an outside circle made from the first strips and a top-to-bottom and right-to-left cross. This is the basic framework for the mask. Now you just carefully run wider strips across the face and forehead horizontally until there is no skin showing. Be careful around the eyes not to get plaster in them or place strips too close to them. Try to form the plaster to look the same around each eye.

I prefer to cover the lips as well, and of course leave two nostril holes. When you are finished, the only holes in the entire mask are the eye holes and nostrils. About ten minutes after you place the final strips, the mask should be strong enough to come off. Have the boy simply look down and wiggle his facial muscles. The mask should almost fall off, or need just a little careful help with the hands. Masks need to sit for at least a couple of hours to dry.

Once dry, they can be decorated in just about any fashion you like. Besides various paints, I also supply feathers, sequins, yarn, leather, and a myriad of other art supplies to give boys as much freedom to express themselves as possible. I typically coat the finished mask with Sobo glue, available at any craft store. Sobo glue dries clear and hard, acting like a varnish to protect the mask and artwork. It also serves well as a glue for applying sequins and buttons, for example.

The best illustrated, step-by-step example I have seen for building masks with teens appears in David Oldfield's *Journey* workbook (www. midwaycenter.com). You can also do an Internet search and find numerous articles on how to apply the strips.

Mask making, particularly for boys, helps develop sensitive and intimate touch, two taboo dynamics in the world of boys. To make a great mask, you really have to get in close to get the dimples and special features of each face. I always have one group of boys form the mask on the second group of boys, then switch. This exercise allows boys to get inches from each other's faces without any sexual innuendo or antagonistic feelings.

Drum Building

Drums have become another of my favorite, most successful tools in working with teen boys of all kinds. Drumming can be just for fun, have a therapeutic purpose, or may simply help boys channel energy in an appropriate way. Indeed, I know of many families that drum together and participate in organized drumming activities such as celebrations on Earth Day and the solstices, or any other occasion when folks gather and make music. Drums are used throughout the world, and are one of the most ancient, archetypal instruments on the planet. For many cultures they represent the heartbeat, the rhythm of the world, and connection to Spirit.

For boys they are really fun and really loud. But with some guidance, boys will find there is more to drumming than making noise. Drumming with older men or adults can make them feel like part of the tribe. We used to take some group-home boys down to the local coffee shop on summer Friday nights. After the coffee shop closed, the owner brought out his conga and pretty soon we had ten to twenty adult drummers with as many children and dancers. The boys would be shy for a while, then someone would offer a boy his drum, and he'd tentatively begin to play. Pretty soon all six "bad" boys were forgetting to be bad, jamming with grown-ups who knew how to have fun legally, and getting treated like young men who were not on probation. For many modern Americans, making music, the original form of entertainment, before radios, TV, CD players, and the like, is a lost art. Making their own music from scratch is a fulfilling experience for boys who may not yet be aware of their creative capacity.

In Ireland, at our Youth Conference, we played drums not only with the teens, but with children of all age groups. We also built rattles, something like those babies use, to supplement the drums, and every child helped construct a two-foot ceremonial drum that was played at the final ceremony and then presented to the main conference as a gift. Return and Contribution has never been so much fun.

I taught one group of boys how to build hand drums for a planned camping trip to Death Valley. To make a drum, we had to use items from nature: wood to construct a hoop (drum frame), tree limbs for mallets, cow leather to make the mallet head, and a piece of horse hide for the drum's "skin." The process of making the hoops and cutting up an animal hide was powerful for the boys. Seeing the outline of the horse's body lying flat on the ground before it was cut up helped the boys see the sacrifice the animal made so that an instrument could be created. It gave them an appreciation for the materials that they would not get if they'd bought the supplies at a store. They also learned that many Native tribes were noted for using the hide after killing an animal for meat, so little of the animal was wasted.

Each boy chose a certain part of the hide to cover his drum, and no two mallets turned out alike. Making the drums and mallets pushed a few boys' buttons as far as eye–hand skills (often an issue with fatherless boys), and pushed their hyperactivity boundaries, but they all got through it and soon owned a drum they made themselves. In Death Valley they were allowed to walk up a canyon alone and drum up a storm. They loved it and talked about it for weeks.

Some serious research has been done on the effects of drumming. In its simplest form, drumming for more than about fifteen minutes puts most people into a theta state—a state of consciousness common between dreaming and waking. The theta state is very conducive to creativity, and can bring lucid insights. With many of my stubborn, closed boys, this effect of drumming has helped open a window in their defensive walls. Let a boy drum some of the energy out of his system and, between the exercise and the shift in consciousness to a more malleable theta state, you've got a boy more open to talking and counseling.

Power Shields

Power shields are symbolic shields that look like those held by medieval warriors. Built in a ritualistic manner, they represent a boy's strengths and blend well with mask work. Many cultures use shields for protection and ornamentation. The shield is best constructed from raw materials such as rawhide and leather, or perhaps tree bark. Often, the shield's bearer will decorate the shield with "power animals": animals he especially likes or that came to him as a vision in a guided imagery or sweat lodge. Visions, dream symbols, and other images can be depicted on the shield or attached to it, to symbolize what makes a boy feel strong and powerful. Metaphors for strength (I was a tiger) can be drawn or painted on it, as well as single words like *power, honor,* and *courage.*

As in many of the transpersonal approaches, ceremony and ritual should be woven into the construction of power shields. Before making one, for example, your son could make a string of prayer ties relating to aspects of power he wants to include in his shield. He may want to take some "clues" or other lines of text from his bundles or boxes to use on his shield. The point is to make the process as deep and meaningful as possible at every juncture.

Having this literal, tangible reminder of a boy's strengths helps him stay focused on his healthier and stronger parts. A group home I know is using power shields simply drawn on poster board to help its boys create, visualize, and honor the positive intentions or images they have created for themselves. They're on prominent display in the home, where they can be a constant reinforcement of the boys' aspirations.

Power shields can be made of anything that is firm enough to support itself, like cardboard, bark, sheet metal, or rawhide (this can be purchased from a local or online taxidermy shop). As with masks, collect a variety of craft materials to allow for the broadest range of decorating options. You'll want to have the boy cut or sculpt the power shield to look like a classic shield, as in the movies. If possible, some handles or loops of some sort should be attached so the boy can carry it around or hang it. This is a symbolic representation, and while almost any material will do, I believe the more the shield looks and feels like the real thing, the more power it will carry.

Creating a new power shield each year will give you a chronology of your boy's evolving understanding of what makes him strong. He can keep the shields on his wall, or, if he chooses, release the shields in any of the methods described in this chapter.

PUTTING IT ALL TOGETHER

I hope by now you have decided that it is important for you to begin offering the boy or boys in your life some initiation activities in an effort to help ease the transition from adolescence into adulthood and manhood. Boys are in crisis all over our country on numerous levels. Not all boys are criminals and gang members, nor are they all addicted to drugs or school dropouts. Many boys are good kids who simply want to move forward as best they can, but they struggle with the conflicting and confusing messages they get about what it means to be a man in this time and culture.

I have a good reputation for getting difficult teen boys to do many things most adults do not think the boys can or will do. I'm convinced that most boys want to be good, strong adults. Sometimes, it is just not clear how to get there.

I realize it may be difficult for some of you to begin using the practices I've described. I know how you feel. I had to try each of them for myself. Many times I experiment with an approach that fails miserably. I'll try it again a couple of more times to see if maybe an adjustment for age or a different setting will help. If the approach still does not work for me, even though logic says it should, I let it go. I've tried to share what works for me and why. The practices and information in this book are the best I have found.

By using some of these approaches together or blending approaches, you can transform a simple camping trip into an initiatory experience. Trials and ordeals your son goes through can be reframed to make him feel stronger and wiser rather than like a victim. The Hero's Journey can help you figure out together where he is stuck on a certain issue and how to get him back on track. Because this is a family and community process, these practices will bring all participants closer together in a unified effort to help the boys in your life not only survive but thrive as well.

I once helped facilitate a men's weekend workshop that included teen boys so the men could give back what they had been learning. The boys participated in many of the same exercises as the men, such as drum journeys, storytelling, guided imageries, and meditation. Many of the men acknowledged their uncertain feelings about whether they were really men, and voted to create a ceremony to initiate themselves. It was decided also to initiate the boys, who were all eager to participate in the initiation ceremony.

We began the boys' initiation by leaving them in an unused conference room, saying we'd be back for them in a few minutes. We actually took about half an hour to get them, as we wanted them to be a little on edge to make the experience more powerful. Interestingly, none of the boys left the room or complained. When we came back, we told them we'd be taking one of them out at a time for initiation, which served to slowly break down the safety of their group of about six. One boy was chosen to go first and told he would begin by walking a gauntlet to get to the sacred site. The boy was blindfolded to heighten his senses and add drama to the scene. All of us men formed a crooked and moving line with our drums pounding. The initiate walked slowly and stumbled through the gauntlet of drums for about five minutes, until he finally arrived at the sacred spot.

We stood him up, still blindfolded, on a huge boulder overlooking a lake. We tied a length of purple yarn around his waist and secured the other end of the yarn to a tree. This symbolized his attachment to his mother. We gave the boy a knife and told him that when he was ready to cut the yarn and his attachment to mother and nurture, he should take off his blindfold and do so. All of the men stood behind him in two rows, ready to catch him in a "trust fall." (A trust fall is when someone falls backward into the safe arms of two rows of people). After he "cut the cord," he would fall backward into the waiting arms of men who supported him.

The lake waves were crashing against the shore and the drums kept pounding. After a few minutes of working up his nerve, he took off the blindfold and took in the spectacular view of the lake at his feet. He cut the yarn and fell backward. We caught him safely, then raised him above our heads as people do at rock concerts. We held him up, swaying quietly, for five minutes, which is a long time to just lie there six to seven feet off the ground; fear of falling is universal and instinctive. When we put him safely on his feet, the eldest man in our group held the boy by the shoulder and said, "Welcome to manhood."

One of the boys was the son of one of the men involved. When it was that boy's turn, everything was repeated as before except that once he was on the ground, it was his father who held him and welcomed him to manhood. This was an extremely intense moment for both the boy and father, as well as for the rest of us guys. I had a sense of how the process worked in Native cultures in other times, and we all left feeling very empowered and complete in our new identities.

Stephen Larsen, who helped me at the Santa Clara Youth Conference, told me how he initiated his own children. Larsen's son ran into the ancient problem: he had no menstrual cycle to kick off the process. So, as in many other cultures previously, they had to pick a time and work around that.

Part of the son's responsibility throughout the years prior to this initiation had been to care for his sacred space and keep it ready for use. He weeded the area to make it feel clean. He kept firewood and kindling nicely stacked and dry. His investment in the ceremony went back years, so it could build up to this crescendo.

The men welcomed him into manhood with stories, mentoring, and instruction, while the women held sacred space back at what would later be the site of his sister's initiation. For a week the men drummed with him, taught him about relationships with girls and women, told him stories, and started treating him like an adult. He was given solo time so he could ponder all the upcoming changes and integrate the new information he was receiving. Most important, after the ceremony concluded, all of the adults treated him like a young man rather than a kid. He was one of the more mature teens I have ever met.

For Larsen's daughter he and his wife, along with their community of relatives and other supporters, created a ceremony that was about a week long. As was the custom in most older cultures, the celebration was to kick off when she began her menstrual cycle. Since her family had no idea when this would occur, they had to make plans and then wait.

Larsen told me it was critical that when she did start her cycle, the family did not wait until a more convenient time. That might diminish the impact of the process, and would perpetuate the thinking that our daily schedules are more important than our children's welfare. When she finally did begin her menses, her parents dropped everything they were doing, set the phone tree in motion, and moved to their respective places.

For about a week, all the women supported and nurtured her in an outdoor setting, where everyone camped out. They explained sex, relationships, and family. They prayed and gave her gifts. In essence, they made this experience the most important thing in her life since she was born. The men and the boys were a mile or so away, holding sacred space for her. They drummed, prayed, maintained an ongoing sacred fire, and honored her transition into womanhood. When I met her at sixteen, she was already traveling alone internationally, and had just flown into the youth conference from Israel, where she was learning dance. She was a most remarkable and mature young woman.

I have designed a number of coming-of-age ceremonies for some men who wanted to honor their son's passage through adolescence. One Jewish father had already had a bar mitzvah for his son, but wanted something unique and connected with the West Coast mountains we live in. I helped him structure a weekend outing with his son and a handful of men who had agreed to support Jacob. I spent time teaching the dad how to make prayer ties and create a sacred fire setting. I gave him a couple of stories that spoke of boys trying to do things on their own without asking for help, how to let go of the mother to look for a mate, and selling honor for money, among other topics.

Prior to going out for the camping weekend, this man had made a mask and power shield with his son. These items, now considered sacred, went with the boy into the woods. He was taking his power and identity with him. The men told him stories, explained about relationships with girls and how they would now change, and offered as much insight into manhood as they could. I never met the boy but his father has told me a number of times throughout the years how powerful that weekend was not only for his son, but for him as a father as well. The dad said he really felt like a good father for passing along such vital learnings, and told me he wished (like most of us guys) that someone had done this for him when he was young. The boy is now well into his twenties and I hear he is a caring, mature man.

I'll end this chapter with another story from Stephen Larsen. He recently shared with me this account of a group initiation that he and other concerned parents decided to arrange for their sons when they noticed the boys starting to dabble in risky behaviors. His commentary on what this initiation experience meant to the boys and their dads really says it all.

"When Merlin was about sixteen, he and some of his close friends were getting into trouble of one kind or another—raiding one parent's liquor cabinet, smoking pot, getting picked up by the police for mischievous pranks, and so on. His mother and I talked about it with some of the other parents who shared similar values. We decided that what the boys needed was a rite of passage.

"We started preparing the boys about two weeks ahead of time, and the dads and I got together a couple of times to plan the event. We had meetings with the boys and told them what was up. They were nervous but agreed to join us in what we had in mind.

"On the first morning of the chosen weekend, we asked the boys to meet us with a backpack, outdoor clothing, and sleeping bag. We piled into cars and went to the Shawangunks, local cliffs renowned for rock climbing. There we met an expert climbing guide. The group was instructed on safety procedures and how to make knots, and familiarized with the technical gear. Then we were separated into dyads, a boy and his dad or stepdad.

"There were experienced climbers among us, so those of us who could led the climbs up the vertical cliffs. Each party was told, 'The life of your son or dad will be in your hands, literally, as you watch and belay him as he climbs the cliff.' (Belaying is preventing a climber from falling by means of a belay device. The rope attached to the climber is run through the device, which 'locks' the rope in place if someone pulls on the other end of the rope.) The young men were extremely attentive, and so were the dads. It is hard to say who was more anxious. After climbing a number of pitches in this way, some easier, some more difficult, we all did a hundred-foot rappel [sliding down a steep face on a rope], again with dads belaying sons for safety and vice versa.

"Afterward we gathered to share our responses to the experience. Some of us wrote about it in personal journals. You could almost feel the bonding taking place.

"Upon our return home, some of us dads went ahead to a spot we had chosen in the deep woods, hiking through some rough terrain and finally emerging at the top of some two-hundred-foot-high rocky slabs where there would soon be a great view of the sunrise. The rest stayed behind with the boys. One by one, the boys had to make the journey through the dark woods alone, with a candle, some tin foil, and a few matches. Each boy was met by his dad in the dark, and warmly welcomed to the 'vision quest spot,' as we called it. When all had arrived, there was much joy and celebration. A campfire was lit, and we cooked out together.

"Then one of the dads broke out a bottle of red wine. With parental permission, all were allowed to partake, at the same time receiving stern lectures about the indiscriminate use of alcohol and its dangers. As the evening wore on, a very natural all-night storytelling ensued under the stars, centered on escapades the dads had engaged in when they were young. The young men sat around the fire in wide-eyed amazement. There was laughter and much camaraderie.

"Most of us got up to greet the dawn, which came rosy-fingered and splendid above the forest. A breakfast of slightly burnt pancakes did not diminish the spirits. Those who remembered dreams shared them. The rest of the morning was spent processing, and a solemn vow was made by each of the dads to each of the boys. 'If you've done something stupid, or that you're ashamed about, or gotten in trouble, all of us will be there for each of you. You can call any one of us, even if your dad is not around or you're scared to call him. Each is there for the other. We won't be mean and judgmental, but on the other hand, you may be asked to face the consequences of what you do, in a grown-up way.'

"That promise was made good over the next few years as the boys turned into increasingly emancipated young men. It was incredibly bonding, and also freeing, for the boys to have older males other than a biological father they could turn to for advice or counsel—or even help in a tight spot. All of us became quite good friends, and as they grew up, the young men became substantial mentors in their own right to younger boys (and girls).

"After our little venture into tribalism, there were dozens of incidents in which we were there for each other, in countless small ways. I think the dads took in some of the wise and measured advice they had given the young men, and were less reactive and judgmental with their own sons, and this allowed the young men to be less polarized or antagonized. Later on, my wife Robin took the initiative and made sure our younger child, Gwyneth, had a marvelous and moving initiation into womanhood.

"One of the young men, Morgan, has come back to our farm to live, and is now the father of two small boys. He is a marvellously interactive, playful, and loving dad with them, and his best friend, our son Merlin, now thirty-seven years old, has just told us he is going to be a dad himself. Robin and I have absolutely no doubt he will be a wonderful one. There can be no doubt that a lot of love and a little touch of wisdom are never lost on the young—these gifts keep on giving, down through the generations."

9
The Last Resort

Why we doin' this?

JAMES DEAN AS JIM STARK IN
REBEL WITHOUT A CAUSE

You gotta do something!

BUZZ, WHO DIED MOMENTS LATER
IN THE FATAL GAME OF
AUTOMOBILE "CHICKEN" AT THE CLIFF

The title of this chapter is "The Last Resort" for good reason. It's about where many boys end up when their journey toward initiation has gone completely off-course, and the resources of their families and communities have been exhausted. Readers will no doubt find some of the stories that follow disturbing, because they reflect a harsh reality of kids who are at the end of society's rope.

Here you will see what happens when the adolescent spirit is perverted as a result of neglect or abuse. Treat it with disrespect, and it will haunt you. Abuse and neglect it, and it will come after you.

Early in my career, I worked in one of the first boot-camp-type programs for incorrigible boys. I respect the intent and the dedication of the people who work at these programs, and I believe that here and there they get through to a boy and make a real difference in the direction his life will take. But the sad fact is that for most of the boys who arrive at a facility like this, the abuse and neglect they have suffered have irrevocably distorted and cemented their behavior and attitudes.

By the time boys arrive at a "last resort" facility, they have usually become alienated, highly resistant, and often violent individuals. As you will see in the details that follow, working with these desperate, defiant young men pushes adults to their limits physically, mentally, and emotionally. The toll this work takes on the people trying to help these boys makes it very hard to exemplify the behavior and values we want them to emulate. The reality of their distorted perspective on life can be overpowering, especially in an isolated facility where they outnumber the adults.

The purpose of sharing my experiences with readers is not to elicit sympathy or admiration for the adults who do this difficult work, or to excuse the mistakes they may make. The point I am trying to underscore is that once a boy has reached this last resort stage there are undeniable limits to what institutions can do for him. What I hope readers will take from this chapter is the conviction that we as a society should do everything we can to prevent the need for such institutions.

The majority of events recounted in this chapter happened during my first three years at Rite of Passage, which gave me insight no graduate program will ever be able to match. To its credit, Rite of Passage did, and still does, an admirable job trying to work with and help so many troubled youth. However, facilities like these adhere to strict behavioral and sociological models that, in my opinion, miss the deepest component in the "whole person" spectrum: spirit. This gap in their treatment approach is illustrated very clearly by the following incident.

A few years ago, ROP's director of human resources contacted me about building more ceremony and ritual into its program. One day as he and I were discussing this, we noticed a student working in the office. Almost a graduate, he was trusted enough to do menial work and filing. We asked him about his program in general, and he immediately answered in the speeches and prose he had been taught. I literally saw his eyes searching for the canned response to the questions.

It became clear that he had more to say, but was hesitant to do so.

Both of us adults encouraged him to speak openly, and soon he did. He said that, while he appreciated the structure he had learned through the behavioral program and the perspective he had gained about being removed from his old gang, he really had wanted more of a celebration of that feat. He said he wished the "jumping out" of his gang was seen and celebrated as importantly as his original "jumping in" had been. Ceremony and ritual are important to adolescents, as well as all humans, and this kid wanted and needed a more spiritual grounding and cementing of his decisions. The program did not fulfill that crucial need.

A DESERT CAMP FOR DESPERATE BOYS

In the grand scheme of things, it was surely not an accident that my first experience working with troubled boys, which would become my passion and my career, was actually at an organization called Rite of Passage. Rite of Passage tried to give troubled boys an experience and opportunity akin to a real initiation from which they could emerge a new and better person. My own internal rite of passage began there, for the challenges of this job were beyond anything I was ever trained or prepared for.

Rite of Passage started in 1984 with half a dozen boys and a couple of staff staying in a tepee. More than twenty-two years and ten thousand boys later, ROP has facilities in four states housing more than a thousand boys. The "students" are mostly adjudicated youth on probation, and sometimes social placements (kids with no family to speak of). They are sent to ROP for a period of time because nothing else has worked in their county or town of origin. While placements across the country vary greatly in scope and flavor, most house the boys for a number of months to a number of years.

One of the dynamics that differentiates ROP from other placements or incarceration is that ROP does not operate on a fixed time frame for the boys. For example, time in juvenile hall is true calendar time, such as forty-five or ninety days. The boys call this "dead time." At Rite of Passage the boys have always had to earn their way out with good behavior, so there is no "dead time." Boys have to successfully complete the variety of challenges presented to them to either progress to the next level or, eventually, go home.

Typical boys that are sent to ROP are classic delinquents: gang members, drug users, boys who steal and burglarize, skip school, and get in fights. Most have been arrested more than once, and most have failed multiple other placement opportunities by running away, breaking rules, or fighting. The boys have a long and deteriorating history of negative behavior that makes most people think that without some serious intervention, the boys will end up in prison or dead. The social services youths who make it to ROP may not have a delinquent or criminal history, but they will not stay put in any other foster setting, so ROP takes them because their facility is so hard to run away from.

ROP has always had an athletic treatment model, using sports and exercise to help get the boys physically healthy so they feel good about themselves. Behavioral approaches and sociological models to help change their thinking are integrated into all the boys' activities. The boys also attend school and nowadays get vocational training. Additionally, they will receive various forms of counseling and therapy to help with their emotional and psychological issues.

When I came on board, ROP's Remote Training Center (RTC) was situated in the middle of the Nevada desert, sixteen miles from the nearest tree, water, or town. There were no lock-down facilities at the site, no handcuffs or any other means of inhibiting or restricting a youth who was violent or out of control. Hence, we relied on physical restraints and escorts. To keep a youth from harming himself or others, staff would physically hold him in a "bear hug" until he calmed down—holding his arms so he couldn't hit or flail. If he continued to resist or thrash about, he would be transitioned to the ground, hopefully in a sitting position or possibly a prone position. Once a boy was transitioned from standing to the ground, at least one or two more staff would contain his legs and make this as safe and harmless as possible. Once a boy de-escalated, he was slowly released until he could control his actions. Through the years, this process has gotten much safer and more refined, and as ROP became more adept at choosing which students to work with, restraints decreased considerably.

Largely because of the volatility of the students in the program, when I started at ROP in 1988, the company was experiencing an annual staff turnover rate of 400 percent. That's the equivalent of an entire new staff every three months! Being there a year made you a fixture, or "fossil." Having just traded my lucrative but hollow corporate career for something more meaningful, I was as ill prepared and trained as anyone else. This, of course, does not help youths who need guidance, therapy, mentoring, and parents, but we did the best we could and I was privileged to work with many amazing and caring people who succeeded and persevered. Fortunately, I was a quick study.

Seven-day shifts consisting of eighteen- to twenty-hour days were common. In times of low staffing and/or intensifying problems, there were stretches when I and my coworkers got little or no sleep for days. Not only was the schedule grueling, but this was an athletic treatment model, and we were required to exercise and participate fully with the boys. The strain on the body and senses was quite high, and as you can imagine, decision-making abilities and compassion were diminished as the week wore on.

These dynamics reflected typical macho beliefs about withstanding discomfort and adversity. There was a lot of peer pressure among staff to see who could take the most abuse, stay up the longest, participate in the most restraints. Although I had been subjected to this "get tough" approach for most of my life, I began to see how unhealthy much of it is and how we project it onto our youths.

Add to this scenario the effect of being in the Nevada desert. The temperature frequently reached as low as twenty degrees below zero and one week consistently reached thirty below. The generator froze, shutting off all electricity to the camps. Beds had to be placed next to each other and piles of kids were heaped under all the blankets and sleeping bags that could be found. With the electricity out, the radiophone could not work, nor could the water pump supply water. We actually felt lucky that there was snow on the ground, which the cooks gathered for making soups and hot drinks. Interestingly, this challenge brought the boys together, resulting in one of the least violent, least troublesome shifts ever. This was an early glimmer for me of the understanding that teen boys want and need a challenge to face.

I gained more insight into the fundamental, normal needs of these boys when one of the caseworkers got the idea that the boys needed a graduation rite. We had a cinder cone mountain a few miles from camp, and he chose to take one week's graduates to climb it. The boys, who had previously been runaway threats, were now treated with trust. They had a great time.

I went a few weeks later with another group of boys. It was bitterly cold, and I felt sorry for the boys walking through snow all day in tennis shoes. It was so cold that the canteen I wore around my neck and the gallon jugs of water the boys carried actually froze while we walked. Although the boys complained constantly, once we got back to camp they were heroes, survivors of the ordeal. This was one of the first examples I witnessed of the need for initiation and acceptance afterward. Unfortunately, in summer ROP canceled the graduation hikes when the returning boys bragged of seeing rattlesnakes. ROP mandated that graduation hikes would now take place only in spring and fall to minimize liability. This made the hikes possible for only some of the boys, which diminished the rite-of-passage aspect of these trips. The hikes soon lost impact, and eventually ground to a halt.

Summer temperatures in the desert would soar to one hundred twenty degrees, testing the mettle of both youth and staff. Until about 1990 there were no criteria for not exercising in these conditions, so youths were expected to complete their three-mile runs and do their workouts regardless of the temperature. After some youths died of heat-related problems in a Utah facility, eventually a plan was initiated that had levels of participation based on temperature and conditions.

The radiophone worked sketchily, particularly on windy days. There were a number of shifts I worked where we had no contact with the outside world for an entire week, frustrating staff who needed to communicate with family and friends, and angering residents who worked very hard to earn a three-minute phone call about once a month.

At ROP, every privilege was earned. The local denomination was a twenty-four-hour day. Youth had to "earn" their day by adequately participating in all required elements including sports, workouts, school, and meals. Infractions could lead to a "day loss," which meant that they basically had to stay one more day. It took one hundred good days to exit the RTC and move up to a less stringent facility and closer to gaining their freedom. Days were collected like dollars in a savings account, and they were the keys to the outside world. If memory serves, a youth had to earn about fifteen days to get a short phone call. He had to earn twenty-five days, I believe, to earn a closely supervised family visit.

Thus, rather than a set time of placement, the length of a boy's stay was determined by how long it took him to acquire days. I agree with this part of the program, which allowed youths who wanted to do so to accelerate their rehabilitation and didn't restrict them to an arbitrary time period. A few boys looked around, sized up the program and surroundings, and realized they wanted out fast. They would try hard to get as many days as they could, and would also try to acquire a few extra ones for student of the week, resident of the week, and athlete of the week. Many other boys sat out there for years because of their resistance and reluctance to participate in the program. Sadly, many boys simply had no better place to go, while others simply would not be told what to do. And, of course, there were all the middle-level kids who had good intentions but were so ingrained in their behavior patterns and misguided belief systems that they took two steps back for every three forward.

The most common argument I heard from boys who continually resisted the program was that they refused to be "told what to do." They seldom saw, or understood, the irony that their refusal to follow convention had cost them their freedom in the larger sense. They had no ability to go get a pizza, take a girl on a date, or sleep in on a weekend. They had given up great freedoms in their incarceration, and, once locked up, made it even harder on themselves by refusing to cooperate. This dynamic repeated itself so many times that it led me to look deeper into how adolescents think and feel. I saw countless times that teen boys need to feel pride and without effective parenting or mentoring, they will confuse pride with destructive stubbornness.

Special Treatment Program

"Specials," as the Special Treatment Program (STP) was called, was a fascinating place. Removed from the rest of the complex and hidden among some sand dunes, Specials was its own little universe. Any youths who were violent or noncompliant were taken to Specials, where they were required to cool off, complete some very long exercise sessions, and prepare themselves for entry back into the main camps.

Specials could be a volatile place, since everyone who was there was noncompliant to some degree, and STP staff had to be good at restraints. It tended to have, when possible, the highest staff-to-resident ratio. Boys in Specials were assigned to platforms, which were just a round piece of plywood attached to a shipping pallet to keep them off the ground. In the early years, residents spent all of their time, even sleeping at night, on these platforms. Eventually a couple of small Quonset huts were placed nearby for nighttime sleeping and protection from the elements.

Restraints were rampant in Specials, as the tension was often very high for both youths and adults. Specials tended to bring out the best and worst in both age groups. Boys could spend long periods of time there, often weeks, and for one youth, eight months! For eight full months, one boy simply, passively refused to do the program and sat every day and every night on a pallet, waiting and hoping his probation officer would change his mind. The probation officer never wavered, and eventually the boy went back to his original camp and ran a decent program. Residents in Specials could attend school if they were willing and compliant. In Specials, as we will soon see, one never really knew what might happen.

The Camps

The boys, and the RTC, were essentially broken down into three independently run camps, which for the most part were isolated from each other. In the center of everything was Base Camp, which housed the school buildings, chow hall, caseworker offices, and administration. Central Camp was housed within Base Camp, and National and American Camps were a ten- to fifteen-minute walk in opposite directions from Base Camp. The boys from each camp had little interaction with one another, and an elaborate revolving schedule took them into school, latrines, and the cafeteria without their coming into direct contact. With approximately thirty-eight boys in each camp, at times there were almost one hundred twenty kids walking around going somewhere.

Each camp had two Quonset huts for the boys to sleep in, with about nineteen in each hut. The Quonset huts were traditionally half round, but made of fabric so coaches (the staff who directly supervised the boys) could hear through them. However, so many boys found ways to cut through the fabric and run away that plywood sheets four feet high were installed to inhibit this.

This overall separation of the three camps was very important, as we had representative members from almost all California gangs, and there was also a natural "sibling" rivalry among the three camps. Except for my first five shifts in American Camp, I spent the rest of my career in National Camp, isolated in such a way that none of the other parts of any camps could be seen from our site. Often, in times of crisis and violence, this dynamic was scary, and many times assistance felt like a long way off. One night during one of my first shifts, we received a Mayday call over the radio at about 11 PM that a riot of sorts had broken out in National Camp. Not knowing what was happening, I was told to jump into a truck, and we drove as fast as possible the half mile or so to National Camp.

As we rolled into camp, we saw a number of youths outside arguing with a few staff members. We checked in with the coaches, who said this group was now under control but that the Group Supervisor (GS) was still inside one of the huts alone with eight to ten kids. We stormed into the hut in time to see the GS holding back the angry kids with a chair, as a lion tamer would. He was roaring commands and managing to keep all the kids at bay. With reinforcements, the situation was quickly resolved, and I came to see how important backup was and how quickly we could need it. I instantly wondered if I would ever have the skills, or the guts, to face ten angry boys.

The boys were assigned to a particular camp based on their school grade and ability. As I later learned more about adolescent developmental issues, I understood some of the flaws in these criteria. Central Camp took boys who tested at about seventh to eighth grade, so all of its boys were close developmentally. American Camp took boys who tested at fifth to sixth grade, and then ninth to tenth grade. In National Camp, we had from third- to fifth-grade level and tenth- to twelfth-grade level, thus giving us the greatest split in age and/or intellectual and emotional development. It was not uncommon in National Camp to have a twelve-year-old reading at eleventh-grade level and a seventeen-year-old reading at fourth-grade level. This kind of disparity compounded already inherent problems.

Nightwatch

Nightwatch was a necessary and problematic function at the camps. Direct care staff were required to sleep in the huts with the boys (which was not very restful). Nightwatch staff kept an eye on things to prevent violence in the dark, foil runaway attempts, and protect other staff.

When I first started at the RTC, the Nightwatch position was typically filled by local residents from a nearby town and reservation. They would sit in their cars with the motor and heater running, and check the huts every fifteen to twenty minutes. This system seldom worked, however. Understandably, in the wee hours of the morning the Nightwatch would fall asleep in their cars. Also, as they tended to make hut checks on a consistent schedule, the boys would simply wait until a Nightwatch had made his rounds, then do what they intended to do. With the Nightwatch in his car with the heater running, the boys knew he was not able to hear whatever they were up to. It was for these reasons that sleep was often restless and incidents common.

Occasionally, Nightwatch would not show up at all, and staff would have to increase their stress loads by staying up in shifts. Over seven days and nights, this could certainly add to the exhaustion level. Caseworkers, who were not used in typical daily supervision, were commonly used for this role. There were numerous times when I and my fellow caseworkers put in an eighteen- to twenty-hour day, then had to stay up all night so regular staff could get some rest. The next day we would resume our usual duties, with many of us staying up for forty hours or at a time. We were still required to act as role models, working out and running with the boys in their exercise and athletic activities. During one particular week, I got eleven hours of sleep in four nights. I was so exhausted when I finally got home that I literally slept for twenty-four hours, until my wife motivated me to get up and eat.

Rite of Passage argued, perhaps understandably, that adding three extra Nightwatch positions to protect the camps (for a total of two per camp, one per hut) would wreck the budget. However, an incident occurred that forced them to change their minds. One fifteen-year-old boy claimed he had been sodomized by a seventeen-year-old youth during the night. He claimed that Nightwatch was commonly asleep in the early morning hours, and at this time he would be forced to perform for the older boy in lieu of being assaulted.

I drove him to a town for a medical examination, which failed to determine whether this had really happened. The doctor said too much time had passed. Some boys confirmed that they had witnessed the events while others denied it. In any case, it became clear that the cost of more supervision would be more than offset by the reduced potential for liability, and the Nightwatch team was initiated. As a further sad side note, the young victim was pulled from the program as a failure and returned to juvenile hall in his county. Shortly after that, he hanged himself in that facility.

The new Nightwatch system worked much better. "Exit" lights were installed over the doors, which added some soft light to each hut. The two Nightwatch personnel were now stationed inside, one in each hut, and instructed to walk and count the boys every five to ten minutes.

Then they would switch huts every fifteen minutes. Although this soon became tedious, it minimized the instances of the Nightwatch falling asleep for more than just a few minutes. The biggest problem now came from coaches trying to adapt to a graveyard shift. However, the rest of us slept a little better, although there were still plenty of times when staffing was so short we had no Nightwatch except ourselves again. I remember doing physical exercises at 4 AM in an attempt to stay awake, and reading horror stories to try and stay alert.

If the power went out for some reason, as in when the generator failed, there was no lighting at all. Boys who had to use the restroom located in the camp office couldn't see the building, and if someone tried to sneak out of a hut, there was obviously no way to see him. On one shift there was no power and no Nightwatch, so I parked a truck with the headlights pointed at the two hut doors. It was winter and very cold, so I had the motor running and heater going. I had already done some previous Nightwatch duty that week and I was tired enough to know I could not stay awake, but our hope was that the sound of the idling truck would convince the boys that someone was watching. I set my watch to wake me up every fifteen minutes all night long so I could turn off the truck if necessary to cool it off. I had to wake up and reset my watch something like twenty-four times that night. Other nights I would walk in circles for hours to keep myself from falling asleep.

Staff Hierarchy

The staff hierarchy at ROP, and particularly the RTC, was somewhat like a military organization. With seven-day shifts, there was one site superintendent who overlapped both shifts, although he tended to deal mainly with managerial issues. Below him were two shift supervisors, one for each shift. In charge of each individual camp was a group supervisor, or GS, who had broad and total power over the camp. On an equal (on paper and seldom in reality) power level were the caseworkers, who did all of the residents' paperwork and conducted individual and group counseling.

The group supervisor and caseworker were analogous to Father and

Mother, I came to understand. They also often lapsed into good cop–bad cop dynamics with the boys. Essentially, the group supervisor played the disciplinary part and the caseworker played the nurturing part. Occasionally, we reversed the roles to show that a disciplinary figure could also be compassionate and the usually nurturing caseworker could hold a hard line. For two years, I played the role of nurturing "mom" while the GS played the strict "father." In my third year, my GS was promoted. I didn't want to shift to group supervisor, but management threatened me with a replacement I knew would be disastrous, so they leveraged me to shift roles. This Call to Adventure was unwelcome and difficult, but it was a good learning experience.

When I first started at ROP, staff tried to get all the boys lined up and involved in whatever component of the program was next—school, workouts, meals—as one large group, which was chaotic at best. Someone finally realized that we should divide the boys into smaller groups, similar to platoons. Eventually each camp had four Cottage Groups, with one staff person, or coach, per group of about nine boys. The senior coach acted like a sergeant, overseeing the four groups and the intense schedule the camps followed. Toward the end of my time at the RTC, a lead coach was added; he was essentially an on-site trainer for new staff. The lead coach followed new staff around to help groom them, and walked them through the procedures and more difficult situations.

It's important for me to have set this stage before heading into the anecdotes and stories. What happened at the RTC was a combination of the situation and circumstances, the layout of the place, the buildings and systems we had, a lack of training and/or qualified staff, the inevitable exhaustion, and, of course, some of the wildest boys you could ever imagine.

I will always cherish my memories and my learning from this period. It motivated me to chase all the rest of the material in this book, and more. ROP addicted me to helping wayward boys and prompted me to fill in the many gaps and shortcomings within the system as I experienced it. I do feel that organizations like ROP could do more to create programs to fit the kids instead of forcing the boys to fit the program.

It is not my intention to bring disfavor to ROP or to cause the program any problems. Staff try to manage a very difficult and often violent clientele. There is no historical precedent for dealing with such teen negativity and violence. Scores of treatment programs have come and gone as their approaches did not work or they had the misfortune of experiencing a serious teen injury or death. With no historical model to follow, programs like Rite of Passage have had to invent what they think will work for highly resistant teens.

The next section illustrates how letting boys get out of control in the first place puts them and us on dangerous ground, both physically and emotionally. Adults are forced to do difficult things in order to stop or control such negative behavior, and their own self-control and maturity are constantly tested. If we do not want to keep putting boys and adults into these situations, we need to channel our efforts and resources into preventing the need to incarcerate them in the first place.

WAR STORIES

In theory, when thirty-three staff left for a week off, another thirty-three would step in. Also included in that staff-to-student ratio were the medic, managers, and caseworkers who did not participate in the day-to-day camp activities. I would have to say that probably most of the shifts I was on (about eighty seven-day shifts), we did not have the full complement of staff. There were times I found a colleague or myself alone with anywhere from eight to all thirty-eight residents, which is where I learned the fine arts of trickery, bluffing, and intimidation when all else failed.

I'd been in American Camp just a few minutes when a student asked me to come over for a talk. I looked around for advice from other coaches, and one of them told me to be careful. I walked over to this boy, who was a sixteen- or seventeen-year-old about my size. He said in hushed tones, "You'll never last out the day." Shocked, I acted tough and stepped back outside the group, with him staring at me all the time and smiling a smile I will never forget. One worker from my training session in another camp had already quit within the first thirty minutes and left the compound. This quick exit was common, I came to learn, and I hoped I would have the grit to last at least a little longer than he did.

I somehow sloughed through the next few hours until it was almost bedtime. By nine o'clock, I was mentally exhausted. That's when the same threatening boy said he wanted to talk to me again. I walked cautiously over to him again, and this time he said "You'll never last the night. I'm gonna f— you up tonight!" This certainly put fear in me, but then I was told to go to Base Camp for some meeting or training. I got to bed about midnight, afraid to sleep because I had to do so in the hut with the kids. The Nightwatch outside appeared to be drunk, and I didn't have much faith that he would be any help later on.

Because most of the boys at ROP are multiple placement failures, they have a propensity to run away from their problems (literally and figuratively). Thus, anything that could aid them in escaping had to be locked up or hidden. It was recommended that we sleep in our clothes, put our shoes or boots at the bottom of our sleeping bags, keep our flashlight in hand, and sleep with one eye and both ears open. Add to this situation my personal threat from the teen, and the result, not surprisingly, was that I got no sleep that night, nor in the next two nights. For that entire seven-day shift, I was so busy and exhausted that I didn't even get a shower. There were a couple of other shifts during which many of my colleagues and I took no showers for the whole seven-day shift.

The next morning, the threatening teen called me over once again. I suddenly felt irritated by him, which I later found to be encouraging. This time he told me that I'd "never last out the shift." I walked away without saying anything, and somehow the week passed. A few days into the shift I had to do my first restraint, which was with a smaller boy and there was little drama to it. It was natural, I discovered, to react quickly to the situation, but I forgot all my training and resorted to just being stronger than he was. I had seen some violent restraints, though, and knew they could get ugly. I wasn't sure at all how I would fare in more difficult circumstances.

Just as I was getting ready to leave after my first shift, the same teen called me over one more time. This time, he claimed that I would not come back for another shift. I didn't respond, because I had little desire to come back to this ridiculous situation for thirteen hundred dollars per month. For most of my off-shift, I was unable to decide what I would do. I was raised not to quit, and I like challenges, but not necessarily ones that could beat me up. I remember thinking that for a nickel, I would never go back.

Toward the end of my off-shift, what kept sticking with me on top of all that I had experienced was the way the boy had had to change his threats and perception of me. I wouldn't last the day, then the night, then the shift, and then he claimed I wouldn't come back at all. I realized that this made me angry, and proving him wrong was the sole reason I decided to go back for shift number two. I had also decided that if this counterattack worked, I'd probably quit after the second shift and save some face. Looking back, although I was accepting this Call to Adventure, I was really struggling with the Thresholds of Difficulty in front of me.

When the boy saw me return, and also realized he had some other new booties to terrorize, he ignored me. The second shift was reasonably tame as I recall, but still no picnic, and I could see the potential for violence and injury all around me. I slept a little better, got a shower or two, and developed a terrible cold that made me testy, which I learned was to my advantage. I was already seeing how the overly liberal approach didn't work well with this type of boy.

I'd had one bad shift and one not-so-bad shift, and thought I'd give it one more week. During the third shift, the supervisor commented that my paperwork and writing ability were good, and that would qualify me as a good caseworker. There was an opening in a couple of shifts, and he asked if I'd like to be promoted. Five hundred dollars more per month, no daily schedule with the group, and the ability to do counseling with the boys—all this was highly appealing. After only two more shifts in the trenches, I was moved up to the alleged safety of management.

Being a caseworker meant I got to talk to the visiting psychologist and the clinical people in the organization. I spoke at length with probation officers and quickly expanded my skills. I got to watch the camp workings from the outside, which helped me to sculpt better systems and approaches. Suddenly, the job was fun, although still challenging and dangerous. I found myself participating in more and more restraints, for caseworkers were often called to take a boy to Specials when no other staff could be spared. While this afforded a therapeutic moment, it just as easily offered a chance for the boy to "go off" on me during the process. Still, overall I did pretty well at it, became proficient at restraints, and set about to improve the boys' lives.

Legal Wrestling

As I mentioned before, the RTC had no lockdown facilities at all. When residents became noncompliant or violent, they often had to be physically restrained on the ground or removed. Since many of these boys had been raised to understand that no actually means "maybe," the function of the restraint was often to prove to them that this time no means no, period.

It was this element, the ability to actually physically restrain a youth who was being a threat, that added so much intensity to the job. If a boy simply refused to do something or go somewhere he was directed to go, he would be physically escorted and/or restrained on the premise that allowing noncompliance would set a dangerous precedent for other boys to try to incite more negative or violent behavior. In many ways, I learned this to be true. The program's concept was to encourage boys to make good decisions, which had not been their history. If they refused to make a good decision, consequences, including physical restraints when necessary, would be invoked.

I was involved in hundreds of restraints during my three years at the RTC. Some were quick and easy, some violent and damaging to both parties. Many involved multiple people from both sides. Boys and adults got hurt sometimes, and I believe that statistically more adults were injured than were youths. As there were human beings involved, there was a mix of good and bad restrainers, clean ones and dirty ones.

I spent most of my first two years being a caseworker (counselor) and the third year as a group supervisor (head disciplinarian), which means I was not often involved in the minute-to-minute trench work. Nonetheless, I was surprised to find that I seemed to end up involved in many restraints, and, as a pacifist, I began to wonder why. I eventually learned that many of the boys needed the catharsis that came from a restraint, or they needed to vent pent-up anger and frustration, and this worked best for many of them with an adult they could trust. Boys whom I restrained would not be abused, tormented, or taunted, so the restraint became just that and nothing more. Many of my fellow staff were also good at restraints, and cared deeply about making sure they were safe for all involved.

I remember the first time I restrained a kid who continually refused to calm down and go to Specials. There didn't seem to be a policy for this. Someone finally drove up to my position with a pickup truck, and we lifted up the boy in restraint position and re-restrained him in the back of the truck. We then were driven to Specials, with him yelling, cursing, spitting, and trying to bite us all the while. Once in Specials, we picked him up out of the truck and restrained him again on the ground. The need to resist, against all logic, was something I would spend a lot of time pondering: the adolescent spirit was very angry. Specials staff would replace us and off we would go, back to camp.

Countless times after that, we had to put the boys in the back of some vehicle for transport. It was difficult, painful, and held lots of potential for things to go wrong. Other times we carried the boys, if possible, restraining them again if they resisted. I soon saw that because of the volatile nature of the boys and the large geographic area the camp was on, there was no other way to get a violent and/or noncompliant youth to Specials.

To vent our own fears and frustrations, we often resorted to grading restraints as in an Olympic competition. A noise or blur would catch your attention, and out of a schoolroom, for example, would come some wildly out-of-control boy with a staff person or two attached to him. People would trip, fall, or jump to get the best leverage and the top position in the restraint, which made these incidents fascinating to watch. Staff who witnessed the incident, when it was determined that everything was all right, would hold up the appropriate number of fingers and score the restraint ("Yeah! That's an eight!").

The most spectacular restraint I ever witnessed took place in Base Camp. We had one boy who was allegedly having PCP flashbacks, and would occasionally go completely out of control. He was not always violent or vindictive, but seldom had any control over his thought processes, so sometimes he made no sense or could not understand our requests and commands.

One time he bolted from his group and started running around the compound. Although he wasn't really doing anything wrong, we had learned that allowing any out-of-control behavior incited other boys to act out. This boy, about sixteen, was extremely fast and only one staff member (who had played college football) was able to keep up with him. The boy was creating havoc among the other boys. One of the difficulties with restraints was the impact they had on other youths. Sometimes, for example, if a gang member was being restrained, his "homies" would jump in and more staff would be needed. Typically we tried to remove any other youths from the area when restraints happened. Restraints, and noncompliant boys like this particular one, could easily incite the other residents to defiant and often violent behavior. A riot was our biggest fear, which is one of the main reasons the three individual camps had very little interaction.

This particular boy kept on running from our staff member, who could keep up but not catch him. After a few minutes, they both ran at a full sprint toward the Mess Hall, or cafeteria. The Mess Hall was a half-round Quonset hut about ten to twelve feet high. The boy just used his momentum to run up the sloped side and onto the top of the roof. Once there, for a moment or two he seemed elated, as though he'd achieved some difficult goal.

All of a sudden, our staff member, who also did not slow down, went running right up the side of the hut and came up behind the boy, wrapped him in a bear hug, and off the top of the hut they went. As they fell that ten or twelve feet, the staffer pivoted like a falling cat in the air so the boy was on the bottom. They landed this way in deep sand, which thankfully broke their fall. The impact knocked the wind out of the boy, and moments afterward more staff came to escort him to Specials. The staff member brushed himself off and looked up to see his colleagues signaling what I believe was the only perfect ten score I ever saw while I was at ROP.

Sometimes restraints actually had some therapeutic value, and some were even humorous. One boy who came to us was not on probation, which was highly unusual. He had no case file with him when he arrived, so we knew nothing about him. He claimed to be at ROP on an education scholarship, which made no sense to us. Eventually we learned that his mother had feared he was heading down a self-destructive track like his older brother and had convinced the principal of his school to fund the placement, hoping the boy would see that it was no picnic to walk on the wild side. Mother acted as his probation officer, and to her credit she did not listen to his pleas to leave and forced him to do the program. He never agreed with his placement and spent a lot of energy in trying to get out of performing. We soon saw why his mom had put him in ROP.

One day he "went off" in National Camp and was restrained. We had no vehicle to drive him to Specials, so I was nominated to push, pull, and drag him there, about a ten-minute walk away without a struggling boy in tow. He refused to go peacefully, so I bear-hugged him and started walking slowly toward Specials. He was a small fourteen-year-old, but he certainly got heavy in a hurry as he resisted every move I made.

I had previously broken my glasses in a restraint (a constant occupational hazard), and once while we were struggling, they broke again. When he realized this fact, he quit struggling and became passive. He promised to not move while I pulled out my Super Glue and tried to make repairs. Wary of his promise, I slowly released him and worked on my glasses. He calmly sat down and talked of mundane things while I fixed my glasses. Once I had them back together, I asked him to continue walking to Specials. He refused, and I had to carry him again.

Three more times my glasses broke during our "wrestling match." Each time he calmly sat down and waited for me to get ready. And each time, as soon as I was finished, he became noncompliant again, and off we'd go. I eventually got him to Specials, exhausted from the effort, and went back to my camp.

This was one of the incidents that showed me how many of these boys used restraints to get personal attention from the staff, particularly the men (we occasionally had a few women on staff). There was some need this boy obviously had but could not express in words or feelings, so his unconscious helped set him up to get what he wanted.

One time a gang member from Southern California was "going off." Screaming, yelling, and throwing things, it was apparent he needed to be restrained. As I moved toward him, he spun around to run the other way just as a very large staff member was coming out of a hut to assist. He bear-hugged the oncoming boy and down they went. The boy vented for a while, and when he seemed calm, the staff member released him. The boy stood up, brushed himself off, walked over to the staff member, and said, "Thanks, man, I needed that." Then they shook hands.

I started paying attention to how often these boys set themselves up to be restrained. Caseworkers were involved in a number of restraints, as we were often used for transporting a youth from camp and the restraint would happen on the way to Specials. Not often, but occasionally, a boy thanked me for my participation. Of course the goal became to teach the boys to attract attention for positive behavior, but many youths had such ingrained destructive belief systems that this seldom happened.

It is obviously dangerous to perform physical restraints. And though I believe there were actually more serious injuries to staff than to residents throughout the years, it was the occasional injuries to youth that caught everyone's attention. Many of us had scraped and bruised knees and elbows almost constantly, my hands were often marked with fingernail scratches, and occasionally some boy bit me or pulled my hair, among other things. I now see the folly in much of this, but I remember vividly the feeling of rising to the challenge, which is a key ingredient in initiations and traditional rites of passage. It's apparent now that this three-year experience was a rite of passage for me, and I wish I'd had some frame of reference or guidance regarding it at the time.

One boy I saw being restrained tried to put his arm out to stop his fall, and broke that arm in the process. It wasn't anyone's fault, but it happened just the same. Another boy had a habit of tucking in his arms under his chest, which gave him leverage and made it extremely difficult to keep him still. He often wrapped himself up like an octopus around his desk, more than once forcing us to carry him and his school desk outside, where we could try to separate the two. We were instructed to get a boy's arms out to the sides of his body, with the palms up if possible. This took away all leverage and made him much easier to handle. As I tried to pull his arm free, I heard a terrible sound in his shoulder. He let out a scream, and later it was confirmed I had separated his shoulder. The damage was actually minimal, but it makes me sick to my stomach to remember it, and I'll always feel bad about that incident. This boy constantly set himself up to be hurt, a dynamic common in his upbringing.

Another time, one of my students had gone noncompliant in school and was being sent to Specials for a workout. He was highly agitated, and I was certain he was going to strike the staff person who had done the intervention. I stepped in, and began escorting him to Specials. Everything went well for a hundred feet or so, when suddenly he stopped, yelled "F— this!" and turned to hit me with his fist. I had been following right behind him just for this possibility. When he spun to his right, I came in on the left side from behind and started to wrap him up in the restraint. As we spun, I heard a great *snap* and felt my right leg give way, and we tumbled to the ground. As I fell, I knew I had broken my leg.

We rolled around on the ground as he tried to assault me and I tried to contain him without mangling my leg any further until help arrived.

After a very long minute, staff came running to assist. They pulled him off and continued on to Specials. As I felt myself slipping into shock, my friends carried me to the medic's office. I was first driven to a local hospital, bouncing painfully over our sixteen-mile dirt road, then moved up to an orthopedic clinic as it was discovered I had two breaks: one low on the tibia and one high on the fibula.

In hindsight, I see restraints as a double-edged sword. On the one hand they were absolutely necessary in those circumstances; however, it was too bad that's how we had to deal with troubled youth. If our judicial system worked more effectively, we would not be creating such incorrigible youth who need to be manhandled. Since my time at ROP, California has passed legislation basically eliminating out-of-state placements. A generation of bureaucrats later, in an effort to keep treatment money at home, the state that created the need for these types of treatment centers has brought all those bad boys back into California. Rite of Passage Inc. has moved on to other states' boys, and now is, I believe, the largest treatment center in the country.

Devil Worshippers

Devil worshippers, known at the camps as D.W.'s, were an interesting group. During my three years at ROP, I'd have to say I met only one boy who I felt really believed in devil worship. Most kids floated in and out of the group. At first I was uneasy about them, but after I watched them for a while, I began to understand how this unique group of kids worked.

The most obvious thing about them was that they were almost always white, and usually young and/or small. I learned that the Latino boys typically were protected by affiliation in their gangs. Also, most Latinos tended to be Catholic, so the D.W. stuff bothered them in a religious sense. The African American youths were also protected by their gang affiliations and they tended to be superstitious about the devil. Thus, the D.W. stuff also kept them at bay. The young white boys seemed to use the D.W. identification mostly to keep other boys off their backs.

I mentioned that there was only one boy I ever really felt was a true believer in the devil. Besides this, he was a sociopath who had what I call "shark eyes": kind of dead and lifeless. This boy spent more than two years, I believe, in the RTC alone.

RTC youth were never allowed out of sight of the staff. Any time they went to the bathroom, or ran back to the hut to get a coat, they were accompanied by staff. One day it was discovered that this youth had somehow not only caught ten lizards, which should have been impossible under constant supervision, but he also had made sacrifices of them. The lizards were lined up in a row behind the hut, an absolutely out-of-bounds area, and placed on the ground on their backs. They had been dissected vertically through their bellies in a sacrificial manner. He had even constructed ten upside-down crosses and placed them in the ground at the head of each lizard. This was one of the scariest boys I ever met. (As is the case with most of the boys I've worked with through the years, I have no idea what became of him.)

Another devil worship incident involved a boy had been terribly stressed for some reason. He became out of control and was removed to Specials. Once there, his behavior was getting worse and I got a call from some staff who wanted me to try and talk to him. As I arrived in Specials a few minutes later, I saw him come blasting out of the hut and running away up a large sand dune. He kept screaming that a staff member had been "dissing" (disrespecting) his mother, and he couldn't take any more of it.

Two of us caught him running up the sand dune and restrained him. He was hysterical, screaming, yelling, crying, and writhing on the ground. What makes this particular incident so interesting is that in the middle of being essentially senseless, he started growling and "throwing horns" with his hands. Throwing horns involves holding up only the first and little fingers on a hand to look like horns. I have to admit that it made me very uncomfortable, and to this day I believe that he was so emotional that this was not planned. We learned later he had recently lived with a man who took in young runaways. In exchange for sexual favors and stealing for him, he provided a "safe" place to stay and, based on what I had seen, perhaps some training in the occult.

Gangs

Without a gang, you're an orphan.

MEMBER OF THE JETS
GANG IN *WEST SIDE STORY*

Many of the boys at ROP came from gangs. Of all the different types of boys I have worked with through the years, I've had the least success with gang members. This comes, I believe, from the fact that once they join a gang, they anticipate that they will "do some time" along the way. Also, there is an ethical shift that youths go through when they enter the gang life, a kind of irreversible decision to abandon decent behavior. Gang members, as we all have read about, are commonly involved not only in drug or turf-related acts of violence, but also random ones, including drive-by shootings.

The bond that gang members create among themselves never fails to amaze me; it's comparable to that of soldiers in combat. Most gang members, as well as most adults working with gang kids, will tell you that the main reason they get together is that the gangs make them feel special and needed and give them a feeling of belonging. And as we saw in the Loss of Initiation and Rites of Passages chapters, gangs are actually engaged in the kind of archetypal initiation dynamics that are so sorely missing from boys' lives, albeit in a twisted form. In terms of symptoms versus causes, it has become clear to me that force and incarceration will not stop gangs. What is needed is for a child not to have to look outside of his home to feel needed. Community-based initiations and more male mentors would also help prevent the need or desire to join gangs. I mention the "need" to join gangs because many boys grow up in very dangerous neighborhoods where they feel pressed to join one gang or another for protection. Like soldiers in a time of war, they are essentially drafted.

Gangs are their own little world with their own laws and rules, as well as their own jargon, hand signs, and other behaviors that separate them from other youths. They live outside the law, but adhere strongly to the rules of their own culture. The rules and signs vary in different parts of the country—what I describe here is common for the western United States.

African American teens tend to split into two separate gangs, the Crips and the Bloods. (It was estimated back in about 1993 that nationwide the Crips had more firepower than the Mafia.) Each gang will have many sub-gangs, called sets, which usually have their own territory, local rules, and a name that identifies their particular boys. Crips gangs tend not to have disputes with other Crips gangs, but aggression between groups is becoming more common each year. Perhaps this is because the economy of gangs is based on drug sales, and the lure of more money eventually overrides loyalty to the main gang. Latino gangs are generally separated into two sects also, commonly known as Norteños (Northerners) and Sureños (Southerners). Generally speaking, Crips and Bloods hate each other, as do Norteños and Sureños.

Crips generally claim the color blue and sometimes black. Their clothing and cars will reflect this. Bloods claim red. These color distinctions usually make it relatively easy to determine a youth's gang affiliation. The Latino gangs vary in their color preferences, but are getting more specific each year. Latino gangs claim the number thirteen and the color blue (Sureños); the number fourteen and the color red are claimed by the Norteños. Explanations abound for their attachment to these numbers. The one I hear most often is that the Mexican Mafia, one of the toughest prison gangs, adopted thirteen because the letter *m* is the thirteenth letter of the alphabet. The letter *n* is the fourteenth letter of the alphabet, which works well for Norteños.

A gang member's level of involvement or belief is often indicated by how serious his attachment is to his color. Crips avoid the color red at all costs. They avoid, if possible, strawberries, Coca-Cola in its red can, Hanes underwear because of the red stripe, and even coming in contact with the color. This was difficult at the RTC, for the boys wore red sweats and shorts with blue T-shirts and sweatshirts. If a Crip brushed up against someone wearing red, he would actually flinch.

Crips really struggled with this at times in school, especially in biology, where they studied the cardiovascular system. I can't tell you how many boys flunked assignments and classes because they refused to color blood in its natural color, and they would never write the word *blood* itself. In other classes, they would put a slash though any letter *b* on their homework, which served to disrespect it. They would alter the word *blood,* or disrespect it by writing the word *slob,* which everyone knew meant a Blood. Instead of saying *red* they would say *ded,* and recycled the old saying from the cold-war days, "Better dead than red."

Bloods had the same issues with the color blue. They would avoid it, or disrespect it any way they could. Refusing to use the word Crip, they altered it to the word *crab.* Since the clothing forced each gang to wear its rival color, the boys were tricky in how they handled it. They would try to wear part of the offensive clothing inside out, or they would put a hole in it. Bloods also changed the common term *kicking it,* which means just resting or hanging out, to the term *bicking it,* which stands for "Bloods is Crip killers." The boys from Latino gangs had similar approaches with respect to their number associations.

We had to screen all of their correspondence in and out of the RTC, as well as their homework, to prevent this kind of gang provocation. Every time a boy was caught doing any gang behavior, he would lose not just a day, but instead 10 to 25 percent of all his accumulated days. We had to make gang associations expensive or boys would continue to adhere to them.

Members throw gang signs to brag about who they are and to see who the other person or group of people are. They get very good at it, and the signs change and evolve, making them difficult to spot. Anyone who has seen gang graffiti, or tagging, as it is called, knows that gangs have invented their own alphabet, which is very difficult to read unless you are well practiced.

Even their baseball hats and other clothing reflected this obsession with their gang. For example, a boy wearing a UNLV (University of Las Vegas) hat might really be using the acronym to mean Us Norteños Love Violence. The L.A. and Sacramento Kings hats were used as an acronym for Krazy Insane Norte Gangsters. A hat with the NFL logo could stand for Norteños For Life. Numerous variations come and go.

I've noticed as the years pass that more and more teen clothing is designed around these gang preferences. I've seen, for example, almost every professional sports team, regardless of its official colors, come out with official team gear in red or blue but often no other colors. For example, the Cincinnati Reds baseball team, historically wearing a red hat for obvious reasons, now produces a blue hat with the C for Cincinnati on it. This is great if you are a Crip desiring blue. The Oakland Raiders football team, one of the first to market clothing that was adopted by kids as "gang-style," has a black-and-silver logo. But now it is marketing hats in both blue and red. Not orange, purple, or yellow, but the two major gang colors in the San Francisco Bay Area, where the Raiders are located. A coincidence?

Here again we see how the marketing people seem not to care about the impact or influence their products have as long as they sell. Nike does a lot of its teen marketing research in the inner cities.

At ROP, we had opposing gangs within the same camps, which seemed ludicrous to me. Kids who were willing to kill each other on the outside had no qualms about fighting each other at the RTC. Sometimes, especially with new residents, gang signs and blatant fights broke out. As we adults slowly leveraged the gang kids out of clear participation, they became more subtle. For example, as the kids walked and stood a lot of the time in the desert sand, they would often, very subtly, draw an opposing gang sign on the ground with their toe as if they were just goofing around. Then, they would either spit on it or stamp on it and rub it out. Their adversaries did not miss this disrespect and symbolism, and fights would begin almost instantaneously. It was in this space that I learned to watch hands and feet closely.

Some of the most unnerving times I had at ROP involved gang members, because of their propensity for violence and for backing each other up. Often, if we needed to restrain one boy who was a gang member, you could expect his homies to jump in at any moment.

The most challenging incident happened one weekend day, when nine Crips banded together, broke into a janitor's room, and came out with brooms, shovels, and other weapons. They walked out of Base

Camp and headed toward National Camp, where they added to their impromptu arsenal.

Short-handed as usual, we were only able to come up with eight staff to deal with the situation, as there were another 110 boys to be supervised in the other camps. We picked the biggest, the strongest, and the ones with martial arts experience, and headed for National Camp.

The nine boys were situated on a sand dune so they could see if anyone was trying to sneak up on them. They had formed a circle, standing back to back with their weapons in front of them. When we eight grown-ups arrived, we didn't really know what to do. As we stood there talking, our indecision encouraged the boys, who began to talk to us and taunt us. The biggest, the ringleader, asked us what were we going to do, try to restrain nine armed kids with only eight adult bodies?

Not knowing the answer to that question, I was getting more and more concerned that this was not a good intervention and we needed more bodies. During a couple of really dangerous incidents in the past, additional staff actually had to be brought in from other sites to help out. One of our men stepped out of our circle and walked closer to the boys.

He laughed at the boy, then responded with something like "Hey, there aren't going to be any restraints here today, boys. You all have weapons, which means we don't have to play by the rules anymore either. We're just going to walk up there and start beating the shit out of you, one at a time, until we teach you a lesson." The boy argued, but there was definitely fear in his eyes and voice. Our spokesman simply replied, "There are no witnesses, except for us, and we've already agreed on how we'll make this all look afterward. Everyone knows you started it by picking up those weapons."

The rest of us started spreading out, slowly surrounding the boys, who were looking less and less brave with each passing moment. "Well," said our new leader, "what's it going to be? Ya wanna stop this silliness right here and now or do we keep coming and shove that rake right up your ass?" That seemed to make up the minds of the smaller, more fearful boys. A couple dropped their weapons and stepped away from the circle of boys. All of a sudden, the incident was over, as the shrinking group of boys slowly relinquished their weapons and surrendered.

That incident, like so many others, could very easily have ended up with a violent resolution. Testing and challenging angry teen boys is seldom a good idea. Even if the adults "win," we have simply reinforced for the boys the old concept that might makes right, or whoever is toughest prevails. As always, in hindsight we wish for a better solution to situations like this, but when you are isolated in the desert with no assistance and usually outnumbered at least eight to one, you do what you think will work.

WHAT BEHAVIOR MANAGEMENT DOESN'T TEACH

Successes are difficult to quantify in my work, but there have been many. We do a lot of "seed planting"—leaving little seeds of growth and possibility in each boy, hoping that later on in life they will sprout and blossom and help the boy make better decisions. Every once in a while you see a kid make a total turnaround, or as I like to put it, "turn on the lightbulb." But many of the boys had lived with so much abuse that I doubted a million push-ups, three-mile runs, or other consequences could begin to have an impact on them. Many kids laughed at our attempts to enforce consequences, challenging us to hurt them after all the other things they had been through. I learned that as useful as behavior management can be, it often stalled when it hit a high level of prior abuse.

For example, there was the boy at the RTC who had been stealing cars at home. Quite simply, he had been trying to get his workaholic father to pay him some attention. When just being good failed to get a response from his dad, he did what so many kids do: he acted negatively, and got lots of attention. One day this boy came up to me and said, "Hey, Bret, guess what?"

"What's that?" I replied.

"I don't think I'm going to steal any more cars!"

"Great," I said. "Why is that?"

"Because I miss being with my family and this has been an embarrassment to them."

"Oh," I said, "I see." Noticing my lack of enthusiasm, he said, "What's the matter? Isn't that good?"

"Yes, of course it is," I said. "I just think there's more to discover if you look a little deeper."

A few weeks later he came up to me and said once again that he was finished stealing cars. Once again, I asked him why. He told me, "Well, I'm costing my parents a lot money being here, and it's not a good thing being locked up."

I agreed with him once more, but with some reservation. Frustrated, he asked me why I wasn't pleased with his reasons. "Because," I said, "you are looking outside yourself for the reasons. Look inside and tell me why."

Not too long after that, he walked back up to me for a third time. He had a peaceful look and a positive smile on his face, and I asked him what was going on. He calmly said, for a third time, "I'm not going to steal any more cars." And as usual, I asked him, "Why?"

"Because," he said calmly, "it's wrong."

I smiled at him, as I couldn't think of anything better to say than what he had just told me. Finally, I said, "There you go; it's that simple."

He nodded his head and returned to camp. He earned his days quickly and made short work of completing the program.

Earlier I spoke of a boy who had been beaten by his father with a hammer and beer bottles. This was the same boy whose shoulder I had accidentally separated in an ugly restraint. He called me a couple of years ago. He was one of only three non-probation youth I'd ever seen at the RTC. He was a social services case, but his behavior was so bad they couldn't keep him in any foster homes or group homes. His social worker implored us to keep him as long as possible, for his county had no options left except to lock him behind bars somewhere. We were concerned about keeping him longer than we would have liked to, but as it turned out, we couldn't get him to leave. He'd self-destruct every time he got close to graduating, and we knew that deep down, although he claimed otherwise, he really had no better place to go.

In this business there is little that feels as good as a kid calling from down the road and telling you he is doing well. He told me he had indeed heard all of the lectures and advice my counterparts and I had given him during his years in the desert. He said he knew he couldn't return home to his mother/sister, but he didn't want the other boys to know that. He told me that we had given him more support and structure, as well as love, than he had ever received at home. He simply had no better place to go. That dynamic is a sad fact in my business.

But he told me he was doing really well, and had found the perfect vocation for his temperament, his resistance to authority, and his funny view on life. He said he was happy, and was actually working with another one of my favorite boys from National Camp who also had nothing better to return home to. When I asked what they were doing, he laughed and said, "I work in the circus, where they call me Lord Psycho. Can you believe it, these guys are paying me to be crazy!" We spoke a few more minutes before he had to go. I hung up the phone with a smile on my face and tears in my eyes, and went to work on the next boy in my life.

Behavior management is a standard tool in working with high-risk, adjudicated teens, because their behavior must be controlled before they can be receptive to learning new attitudes and strategies for life. But behavior management has serious limitations. In my experience, it is hard to implement effectively with severely abused boys, which is why boot camps and residential treatment centers like ROP have little success. Behavior management is good at teaching that actions have consequences: if I steal, I get locked up. But it does not teach issues of conscience, what a boy really believes is right and wrong as opposed to what is allowed or not allowed. To get to that level with our young men requires multidimensional approaches as diverse as the boys we are trying to reach.

Afterword

*The function of answers is merely to hold things together
until a better round of questions is thought up.*

THOMAS KELLY

Once a problem is solved, its simplicity is amazing.

PAULO COELHO, *THE PILGRIMAGE*

This book was originally published under the title *Slaying the Dragon:
The Contemporary Struggle of Adolescent Boys*. Metaphorically, it is
a dragon that boys are trying to slay on their quest to become men.
Through the years, I've come to look at dragons as symbolic of all the
challenges boys must face in their lives.

The dragon that modern American teens battle is bigger and more
fierce than any mythical dragon. The dragon of today is modern culture, a challenge our teens keep trying to rise to, only to get knocked
back down time and time again. Our boys are dying of atrophy and
neglect, and will resist any attempt to feminize them into being anything but boys. Where we used to love boy energy, in modern culture that boy energy is too often deemed inconvenient, medicated into
submission, and incarcerated into oblivion. Boys are at the mercy of
mega-million-dollar advertising campaigns designed to make them
want irresponsible and inappropriate things, which is unhealthy for

them and frustrating for the adults who care about them.

Boys are built for risk and hungry to be initiated, whether or not we want this. Just because we removed initiations from their lives does not mean we have removed their craving for this healthy nudge into adulthood, and hopefully manhood. While I admit I spend a lot of time with "bad boys," I've discovered they are not all bad. Their behavior may indeed be deplorable at times, but many of the boys I work with are simply sailing without a map or rudder. Many have had little or no positive parenting or safe communities to grow up in, and they face a growing cultural animosity that seems to view adolescence as an inconvenience.

I work with lots of "good" boys as well, kids who don't need counseling so much as a male mentor or elder in their lives. Boys who get good grades and help out around the house. Boys who have wonderfully caring single moms who are working overtime on numerous levels. Boys who are afraid of drugs and gangs yet fear ostracizing or even violent recriminations from tougher boys. My point in this book has been that if we provide healthy initiation for our boys, fewer of them will join gangs and become violent, take and sell drugs, or abuse their spouses, lovers, and children. They will generally live better lives. Is that too much to ask for our children, who are indeed our future?

When we stop putting men out of work to increase our profits, our children will prosper, not financially but spiritually and emotionally. When men are considered a success for staying at home and remaining in relationship, our divorce rate will drop and our children will thrive. When we start putting our energy and resources into effectively sculpting our boys into men, we will see an influx of healthy masculinity that will benefit us all.

Whoever said work with troubled boys has to be clinical to be effective was wrong. Every time I treat my boys like they are from a thousand years ago, they seem to meet me halfway, which is pretty fair for an adolescent. I've been working with "bad" boys for about eighteen years now, and while many of my newer counterparts burn out after a year, I can't wait for tomorrow.

The adolescent spirit is a beautiful thing, and it should not and cannot be legislated, processed, incarcerated, or medicated into a more suitable model for modern times. The adolescent spirit needs to be tempered into a stronger substance, honed to a sharper edge. The way we work with our teens must be approached as an art, not a science.

I understand we can't go back a hundred or a thousand years, but that doesn't mean we can't use older approaches that still have value. One of my favorite quotes, which I used earlier in the book, is most appropriate here. Ever idealistic yet realistic, George Washington Hayduke in Edward Abbey's *The Monkey Wrench Gang* declares, "I don't want the world to be the way it used to be, I just want the world to be the way it is supposed to be."

Here's hoping we do a better job for our teens in the new millennium. I hope that you have found useful information and inspiration for that work.

Bibliography

Abrams, Jeremiah. *The Shadow in America: Reclaiming the Soul of a Nation.* Novato, Calif.: Nataraj Publishing, 1994.

Aichhorn, August. *Wayward Youth.* New York: Viking Press, 1935.

Artress, Lauren. *Walking a Sacred Path: Rediscovering the Labyrinth as a Spiritual Tool.* New York: Riverhead Books, 1995.

Bierhorst, John. *The Mythology of North America.* New York: William Morrow and Co., 1985.

Blankenhorn, David. *Fatherless America: Confronting Our Most Urgent Social Problem.* New York: HarperPerennial, 1995.

Bly, Robert. *Iron John: A Book About Men.* New York: Vintage Books, 1990.

———. *A Little Book on the Human Shadow.* New York: Harper & Row, 1988.

———. *The Sibling Society.* Reading, Mass.: Addison-Wesley Publishing Co., 1996.

Brokaw, Tom. *The Greatest Generation.* New York: Random House, 1998.

Bryan, Mark. *The Prodigal Father: Reuniting Fathers and Their Children.* New York: Clarkson Potter Publishers, 1997.

Campbell, Joseph. *The Hero with a Thousand Faces.* Princeton, N.J.: Princeton University Press, 1949.

———. *The Power of Myth.* New York: Doubleday, 1988

Canada, Geoffrey. *Fist, Stick, Knife, Gun: A Personal History of Violence in America.* Boston: Beacon Press, 1995.

Chinen, Allen. *Beyond the Hero: Classic Stories of Men in Search of Soul.* New York: Tarcher/Putnam, 1993.

―――. *Once Upon a Midlife: Classic Stories and Mythic Tales to Illuminate the Middle Years.* New York: Tarcher/Putnam, 1992.

Cohen, Albert K. *Delinquent Boys: The Culture of the Gang.* New York: Free Press, 1955.

Corneau, Guy. *Absent Fathers, Lost Sons.* Boston: Shambhala, 1991.

Cose, Ellis. *A Man's World: How Real Is Male Privilege—and How High Is Its Price.* New York: HarperCollins, 1995.

Coupland, Douglas. *Generation X: Tales for an Accelerated Culture.* New York: St. Martin's Press, 1991.

Diamond, Jared. *Guns, Germs, and Steel: The Fates of Human Societies.* New York: W. W. Norton & Co., 1999.

Eliade, Mircea. *Rites and Symbols of Initiation: The Mysteries of Birth and Rebirth.* Woodstock, Conn.: Spring Publications, 1958.

Faludi, Susan. *Stiffed: The Betrayal of the American Man.* New York: William Morrow and Co., 1999.

Friedenberg, Edgar Z. *Coming of Age in America: Growth and Acquiescence.* New York: Random House, 1963.

―――. *The Vanishing Adolescent.* New York: Dell Publishing, 1959.

Fulce, John. *Seduction of the Innocent Revisited: Comic Books Exposed.* Lafayette, La.: Huntington House Publishers, 1990.

Garbarino, James. *Lost Boys: Why Our Sons Turn Violent and How We Can Save Them.* New York: Anchor Books, 1999.

Gatto, John Taylor. *A Different Kind of Teacher: Solving the Crisis of American Schooling.* Berkeley, Calif.: Berkeley Hills Books, 2002.

―――. *Dumbing Us Down: The Hidden Curriculum of Compulsory Schooling.* Gabriola Island, British Columbia: New Society Publishers, 1992.

―――. *The Exhausted School: Bending the Bars of Traditional Education.* Berkeley: Berkeley Hills Books, 1993.

Gesel, Arnold. *Youth: The Years from Ten to Sixteen.* New York: Harper & Row, 1956.

Gilmore, David. *Manhood in the Making: Cultural Concepts of Masculinity.* New Haven, Conn.: Yale University Press, 1990.

Gladwell, Malcolm. *The Tipping Point: How Little Things Can Make a Big Difference.* New York: Back Bay Books, Little Brown & Co., 2000.

Goldman, Paul. *Growing Up Absurd: Problems of Youth in the Organized System.* New York: Random House, 1960.

Grof, Christina. *The Thirst for Wholeness: Attachment, Addiction, and the Spiritual Path.* San Francisco: HarperSanFrancisco, 1993.

Gurian, Michael. *A Fine Young Man: What Parents, Mentors and Educators Can Do to Shape Adolescent Boys into Exceptional Men.* New York: Tarcher/Putnam, 1998.

———. *The Prince and the King: Healing the Father-Son Wound.* New York: Tarcher/Perigree, 1993.

———. *The Wonder of Boys: What Parents, Mentors and Educators Can Do to Shape Boys into Exceptional Men.* New York: Tarcher/Putnam, 1997.

Hall, G. Stanley. *Adolescence: Its Psychology and Its Relations to Physiology, Anthropology, Sociology, Sex, Crime, Religion and Education,* Vols 1 and 2. New York: Appleton and Company, 1904.

Harris, Bud. *The Father Quest: Rediscovering an Elemental Psychic Force.* Alexander, N.C.: Alexander Books, 1996.

Hersch, Patricia. *A Tribe Apart: A Journey Into the Heart of American Adolescence.* New York: Ballantine Books, 1998.

Hine, Thomas. *The Rise and Fall of the American Teenager.* New York: Avon Books, 1999.

Howard, Philip K. *The Death of Common Sense: How Law Is Suffocating America.* New York: Random House, 1994.

Jastrab, Joseph. *Sacred Manhood, Sacred Earth: A Vision Quest into the Wilderness of a Man's Heart.* New York: HarperPerennial, 1994.

Johnson, Robert. *The Fisher King & the Handless Maiden.* San Francisco: HarperSanFrancisco, 1993.

———. *He: Understanding Masculine Psychology.* New York: Harper & Row, 1974.

———. *Lying with the Heavenly Woman: Understanding and Integrating the Feminine Archetypes in Men's Lives.* San Francisco: HarperSanFrancisco, 1994.

———. *We: The Psychology of Romantic Love.* San Francisco: Harper & Row, 1983.

———. *She: Understanding Feminine Psychology.* New York: Harper & Row, 1976.

Jung, C. G. *Four Archetypes: Mother/Rebirth/Spirit/Trickster.* Princeton, N.J.: Princeton University Press, 1969.

———. *The Undiscovered Self.* New York: Mentor Books, 1958.

Kaplan, Louise. *Adolescence: The Farewell to Childhood.* New York: Simon & Schuster, 1984.

Keen, Sam. *Fire in the Belly: On Being a Man.* New York: Bantam Books, 1991.

Kett, Joseph. *Rites of Passage: Adolescence in America 1790 to the Present.* New York: Basic Books, 1977.

Kindlon, Dan, and Michael Thompson. *Raising Cain: Protecting the Emotional Life of Boys.* New York: Ballantine Books, 1999.

Kipnis, Aaron. *Angry Young Men: How Parents, Teachers, and Counselors Can Help "Bad Boys" Become Good Men.* San Francisco: Jossey-Bass, 1999.

———. *Knights Without Armor: A Practical Guide for Men in Quest of Masculine Soul.* New York: Tarcher/Perigree, 1991.

Kipnis, Aaron, and Elizabeth Herron. *Gender War, Gender Peace: The Quest for Love and Justice Between Men and Women.* New York: William Morrow & Co., 1994.

Kupers, Terry. *Revisioning Men's Lives: Gender, Intimacy and Power.* New York: Guilford Press, 1993.

LaRossa, Ralph. *The Modernization of Fatherhood: A Social and Political History.* Chicago: University of Chicago Press, 1997.

Larsen, Stephen. *The Mythic Imagination: Your Quest for Meaning Through Personal Mythology.* New York: Bantam Books, 1990.

Lightfoot, Cynthia. *The Culture of Adolescent Risk-Taking.* New York: Guilford Press, 1997.

Mahdi, Louise. *Betwixt and Between: Patterns of Masculine and Feminine Healing.* LaSalle, Ill.: Open Court, 1987.

———. *Crossroads: The Quest for Contemporary Rites of Passage.* LaSalle, Ill.: Open Court, 1996.

Mead, Margaret. *Coming of Age in Samoa.* New York: American Museum of Natural History (William Morrow & Co.), 1973.

Meade, Michael. *Men and the Water of Life: Initiation and the Tempering of Men.* San Francisco: HarperSanFrancisco, 1993.

Moore, Robert, and Douglas Gillette. *King, Warrior, Magician, Lover: Rediscovering the Archetypes of the Mature Masculine.* San Francisco: HarperSanFrancisco, 1990.

Nikkah, John. *Our Boys Speak: Adolescent Boys Write About Their Inner Lives.* New York: St. Martin's Press, 2000.

Nuwer, Hank. *High School Hazing: When Rites Become Wrongs.* New York: Franklin Watts, 2000.

Oldfield, David. *The Journey: A Creative Approach to the Necessary Crises of Adolescence.* Washington, D.C.: Foundation for Contemporary Mental Health, 1987.

Peltzer, Dave. *A Child Called "It."* Deerfield Beach, Fl.: Health Communications, 1995.

———. *The Lost Boy.* Deerfield Beach, Fl.: Health Communications, 1997.

Pipher, Mary. *Reviving Ophelia: Saving the Selves of Adolescent Girls.* New York: Ballantine Books, 1994.

Pittman, Frank. *Man Enough: Fathers, Sons and the Search for Masculinity.* New York: Putnam, 1993.

Ponton, Lynn. *The Romance of Risk: Why Teenagers Do the Things They Do.* New York: Basic Books, 1997.

Prechtel, Martín. *Long Life, Honey in the Heart: A Story of Initiation and Eloquence from the Shores of a Mayan Lake.* New York: Tarcher/Putnam, 1999.

Pollack, William. *Real Boys: Rescuing Our Sons from the Myths of Boyhood.* New York: Henry Holt, 1998.

Raphael, Ray. *The Men from the Boys: Rites of Passage in Male America.* Lincoln, Neb.: University of Nebraska Press, 1988.

Robinson, John. *Death of a Hero, Birth of the Soul: Answering the Call of Midlife.* Tulsa, Okla.: Council Oaks Books, 1997.

Smith, Laura, and Charles Elliott. *Hollow Kids: Recapturing the Soul of a Generation Lost to the Self-Esteem Myth.* New York: Forum/Prima Publishing, 2001.

Somé, Malidoma. *Of Water and the Spirit: Ritual, Magic and Initiation in the Life of an African Shaman.* New York: Tarcher/Putnam, 1994.

———. *Ritual: Power, Healing and Community.* Portland, Ore.: Swan, Raven and Co., 1993.

Sommers, Christina. *The War Against Boys: How Misguided Feminism Is Harming Our Young Men.* New York: Simon & Schuster, 2000.

Tart, Charles. *Altered States of Consciousness.* San Francisco: HarperSanFrancisco, 1972.

———. *States of Consciousness.* El Cerrito, Calif.: Psychological Processes, 1975.

Thompson, Keith. *To Be a Man: In Search of the Deep Masculine.* New York: Tarcher/Perigree, 1991.

Van Gennep, Arnold. *The Rites of Passage.* Chicago: University of Chicago Press, 1960.

Wallerstein, Judith. *Second Chances: Men, Women, and Children a Decade After Divorce.* New York: Houghton Mifflin, 1996.

Walsh, Roger. *The Spirit of Shamanism.* New York: Tarcher/Perigee, 1990.

Zimmer, Heinrich. *The King and the Corpse.* Princeton, N.J.: Princeton University Press, 1948.

Zweig, Connie. *Meeting the Shadow: The Hidden Power of the Dark Side of Human Nature.* New York: Tarcher/Putnam, 1991.

Suggested Reading

Abraham, Ralph. *Trialogues at the Edge of the West.* Santa Fe, N. Mex.: Bear & Co., 1992.

Abrahams, Roger D. *Afro-American Folk Tales: Stories from Black Traditions in the New World.* New York: Pantheon Books, 1985.

Achterburg, Jeanne. *Imagery in Healing: Shamanism and Modern Medicine.* Boston: Shambhala, 1985.

Bierhorst, John T*he Mythology of North America.* New York: William Morrow and Co., 1985.

Bridges, William. *Transitions: Making Sense of Life's Changes.* Boston: Addison-Wesley, 1980.

Chagnon, Napoleon. *Yanomamo: The Fierce People.* New York: Holt, Rinehart & Winston, 1968.

Crisp, Tony. *Do You Dream: How to Gain Insight from Your Dreams.* New York: E. P. Dutton, 1972.

Delaney, Gayle. *Living Your Dreams.* San Francisco: HarperSanFrancisco, 1988.

Erdoes, Richard, and Alfonso Ortiz. *American Indian Myths and Legends.* New York: Pantheon Books, 1984.

Fadiman, James. *Personality and Personal Growth.* New York: HarperCollins, 1994.

Fox, Matthew. *The Reinvention of Work: A New Vision of Livelihood for Our Time.* San Francisco: HarperSanFrancisco, 1994.

Harner, Michael. *The Way of the Shaman.* San Francisco: HarperSanFrancisco, 1990.

Heider, John. *The Tao of Leadership*. Atlanta: Humanics New Age, 1985.

Hill, Norbert. *Words of Power: Voices from Indian America*. Boulder, Colo.: Fulcrum Publishing, 1994.

Houston, Jean. *The Search for the Beloved: Journeys in Mythology and Sacred Psychology*. New York: Tarcher/Perigree, 1987.

Ingerman, Sandra. *Soul Retrieval: Mending the Fragmented Self*. San Francisco: HarperSanFrancisco, 1991.

Johnston, Charles. *Necessary Wisdom: Meeting the Challenge of a New Cultural Maturity*. Berkeley: Celestial Arts, 1991.

Jung, Carl G. *Man and His Symbols*. New York: Dell Publishing, 1964.

Kuper, Hilda. *The Swazi: A South African Kingdom*. New York: Holt, Rinehart & Winston, 1963.

Levine, Steven. *A Gradual Awakening*. New York: Anchor Books, 1989.

Mindel, Arnold. *The Leader as Martial Artist: Techniques and Strategies for Resolving Conflict and Creating Community*. San Francisco: HarperSanFrancisco, 1992.

Nicholson, Shirley. *Shamanism*. Wheaton, Ill.: Theosophical Publishing House, 1987.

Noble, Elizabeth. *Primal Connections: How Our Experiences from Conception to Birth Influence Our Emotions, Behavior, and Health*. New York: Simon & Schuster, 1993.

Prechtel, Martín. *Secrets of the Talking Jaguar: A Mayan Shaman's Journey to the Heart of the Indigenous Soul*. New York: Tarcher/Putnam, 1998.

Roberts, Elizabeth. *Earth Prayers from Around the World*. San Francisco: HarperSanFrancisco, 1991.

———. *Honoring the Earth: A Journal of New Earth Prayers*. San Francisco: HarperSanFrancisco, 1993.

Sams, Jamie. *Earth Medicine: Ancestors' Ways of Harmony for Many Moons*. San Francisco: HarperSanFrancisco, 1994.

———. *The 13 Original Clan Mothers*. San Francisco: HarperSanFrancisco, 1993.

Shostak, Marjorie. *Nisa: The Life and Words of a !Kung Woman*. New York: Vintage Books, 1981.

Tart, Charles. *Open Mind, Discriminating Mind: Reflections on Human Possibilities*. San Francisco: Harper & Row, 1989.

————. *Transpersonal Psychologies: Perspectives on the Mind from Seven Great Spiritual Traditions.* San Francisco: HarperSanFrancisco, 1992.

————. *Waking Up: Overcoming the Obstacles to Human Potential.* Boston: New Science Library, Shambhala, 1986.

Vaughan, Frances. *Awakening Intuition.* New York: Anchor Books, 1979.

Wall, Steve. *Wisdom's Daughters: Conversations with Women Elders of Native America.* New York: HarperCollins, 1993.

About the Author

Bret Stephenson has been a counselor of at-risk and high-risk adolescents for more than eighteen years. He has a master's degree from the Institute of Transpersonal Psychology in Palo Alto, California, and has worked in residential treatment, clinical counseling agencies, group homes, private counseling, foster parent training, and independent living programs, and managed mentoring and tutoring programs. He has been a presenter and speaker at numerous national and international conferences and workshops that have him with teens from more than one hundred countries, including the International Transpersonal Association's Youth Conferences in America and Ireland, the United Nations World Peace Festival, the Institute of Noetic Sciences, and the World Children's Summit.

Presentations at the Association of Transpersonal Psychology's annual conferences include Transpersonal Approaches to Working with High-Risk Youth and Western Adolescence: Shadow of the Patriarchy. He has been a presenter at multiple state and national Foster Parent Association conferences, and is a Global Program Faculty Mentor for the Institute of Transpersonal Psychology. As a men's group facilitator, he has led workshops in Switzerland as well as the United States.

Bret Stephenson is the founder and executive director of Labyrinth Center, a nonprofit organization dedicated to adolescent services and programs based in South Lake Tahoe.

For more information or to donate to Labyrinth Center, please contact: **www.labyrinthcenter.org** or **www.adolescentmind.com**.

Index

Books of Related Interest

THE SAILFISH AND THE SACRED MOUNTAIN
Passages in the Lives of a Father and Son
by Will Johnson

THE THUNDERING YEARS
Rituals and Sacred Wisdom for Teens
by Julie Tallard Johnson

SPIRITUAL JOURNALING
Writing Your Way to Independence
by Julie Tallard Johnson

FROM MAGICAL CHILD TO MAGICAL TEEN
A Guide to Adolescent Development
by Joseph Chilton Pearce

CHILDREN AT PLAY
Using Waldorf Principles to Foster Childhood Development
by Heidi Britz-Crecelius

MOTHER AND CHILD
Visions of Parenting from Indigenous Cultures
by Jan Reynolds

ABORIGINAL MEN OF HIGH DEGREE
Initiation and Sorcery in the World's Oldest Tradition
by A. P. Elkin

MEN'S BUSINESS, WOMEN'S BUSINESS
The Spiritual Role of Gender in the World's Oldest Culture
by Hannah Rachel Bell

Inner Traditions • Bear & Company
P.O. Box 388
Rochester, VT 05767
1-800-246-8648
www.InnerTraditions.com

Or contact your local bookseller